THE TREASURY OF HIS PROMISES

THE TREASURY OF HIS PROMISES

*366 Daily Bible
Readings*

Graham Miller

THE BANNER OF TRUTH TRUST

THE BANNER OF TRUTH TRUST
3 Murrayfield Road, Edinburgh EH12 6EL
PO Box 621, Carlisle, Pennsylvania 17013, USA

★

© Graham Miller 1986
First published 1986
ISBN 0 85151 472 3

★

Set in 11/12½ Plantin at
The Spartan Press Ltd, Lymington, Hants
Reproduced, printed and bound in Great Britain by
Hazell Watson & Viney Limited,
Member of the BPCC Group,
Aylesbury, Bucks

CONTENTS

[v]

BIOGRAPHICAL INTRODUCTION

John Graham Miller – usually known as Graham Miller – was brought up in a Presbyterian manse in New Zealand, the second of seven children who were covenanted to God from infancy and prayed for daily. His father, Thomas, was born in Stirling and his mother, Marion (Strang), in Glasgow, but both grew up in New Zealand and took M. A. Honours degrees from the University of Otago, Thomas gaining his in Philosophy and Marion hers in English and French. Psalms 127 and 128 formed the basis of their understanding of Christian family life, and the children were reared in an atmosphere of disciplined happiness, family worship morning and evening, reverence for the house of God and the Lord's Day, moral earnestness, and stimulating table-talk. What Henry Thornton wrote of the family life of John Venn might also have been written of that of Thomas Miller: 'Breakfasted yesterday with Venn . . . attended his family prayer . . . if there be happiness in this world this is it.' To everything there was a season, however, and the month of January was spent at the seaside where the father diligently taught his sons how to catch fish. Later he was to teach them how to become fishers of men.

At a time when the Presbyterian Church of New Zealand had drifted from its anchorage in Reformed truth, Rev. Thomas Miller remained 'fastened to the Rock which cannot move', and in due time became the acknowledged leader of the evangelical body within the New Zealand Church. His family grew up to respect his convictions and follow his testimony. The four daughters all married ministers of the gospel, one son became an eminent surgeon and elder of the Church, while the other two sons, Graham and Robert, completed law degrees and qualified for the Bar before going on to train for the ministry. At the time of his death in 1981 Robert was Professor of Church

History at the Presbyterian Theological Hall in Melbourne, Australia. The whole family story is an illustration of the truth of Pierre Marcel's claim that 'The covenant of grace reveals . . . that God does not choose His elect just anywhere . . . The covenant is the seed-bed at whose centre election to life eternal is realized'.

The turning point for Graham had come at the age of fourteen when his father called him up to his study for a heart-to-heart talk on the need for personal faith in Christ. The father pressed upon the son the truth of the atoning work of Christ as set out in Isaiah 53: 'All we like sheep have gone astray; we have turned everyone to his own way; and the Lord hath laid on him the iniquity of us all.' (v.6) Graham's heart was convicted, and the Saviour drew him to Himself. Assurance of salvation came some months later. From that time he became his father's 'curate' in a remarkable work among young men in Dunedin. Graham Miller has consistently maintained that he learned more genuine theology from his father's conversation, example and preaching than from any formal lectures.

The Inter-Varsity Fellowship had been formed in New Zealand under the influence of Dr John Laird of Scripture Union in 1936. The Miller family gave it every support in those days of small things. Graham was elected president of the Evangelical Union of the University of Otago and later became first travelling secretary of the I.V.F. in New Zealand in 1938. A strong sense of call to missionary service sent him to the Presbyterian Theological Hall in Dunedin in 1939. In 1941 Graham was appointed with his fiancée Flora McDonald – remembered by Neil MacLeod as 'A bonnie fair-haired lassie' – to the Church's oldest mission field, the New Hebrides, now known as Vanuatu. 'A prudent wife is from the Lord,' says Proverbs 19:14, and so it proved in Flora McDonald's case. She became Flora Miller in 1941 and throughout her life has showed herself to be a woman of grace, gifts and prayer.

Graham and Flora Miller were sent first to Tongoa, the centre of the island group, where they remained for six years. Graham was convinced that the three-self formula of self-support, self-government, and self-extension, understood within a framework of Reformed orthodoxy, was the Biblical solution to the problems of stagnation and nominalism in the island Church. Hence he worked towards the establishment of an indigenous Presbyterian Church of the New Hebrides. This was achieved in 1948 – the first self-governing Church in the Western Pacific. It was entirely appropriate that Graham should be elected first Moderator of the new General Assembly. By this time he had been appointed Principal of the Teachers' Training Institute on the tiny island of Tangoa, off the coast of Santo in the north. Here the Church's evangelists, pastors and teachers were trained. A quickening passed over the whole Church following these developments.

The need to be with their four children as they were educated in New Zealand led Graham and Flora to return to their homeland in 1952. Here Graham became the minister of Papakura, a fast-growing area twenty miles south of Auckland. For thirteen years the work expanded under Graham's systematic proclamation of the Word and prevailing prayer. His father's vision of a revived Church founded upon the Reformation creeds was being fulfilled. Graham worked loyally through the courts of the Church but also served the wider Christian community as chairman of the Rotorua Keswick Convention. This ministry took him to conventions in Australia, India, Portstewart (Ulster) and England (Keswick). In addition, Scripture Union in London invited him to share in the writing of *Bible Study Notes* and later the *Daily Notes* which he did until 1969. Selected portions of these *Notes* in the form of pithy expositions now appear in this book with the kind approval of Scripture Union in Britain and Australia.

Having crossed the Tasman, Graham became Principal of the Melbourne Bible Institute in 1966 (it is now called the Bible College of Victoria), but in 1970 he relinquished this position. The following year saw the Millers back in their beloved New Hebrides in order to set up the Presbyterian Bible College on the site of the old Teachers' Training Institute. It was a delicate time – the islands were moving towards political independence – and Graham played a vital role in preparing the New Hebrideans for national leadership. When Graham left in 1973, after the agreed term of three years, Pastor (now Dr) Titus Path, a New Hebrides pastor on Santo, took over as Principal.

On returning to Australia, Graham was called to St Giles Presbyterian Church in Hurstville, Sydney. Again it was a most significant period in the Church's history. The Presbyterian Church of Australia was preparing for union with the Methodist Church and the Congregational Union – a union which led to the formation of the Uniting Church in June 1977. Taking his stand on the historic Reformed understanding of the Word of God, Graham provided clear-sighted leadership to those Pres- byterians who remained outside the union and who continued in the much smaller Presbyterian Church after 1977.

Week by week Graham opened up the unsearchable riches of Christ in a powerful and much-blessed ministry of expository preaching. The trickle of students for the ministry grew into a steady stream, and the general tenor of the Church at large was changed. The Presbyterian Church withdrew from the World Council of Churches in 1977 and there was a new desire to return to the rock of truth, God's inerrant Word. Graham was greatly used of God in promoting this new spirit within the Church. Not only was he a faithful pastor and teacher, but he served as Convenor of the New South Wales Church's Evangelism Committee and as a most influential member of the Missions Committee, Theological Education Committee and Christian Education Committee. At the revitalized Theological Hall, he lectured on the Westminster Standards.

Arthur Pink once wrote of preachers and authors, 'The one who most profits me is the one whose ministry brings most of the awe of a holy and sovereign God on my heart, who discovers to me my sinfulness and failures, who conveys most light on the path of duty, who makes Christ most precious to me, who encourages me to press forward along the narrow way.' Graham Miller had just such a ministry.

In 1980 the Millers retired from St Giles, and now live in Wangaratta, Victoria. Graham is completing a five-volume *History of Church Planting in Vanuatu*, entitled *Live*, and is still active in preaching and teaching. Graham and Flora have two sons, Graham and Robert, who are both married and who live in New Zealand and California respectively. They also have two daughters, Betty and Sylvia, both married and living in Victoria. A fitting conclusion would be the words of Spurgeon:

'blessed is that ministry of which Christ is all'. But perhaps an even more fitting conclusion would be the words of the Psalmist, so often on Graham's lips: 'Not unto us, O Lord, not unto us, but unto thy Name give glory, for thy mercy, and for thy truth's sake' (Ps. 115:1).

BEGINNINGS

'For man to tell how human life began
Is hard; for who himself beginning knew?'
                    (Milton, Paradise Lost)

Our natural eyesight is so defective that to read the Bible aright
we must put on the spectacles of faith. It is 'through faith' that
we understand that the worlds were framed by the Word of God
(Heb. 11:3). Our reading today has suffered from all kinds of
opinions. We must ask for unencumbered minds as we
meditate upon its oft pondered verses today. 'Accepting the
account of creation as the Holy Spirit's direct revelation, we
acknowledge its absolute credibility in every part. They who do
not so accept it, or who deny the literal interpretation, can have
no voice in the discussion' (Abraham Kuyper). The serious
scientist's comment on Genesis I is 'I have nothing to say. I was
not there.' Verse 2 shows that matter as well as form proceeded
from God. Verse 3 introduces light – 'God's eldest daughter'
(Thomas Fuller). Verse 4 reminds God's people that there must
be a dividing line between truth and error on all great issues.
'The work of God was completed, not in one moment but in six
days, that it might not be tedious to us to occupy the whole of
life in the consideration of it' (Calvin).

DOCTRINE:
*'A miracle of God was necessary if there was to be resurrection; a
miracle of creation by the life-giving God. The resurrection-hope
pre-supposes the faith in creation.'*

'GOD IN THREE PERSONS, BLESSED TRINITY'

We should not hesitate to recognize the triune God in Genesis 1. *Elohim*, the Hebrew word here used for God, has a plural ending. This stands side by side with a *singular* verb (v.1). The root meaning of the verb *bara* is 'to cut'. The Santo island tribes of the New Hebrides describe God as 'The-One-who-cuts' and picture the final act of creation as God's slitting the eyes, ears, mouth etc, of man's clay-like form and then breathing into him the breath of life. The plural pronouns in verse 26 are clearly trinitarian. Before God breathed into man there was the conferring of the three Persons in the Godhead, implying that each Person had a share in the creation of man. These plural pronouns occur in a striking relationship with the singular nouns 'image' and 'likeness'. Compare also 3:22 and Isaiah 6:8 ('I . . . us'). The action of the Holy Spirit in creation is explicit in Genesis 1:2. And the New Testament makes clear the action of the Lord Jesus Christ in creation (John 1:3, Heb. 1:2).

DOCTRINE:
'The image of God (26–27) includes all the excellence in which the nature of man surpasses all the other species of animals. It denotes the integrity which Adam possessed . . . right understanding . . . regulated affections . . . all his senses governed in proper order.' (*Calvin*)

QUESTION:
Underline the six occurrences of 'good' in Genesis 1, and note that the chapter closes with 'very good' (31).

MARRIAGE

There are Four Gospels and how grateful we are for each one! And there are two distinct accounts of creation. In Genesis 1 creation is considered from the natural point of view, in Genesis 2:4 ff. from the spiritual. Hence they together form a unity, the one being complementary to the other. 'The Lord God planted a garden' (8). The old Quakers used to say that there are two fitting hobbies for the children of God – gardening, and the study of history; in the former we see the works of God, and in the latter the ways of God.

Marriage was ordained by God (18) and was not an afterthought. God envisaged this as meeting the nature of man as created on every level of human personality (1: 27–28). God presided as Minister at the first marriage service. We are grateful for the fragment of that first wedding service which has come down to us (2:24), finding endorsement on the lips of the Saviour (Matt. 19:5) and usage in weddings all over the world to this day. If it was 'not good that man should be alone' when he lived in unbroken communion with God, how much more significant is marriage in our society when man lives outside Eden among thorns and thistles? 'Marriage is the most universal duty incumbent on us' (Luthardt).

MEDITATION:
'She shall be called Woman' (23). 'Woman differs profoundly from man. Every one of the cells of her body bears the mark of her sex. The same is true of her organs, and, above all, of her nervous system . . . Women's part in the progress of civilization is higher than that of men. They should not abandon their specific functions.' (Alexis Carrell, Man the Unknown)

[3]

THE FALL

How old does a girl have to be to impersonate Eve? The idiom of our day is different but the voice is still that of the serpent. A generation of seduced teen-agers is in his mind now. Deep in the soul of every boy and girl is the yearning for the tree in the midst of the garden (3), and strangely blended with that yearning is distrust of God's spoken word. It is easier to believe Satan's whispered insinuations (1,4,5) than God's clear declarations (2: 16–17). If this was so for Eve it is tragically more so for us, biassed as we are to choose evil and to believe a lie. Compare the three prongs of the tempter's trident in 3:6 with Matthew 4: 1–11 and 1 John 2: 16–17.

The Fall involved three things: a captivity to Satan by right of conquest (Lk 11:21); a withdrawal of the Holy Spirit (Jude 19); an entire corruption of man's nature, now called 'the flesh' (John 3:6). (George Smeaton)

God sought Adam. His three questions were: Where? (9) Who? (11) What? (13) Show the effect of sin in the evasive answers which were given. Has this not a modern flavour? How often words fall short of an acknowledgement of the truth!

MEDITATION:
'*I was afraid . . . I hid myself*' (*10*).
'*God seeks Adam, not because he is lost from His knowledge, but from His fellowship*' (*Delitzsch*).

[4]

SIN

Guilt is inseparable from sin; and guilt demands punishment. In the case of Adam this had been foretold (2:17) and fully understood (3:3). But it had also been questioned by a very subtle mind (3:4) and the doubts then sown had sprouted at once, producing the first crop of sin. Have you noted carefully the fact that the very first temptation which confronted man was the temptation to doubt God's word? So soon as Eve has sinned she sees Satan in his true colours as a liar, and says so (3:13). But the effects of sin are always greater than we recognize. The virus of sin then entered the blood-stream of humanity, since Eve is 'the mother of all living' (3:20). Adam and Eve were created. We are born, and to the best of our ability we reproduce in our own lives the distrust, ingratitude, and capacity for being fooled which Adam and Eve displayed. They forfeited the Holy Spirit and came instantly under spiritual death ('in the day' 2:17 refers to this). But the virus of sin did more than that. It promoted all moral disorders of which Cain's violence is a typical example (ch 4). Sin also destroyed man's physical life by steady irresistible decay. God created man to 'live for ever' (3:22), but as a result of sin we read of Adam, 'and he died' (5:5). Romans 5: 12–21 is the New Testament commentary on today's portion.

QUESTION:
Verse 15 is the first prophecy in the Bible. To whom does it point? (cp. John 12:31). What aspect of the Cross does it stress?

[5]

THE FIRST MURDER;
THE FIRST MARTYR

Chapter 4 opens amid thorns and thistles. Eve has not forgotten the prophecy of 3:15. When her first child was born she eagerly applied the promise to him and called him 'Possession', from the Lord. She was soon disappointed. She saw the same passions in his young heart as moved in her own and her husband's hearts. When Abel was born she could only find one name to describe her deep disillusionment, so she called him 'Vanity'. Two tendencies now assert themselves: in Cain the tendency for transmitted sin to become more arrogant and violent; in Abel the tendency for God to break through man's rebellion and restore, by His sovereign grace, the lost righteousness of man. Four times the New Testament refers to Abel. Jesus names him as the first martyr in Matthew 23:35.

Both Cain and Abel were sinners. Both were in need of cleansing. But they reacted to their sinfulness in different ways. 'The bloodless offering of Cain was only a grateful present; or, taken at its deepest meaning, a consecrated offering of himself. But man needs, before all else, the expiation of his death-deserving sins. For this expiation the blood of the slain beasts (of Abel) serves as a symbol'. (Delitzsch) The acceptance of Abel's offering was due (a) to the nature of the offering, and (b) to the faith of the man who offered it (Heb. 11:4). There are those today who, like Cain, make gifts to God and to His work which He cannot 'have respect unto' (4:4) because their gifts do not spring from sin-cleansed and believing hearts.

QUESTION:
Look up Hebrews 12:24. In what sense does the blood of Jesus speak 'better things' than that of Abel?

[6]

LAMECH TO SETH

We have here the first 'hit-song' of recorded history. It is best to regard Lamech's rhyme in this light (23–24). Here is a happy pagan's bravado over his exploit. The R.S.V. reads: 'I have slain a man for wounding me, a young man for striking me' (23b). This hit-song is the typical product of a materialistic age swollen with its own self-importance. Arrogance, insolence, brutality, coarseness of thought and of feeling have become dominant. We note this menacing trend in everyday life in our own time. Remember that this chapter covers one thousand years of steady development and reveals the first flowering of technology among men (17–22). We detect also the differentiation of human life along varying cultural, social, moral and religious lines. Civilization is pressing out from its cradle in Mesopotamia and the Near East. It is an age of endless self-assurance, and God is merely an afterthought, save in the home of Adam. The birth of Seth brought new hope to the hearts of the faithful (25). Through him, and his descendants, God will continue his testimony in the earth. The meaning of v.26b is obscure. It seems that the faithful found it necessary, owing to the growth of false worship and pagan cults, to call themselves by the Name of Jehovah. There is something in common with the New Testament experience at Antioch (Acts 11:26).

QUESTION:
What parallel, if any, do you find in this first 'hit-song' and the 'pop' records of today? And what significance do you find in the fact that the writer is the first polygamist of recorded history (4:19)?

[7]

ENOCH

Through the unnumbered centuries of these long-lived ances-
tors of Noah, a busy, buoyant world grew up to complete
sophistication. Men successfully sought out 'many inventions'
(Eccles. 7:29). Life was as absorbing as it is today, and society
as blasé and as sad. The solitariness of Enoch in his walk with
God hints at what most Christians find – that the narrow way of
which Jesus spoke is never popular. 'Few there be that find it'
(Matt. 7:14). Yet God's people are not 'few' when viewed in the
light of the Last Day and the Heavenly City and the 'great
multitude which no man can number' (Rev. 7:9). Today we
may feel as solitary at our job as Enoch did in the pagan town
where he lived and witnessed. It was harder for Enoch than it is
for us. He had no church, no Bible, no fellow-pilgrim even in
his own home. There is no hint that wife or children shared his
testimony. On all sides was the rising tide of unchecked vice
and violence. Had he made a mistake? Was he deluded after all?
What more can you find concerning Enoch in Hebrews 11:5
and Jude 14–15?

STAFF-ROOM COMMENT:
*'You can't be right! You alone believe this stuff. Look how many of
us differ from you.'*

POSSIBLE REPLIES:
'Truth is arrived at by weighing evidence, not by counting heads.'
(An English Lord Justice of Appeal)
'Faith is not a question of majorities; monks are not reasons.'
(Auguste Lecerf)

[8]

THE DAYS OF NOAH

These tantalizing references to giants, mighty men, men of renown, the sons of God and the daughters of men need not detain us (1–4). They have been variously explained. Whatever they represent, they point to and preface the deepening social disorder and moral perversity in the centuries before the Flood. Such conditions recur as society slumps into its blind life where only the flesh is fed. Jesus said that such days would mark The End. In fact the Flood is a frequent New Testament analogy for the Last Judgment (Matt. 24: 37–39; Heb. 11:7; 1 Pet. 3:20; 2 Pet. 2:5).

The ark was the outward *means* of salvation (14–16). It shows us the place and importance of the organized church. The gopher-wood planking was as full of knots as the visible church of faults but it was the divinely-provided means of salvation when the Flood came. Noah did not look around and say, 'Lord, since I alone have found grace in your eyes (8), why bother about this huge ark? Won't a dinghy do?'

The family was the *object* of salvation. Whom did Noah take with him into the ark (18)? Why did he take them? (Cp. Exod. 12:3; 1 Pet. 3:20; Heb. 11:7 and link up 1 Cor. 7:14).

The covenant was the *ground* of salvation (18,9:9). It originated with God (18); was confirmed in sacrificial blood (8: 20– 21), and was everlasting (9:16).

Was anything else necessary? Yes, Noah's obedience (6:22); and so, too, is our obedience necessary if we are to receive the benefits of God's covenant of grace for us and for our family.

[9]

THE FAITH OF NOAH

This chapter opens on a gospel note with the word 'Come!' Adult conversions seem a little more numerous than in a previous generation. But in general old people find difficulty in change; they grow set and fixed in their ways. Yet here is a solitary man, at the age of 500, embarking upon an act of obedient faith which must have drained his bank account, tried him and his family to the uttermost, and caused his fellow-man to doubt his sanity.

He had faith to *believe* God's word about the threatened judgment (6:13) and about the necessity of the ark (6: 14–16). And he had faith to *obey* God's word (7:5). He revealed his faith by his works, as Christians still do (Jas 2:18), persevering with the building of the ark year after year. Every pit-sawn cypress log, every pot of caulking tar, every pay packet handed to every sceptical shipwright, was a lesson in active faith. And he had faith to *preach* God's word. Peter calls Noah a 'preacher of righteousness' (2 Pet. 2:5). He never rested from seeking the salvation of others. He holds the record for the longest ministry of all time, 100 years (cp. 5:32 and 7:6), and one of the least fruitful. Plenty of dumb animals went in; there were no sceptics among them. But his intelligent, good-natured fellow-men were absorbed in their pleasures. He could not get through to them at all.

QUESTION:
'Come thou and all thy house into the ark' (7:1). What is faith but obeying God's command to come? And what is unbelief?

'GOD REMEMBERED'

'God remembered' (1). Chapter 7 closes with the waters of destruction covering a world under God's judgment (7:23). A tiny speck floats, without sail or rudder, upon the vast expanse of troubled waters. In it are eight souls. They have no chart, no compass, no visibility, no knowledge of what to do next, or how long they are to continue in their strange home. Has God forgotten? Is the ark to become a rotting hulk upon the bosom of a dying world? Doubt lives in the heart of every child of God and suggests such thoughts even in our times of fullest obedience. At all such times our hope is in the constancy of the heart and purpose of God: 'God remembered' (cp. 19:29 & Exod. 2:24).

The dove remembered (9). There are some who value the protection, consolations and friendship of the ark of the organized church whose heart, however, is not in it. The raven, an 'unclean' bird (Lev. 11:15) is a picture of such. It had no heart to return to the ark once it had served its useful purpose (7). But the gentle and inoffensive dove was drawn back as to its true home (8–11). When she returned with the olive leaf (11) Noah at last had evidence to undergird his faith.

Noah remembered (20). It was New Year's Day in a new world when Noah removed the hatch-cover of the ark (13). God planned these details to confirm to Noah that he was as a man alive from the dead, and was called upon to walk in newness of life (Col. 3: 1–3). Noah's altar (20) speaks of atonement, thanksgiving and self-surrender.

MEDITATION:
It is with these three thoughts in our hearts that we, too, 'remember'. See 1 Cor. 11: 23–26.

[11]

THE LIBERALITY OF GOD

We have here a threefold cord, woven by God with the stout fibres of grace. *The liberality of God* (1–3). 'As I gave you the green plants, I give you everything' (3 RSV). That which we took for granted before we trusted Christ we now take as part of God's gracious provision. The food on our plate, the fish in the river and the pheasant on the hillside are all the gift of God. We pay for the food, we purchase a licence to catch the fish and to shoot the pheasant; only the simple-hearted still render their thanks to God. The black-skinned islanders of the Western Pacific would not harvest their yam crop without first giving God his portion, in acknowledgment of the truth, 'I give you everything'. An anaesthetic costs money; but the air we breathe is free – the gift of Noah's God.

The law of God (4–7): God's gifts are linked with God's laws. To abuse the gifts is to despise the Giver. The key phrase here is verse 6b, 'for in the image of God made he man'. Whatever defaces the image of God and engraves upon man the features of Satan is sacrilege and flies in the face of God's intention in our creation. We are to interpret this passage as a clear divine command requiring the judicial execution of the murderer. The death of the murderer is here viewed as an obligation which society must fulfil to satisfy the law of God. Only secondarily is it a question affecting the well-being of society.

The love of God (8–17) is here seen in its length (8–9), breadth (10), height (13) and depth (15).

NOAH'S SONS

We see here, as it were, the reverse side of yesterday's reading.

The abuse of God's liberality (20–21). There is no gift of God which may not be abused. In Corinth even the Lord's Supper became a disorderly party (1 Cor. 11: 21–22). God gave us the vine, but its first appearance here in Bible history is both a judgment and a warning; a judgment upon our proneness to selfish abuse of God's gifts, and a warning that drunkenness is closely linked with moral laxity. Liquor knocks out the linch-pin in man's moral reserve.

The breach of God's law (21–28). There is no such thing as an unrelated sin. Noah's three sons all received the backwash of his sin; Ham, because his dark heart was further corrupted by seeing evil (22). The modern magazine has employed this device with incredible effectiveness for evil. Shem and Japheth were hurt, too, because they found the saintliest person they knew in beastly self-indulgence. Children never forget the event which first rudely shatters the image of godliness which they had made of their parents. Noah's sin struck at the God of the Fifth Commandment. Shem and Japheth's intervention honoured the God of the Fifth Commandment.

The provision of God's love. The name Noah means 'rest'. In the deluge he found rest in God's ark; in his sin he found rest in God's Son; and in the end he found rest in God's heaven (Heb. 11:7, 13–16).

BABEL

On the Lord's days, as we worship in the house of God, we anticipate the consummation of Calvary's redemption when 'all nations, and kindreds and people and tongues' shall stand before the Lamb and cry 'Salvation to our God, . . . and unto the Lamb' (Rev. 7: 9–10). Already at Pentecost we see the reversing of the miracle at Babel (Acts 2: 7–8). And wherever Christians meet there is the common language of praise and prayer, of broken bread and brotherly love.

Babel means literally 'Gate of God'. The ambitions of the builders of these ancient ziggurats can be read in Prof. D. J. Wiseman's article 'Babel' in The New Bible Dictionary. God saw the pride in the builders' hearts (4–6), and he deliberately confused (7 RSV) and scattered (8) them. Why? Here is pagan man, drunk with arrogance and self-confidence, ready to dispossess God of his sovereignty (cp. Gen. 3:5). God now takes their own pet word 'Babel' – Gate of God – and slants it accusingly at their own folly and sin. He plays upon the similarity of Balal, the Hebrew word for confusion, and, by his intervention, says 'Your "Gate of God" will become a monument to your pride and folly.' And so Babel has remained. Babylon appears and re-appears in the Bible as 'the idea of materialistic and humanistic federation in opposition to God.'

MEDITATION:
'Multae terricolis linguae, coelestibus una'; on earth many languages; in heaven one. (Motto of the publishing house of Samuel Bagster & Sons, London)

TERAH AND HIS SON

After Noah the stream of God's church disappears, and from
Shem to Terah the Holy Spirit's work remains hidden. With
Terah, the father of Abram, the stream again appears and flows
down through the lives of his descendants. Whatever promp-
tings of the Holy Spirit stirred Terah to forsake Ur of the
Chaldees (11:31) we have the words of Joshua 24:2 to confirm
the fact that he never yielded decisively to the true God. In this
attitude he resembles the many who are deeply dissatisfied with
their lives, who recognize their bad environment and who try to
extricate themselves from it, but who die without yielding to
Christ. The initiative of God in the call of Abram (12:1) is
vividly emphasized in Joshua 24:3: 'I took your father Abram
. . . and led . . . and multiplied . . . and gave.' That miraculous redemption which appears as prophecy and promise in Gen
12: 1–3, reappears as fulfilled history in Joshua 24:3.

In Galatians 3:8 the Divine promises of today's reading are
referred to as gospel preaching. By comparing Galatians 3: 6–9
and Hebrews 11: 8–10 we find the true ingredients of the gospel
in Genesis 12: 1–5. In view of this, how do you understand
Abram's action in erecting his altars (7,8)? James Strachan says
that the marks of Abram's worship were: It was local, vocal,
simple, spiritual, and reasonable.

QUESTION:
*Compare Abram's worship with Romans 12:1, a verse which has
been entitled 'A Christian doctrine of worship'.*

ABRAM IN EGYPT

Yesterday we saw Abram as God's man of faith. 'He walks through a land of which he is the owner and perfumes it with the odour of his faith' (Calvin). Now, with startling abruptness, we see another Abram, who in the dance of circumstance lives by his wits, launches 'Operation Half-truth', and finally has the unspeakable humiliation of being rebuked by a man of the world and peremptorily dismissed from a land which he should never have ventured to enter (18–20). God sent this famine to bring out what was in Abram's heart (see Deut. 8: 2–3). Into the Bible record leaps the sinister word 'Egypt'. Abram 'went down' into Egypt. This was a moral decline. All through the history of the Hebrews Egypt signifies the land of plenty, of pleasure, of fickle promises, of treachery and of tyranny. Then why go there? The Christian is capable of any folly when he begins to live by his wits (11–13). George Morrison likens the tests which here confronted Abram to our Lord's three temptations – food, favour, and fortune. Abram acted faithlessly (12: 'they will kill me'); selfishly (12: 'me'); presumptuously (see 20: 12–13 for a revealing parallel); basely (15–16). Abram's mouth was shut by the royal gifts (16). This would have been the end of him had God not intervened (17–20). The very land to which Lot has laid claim is now conveyed unencumbered, and in fee simple, to Abram (chap. 13. vv. 15,17).

MEDITATION:

> *'What boots it at one gate to make defence*
> *And at another to let in the foe?'*
> (*John Milton:* Samson Agonistes (*560–1*)

[16]

ABRAM AND LOT

The grand events of this chapter, in which the faith and nobility of Abram shine forth once more, begin with his deliberate return to the altar of consecration (1–4). Abram and his nephew Lot had stayed together all the way from Ur. In trials, hazards and adversities they remained united. It was prosperity that wrecked their friendship (5–6). The wide-eyed Canaanites watched with cynical surprise the strife in the camp of the men of God (7). During the 17th-Century Covenanting struggles in Scotland, Robert Leighton, the saintly and sensitive archbishop of Glasgow, was forced by the fierceness of party-strife to cry, 'I had as soon be a martyr for peace as for truth'. Much strife has neither peace nor truth at heart. Quite often it simply reflects the insubordination of conceited, self-willed souls. How this hurts the church of God, and how the Perizzite rubs his hands in unholy amusement! (7) In the decisive choice which followed, the greatness of the younger man's self-assurance is only equalled by the greatness of the older man's large-heartedness. 'Lot put gain first and lost all; Abram put God first and won all.'

QUESTION:
Consider the significance of the words in verse 14, 'after that Lot was separated from him' (cp. 2 Cor. 6:14).

MEDITATION:
'Lot chose the plain of Jordan because it was well-watered; but his soul was all but withered there.' (Robert Murray McCheyne, 1813–1843)

THE FIRST WAR IN BIBLE HISTORY

Four kings of the east (from beyond the Euphrates) made war on five petty kings of the lower Jordan valley. The invaders came down the eastern side of the Jordan, harrying the settlements of the scattered hill tribes. The five petty kings defended themselves in a valley full of old bitumen pits. What might have been their main defence proved their undoing and they were routed. The victorious invaders retired northwards up the western side of the Jordan, laden with plunder and hampered with captives, including Lot (12). Abram here meets the test of complacency. Lot had only himself to blame for his troubles. By pitching his tent toward Sodom he had asked for trouble. Abram, secure in the isolation of the hills, might simply have shrugged his shoulders and written his nephew's epitaph. The word 'brother' in verse 14 is no mistake. His nephew *is* his brother, and he is his brother's keeper. What follows in the surprise attack at Dan (14–16) dispels the image of Abram as an old man with monk-like robes and soft hands. The first battle-story in the Bible tells us that God is not necessarily on the side of the big battalions. 'It is the redeemed of the earth who are the stokers of History' (D. R. Davies).

THOUGHT:
To accept money from no one is the first principle of moral independence. Illustrate this truth from Abram's contrasted attitudes in ch. 14: 21–24 and 12:16.

[18]

Genesis 15: 1–21

GOD'S COVENANT WITH ABRAM

Abram is now about 85 and Sarai 75. In verse 2 he is not lodging a complaint but is thinking aloud in his bewilderment. Thirteen years have passed since God's initial promise of a great posterity to Abram (12:2). But still there is no son and heir. To Abram this son is God's greatest 'reward' (1). He immediately makes an issue of it. 'I go childless . . . to me thou hast given no seed' (3). The faith of verse 6 is saving faith in the full evangelical sense of that word. It is so regarded in the New Testament (Rom. 4: 3,9,13,22). Then and there Abram was counted righteous on the ground of faith in the bare word of the living God. He saw Christ's day and was glad (John 8:56). At Abram's request God's promise was then corroborated and confirmed in the 'audio-visual' of verses 8–18. The horror of great darkness (12) took its nightmare nature from the foreview it gave Abram of the future afflictions of his descendants in Egypt (13). It is only to the man of faith that God is able to entrust the disclosure of his secrets (14–16). The 'smoking fire-pot and the flaming torch' (as one translation runs) seem to suggest first the fires of affliction (13) and then the torch of deliverance (cp. Isa. 62:1).

MEDITATION:
'And what will you do', Luther was asked, 'if the Duke, your protector, should no longer harbour you?' 'I will take my shelter under the broad shield of almighty God,' he replied.

Genesis 16: 1–16

HAGAR

Every Christian is a bundle of contradictions. It is the Christian's Lord alone who is consistent. After the 'Egypt' episode of chapter 12 there now comes the faithless tangle of chapter 16, centred upon an Egyptian handmaid. There would have been no Hagar to complicate this page but for the earlier backsliding. The old Jewish rabbis tried to justify all of Abram's actions. We cannot do that. But we can profit by his mistakes and see ourselves in most of them. Abram and Sarai, in their eager hopes for a son, have reasoned themselves into the necessity for meddling with God's clock. Whereas in 12:11 Abram was the instigator of their sinful collusion, this time it is Sarai (2). Faith waits; it does not meddle, fret and scheme. Look at the crop of bitter consequences which follow: Sarai hates herself for her folly, reproaches Abram (5) and torments Hagar (6). After verse 7 the narrative focuses upon God's gracious dealings with this outcast from society; and the confession which God's grace drew from Hagar is one of the loveliest in Scripture: 'Thou God seest me.'

MEDITATION:
Sir James Barrie in Margaret Ogilvy *tells how this was his mother's favourite text. 'I read from the beginning of the chapter, but when I come to "Thou God seest me" I stop; . . . for once a body's sure o' that, they're sure of all.'*

FAITH FALTERING

> Faith, mighty faith, the promise sees,
>   And looks to that alone;
> Laughs at impossibilities,
>   And cries, 'It shall be done!'

Is this the laughter of verse 17? Though Abram is everywhere in the New Testament viewed as a man of faith, it is instructive to note that his faith, like our's, was often mixed with questioning and blind self-pleasing. In this instance his laughter seems to arise from self-conscious astonishment rather than steadfast trust, as if he had muttered inwardly: 'That will be the day!' (17b). To save his confusion he then tells God how to make his promise come true (18). Here is Ishmael, the son of his faithless blundering; Abram grasps at his presence as an easy way for God to fulfil his oft-repeated promise (12:2; 13:16; 15: 4–5; 15:18; 17: 4–8). How many hydra-heads has unbelief in the soul of the believer! We marvel here at God's patient answer (18), at the kindly precision which removed all ambiguity by naming the promised child (19), and at the divine liberality which blessed Ishmael too (20). There must have been a smile in the heart of God as he named the child, for Isaac means 'laughter'.

MEDITATION:
Augustine called his natural son, born years before his conversion, Adeodatus, 'not God's gift'. Yet God so worked in both father and son that they were baptized by Ambrose of Milan on the same day (cp. verse 26).

ABRAHAM'S VISITORS

The Lord of the oaks of Mamre (1, RSV) is no other than the Lord Jesus Christ in one of his pre-incarnation appearances. For another instance see Joshua 5: 13–15. As later he found houseroom at Nazareth so here he is given instant hospitality by Abraham. We need not be surprised that Jesus is here called Jehovah (verse 1: the 'LORD': A.V.); but should remember Hebrews 1: 8–10: 'But unto the Son He saith, "Thou LORD (Jehovah) . . . Thou remainest . . . Thou art the same"' (quoting Psalm 102: 25–27 and using emphatic pronouns). For too many hazy Christians the life of the Lord Jesus began only at Bethlehem. Here in Gen. 18 we are reminded that he was 'in the beginning' (John 1:1).

Underline the words in verses 1–8 which picture Abraham's quick obedience. His deep respect is seen in his refusal to eat with his guests; he is simply their serving-man. The visitors reveal their mission (9–10). Abraham is now 99 and Sarah 89. Her self-conscious laugh (12) was inward but overheard (12–13). Her laughter, wrong and faithless though it was, has given us one of the great verses of the Bible: 'Is anything too hard for the Lord?' This is a rhetorical question to which our hearts are meant to make answer as we face today.

MEDITATION:

> *Wait for his seasonable aid,*
> *And though it tarry, wait;*
> *The promise may be long delayed,*
> *But cannot come too late.*
> (*William Cowper, Olney Hymns, No. 7*)

Genesis 18: 16–33

ABRAHAM'S PRAYER

Abraham's prayer has much to teach us. (a) He rests his petitions upon the character of God (25). This is a lesson the Bible prayers consistently illustrate, e.g. Solomon in 1 Kings 8: 22–24; Jonah in 4: 1–2; Nehemiah in 1:5. 'We cannot expect too little from man, nor too much from God' (Matthew Henry). (b) He repeats his petitions, with importunate faith, six times. 'His faith pleads with God, orders his cause, and fills his mouth with arguments' (Matthew Henry). Jesus' teaching about importunity in our prayers is found in Luke 11: 5–8; 18: 1–7. Luther was so bold as to pray, 'Lord, I will have my will of Thee at this time, for I know that my will is Thy will.' (c) Abraham remains in the posture of a humble suppliant, neither falling into familiarity on the one hand, nor becoming a servile beggar on the other. Jonathan Edwards had noticed these dangers in his day in New England and wrote, in *The Religious Affections*, 'There is in some persons a most unsuitable and insufferable boldness, in their addresses to the great Jehovah, in an ostentation of eminent nearness and familiarity'. James Strachan's points are: Abraham prayed with charity, humility, jealousy (for God's glory), reverence, importunity and success (*Hebrew Ideals*).

MEDITATION:
'God did not leave off granting till Abraham left off asking.' (33)

[23]

LOT'S DECAY

Sin works greater havoc in a man's character than any of us ever realize. Lot's stupidity, inaction and feckless hesitancy all point to the decay of his will, and the slow but fatal deterioration of his capacity to make prompt moral judgments. Genial, hospitable to a fault (1–3) and well aware of the rottenness of Sodom's social life (4–5) he still calls these loud-mouthed perverts 'my brothers' (7) and with the basest of mistaken judgments is prepared to barter his daughters in place of his guests (8). Such weakness never wins respect: 'This fellow came to sojourn, and he would play the judge!' (9). To his sons-in-law Lot's sudden seriousness, so much out of step with his easy-going attitudes in the past, 'seemed . . . to be jesting' (14 RSV). Lot was not jesting, but a tragic inconsistency of life had made his attempt to witness to the truth of God look like a farce.

The slow process of decay in Lot's life is vividly portrayed in 2 Peter 2: 7–8. 'God rescued Lot, who was a good man, shocked by the dissolute habits of the lawless society in which he lived; day after day every sight, every sound, of their evil courses tortured that good man's heart.'

Underline the words in verses 1–20 which point to the decay of Lot's power of decision and action.

THE GOODNESS AND SEVERITY OF GOD

The Apostle Paul speaks in Romans 11:22 of 'the goodness and severity of God'. In today's portion both of these terms are vividly illustrated. We see the *goodness* of God in his patient dealings with Lot in spite of his sluggishness, ingratitude and folly. A more sorry sight it is difficult to imagine than this backslidden follower of the true God with his heart locked in Sodom and his feet incapable of flight. All God's urgency (15), vehemence (17) and active help (16) are met by a divided will, 'Oh, not so, my Lord' (18). At every divine command he is ready with his own retort (19–20). This is the fruit of those years of prosperous self-choosing when conscience was all but silenced. Yet the goodness of God toils and wrestles with this man and compasses his loved ones in its saving embrace (16).

We see also the *severity* of God. The two angels came in search of incriminating evidence (18: 2–22). They have it in full measure (19: 4–5). The Judge of all the earth – it is *His* earth – is about to cauterise this plague-spot for the sake of His earth. It is impossible to stand under the blistered cliffs of Qumran, and look with shaded eyes across the shimmering expanse of the Dead Sea without the silent desolation saying, for all who have ears to hear, 'Our God is a consuming fire' (Heb. 12:29 quoting Deut. 4:24).

QUESTION:
Look up Christ's comparison of Capernaum with Sodom (Matt. 11: 23–24). What relevance has this warning for us to-day?

[25]

Genesis 20: 1–18

KING OF GERAR

When our communion with God decays we expose ourselves to danger. Abraham built no altar in Gerar (Philistia). Failing to make a clear-cut witness to his faith he quickly gave way to fear (11) and falsehood (2). Jesus has told us as plainly as can be that even the harboured thought of illicit love is adultery (Matt. 5: 27–28). Here in today's portion God tells us, in a plain object lesson, that the wages of this particular sin is death (3). Sentence has already been passed upon Abimelech. 'Every wilful sinner ought to be told that he is a dead man' (Matthew Henry). The many extenuating features of Abimelech's sin do not affect God's judgment. Note down these features. How often we hear sin excused upon exactly these grounds. The restraining Hand (6) is something for which we can all thank a sovereign God as we remember how near the edge of the precipice we walked in our folly. God's sovereignty was our only innocence (Luke 22:31). Abimelech is remarkable for his sincere and immediate confession (8), his honest rebuke (9), his insistence upon Abraham making a clean breast of everything (9–13), and his immediate restitution and compensation (16).

MEDITATION:
Chrysostom once said, in reply to a threat from an empress, 'Go, tell her that I fear nothing but sin.'

Genesis 21: 1–21

HAGAR AND ISHMAEL

This glimpse into the agonies of Hagar's heart is no accident in
the narrative of God's dealings with Abraham. Only the clear
Word of God could have persuaded Abraham of the rightness of
what he had to do (12). The New Testament has drawn its own
application of spiritual truth from the incident in Galatians 4:
21–31. God knows our *name* (17). How often he reveals this fact
of his intimate understanding of our personality! (cp. Gen.
22:11). God knows our *nature*, with its passionate yearnings
(6–8), threatening jealousies (9–11), and inarticulate suffering
(12–16). God knows our creature *needs*. He knows when the
water is spent in the bottle of our earthly joy (14), and when
despair beats its wings upon the windows of the soul (16). All
that God did for Hagar and her lad he did in the realm of his
common grace. God heard (17); God called (17); God spoke
(18); God guided (19); God protected (20). Could richer reasons
ever be found for responsive love, for obedience and lifelong
obligation to a tender and compassionate God? Yet Hagar
remained an Egyptian to the end, and when she sought a wife
for her warlike son she sought her among her own people (21).
Here is a warning for our hearts. We may see God's timely
interventions in our lives; experience his daily protection;
marvel at his goodness; sense his intimate concern, and even
hear his voice, and yet dwell in the wilderness (21) without ever
coming to the foot of the Cross as penitent sinners crying for
saving grace.

MEDITATION:
'Ishmael' means 'God hears', but his life remained unchanged.

[27]

THE WELL OF THE COVENANT

In this little-known episode in the life of Abraham we see the working out of the Beatitude: 'Blessed are the peacemakers, for they shall be called the children of God' (Matt. 5:9). To speak the truth in love is no easy art. It calls for direct action (25) in which the cause of misunderstanding is frankly stated in the spirit of manly openness and purpose after reconciliation. Perhaps we need to be reminded of this prerequisite of acceptable worship each Lord's Day as we prepare to go to church. It is so easy to allow misunderstanding to trickle underground and flow hidden beneath a show of chatty goodwill. Jesus says 'First be reconciled . . . then bring thy gift' (Matt. 5: 23–24). As often as not, when we obey God in making the overtures for reconciliation, we find that the other person held no such grudge against us as we had suspected (26). Like all sins, this calls for our confession and for God's forgiveness. We have no ewe lambs to offer (27–30). We rest in the atoning work of Jesus as the Lamb of God, and in the blood of a covenant more enduring than that at Beer-sheba (31). Abraham's tamarisk tree (33) was a living witness to the peace and joy and blessedness of restored communion between the sinner and his Lord.

QUESTION:
It was a heathen king who was forced to testify 'God is with thee in all that thou doest' (22). Can my acquaintances say this about me?

MOUNT MORIAH

We have watched the long adventurous years of Abraham's life of faith. 'God first tried him, in leaving his country, whether he loved God better than his father. Now he tests him to see whether he loves God better than his son.' Luther says, 'Temptation is the best school into which a Christian can enter'; and Calvin says, 'This temptation was necessary to the faith of Abraham'. It was the willingness of Abraham, and not the blood of Isaac, which God wished to see. Here we have vividly set forth for the Old Testament church what was finally realized on Golgotha over 1600 years later. 'Thy son, thine only son, Isaac, whom thou lovest'. Each word was a knife-wound in the father's soul. 'Here God *seems* to contradict God' (Chrysostom). To know Abraham's true mind under this extreme test we need to read Heb. 11: 17–19. He was certain he would receive Isaac back – even if this meant a literal resurrection from the dead. The deed was virtually done when Abraham raised the knife. Faith and obedience were complete. The voice that stayed the hand of Abraham did not later stay the hand of Judas, of Caiaphas, of Herod, of Pilate, of the Jews, and of the Roman execution squad. Christ's pierced hands were the silent answer to his Gethsemane prayer, 'Father, if it be possible, let this cup pass from me'.

MEDITATION:
When Ignatius of Antioch (early 2nd century), at the close of a life of service for Christ, was being led to Rome, to be torn by wild beasts in the Colosseum, he exclaimed, 'Now I begin to be a disciple!'

A SEPULCHRE FOR SARAH

Sarah is the only woman whose age at death is mentioned in the Bible. There is therefore some apparent justification for a woman's reticence in disclosing her age. Isaac by this time was 37. The long-drawn-out courtesies over the burial-plot are not to be lightly passed over. 'Honesty as well as honour forbids us to sponge on our neighbours . . . Religion teaches good manners [as in Abraham]; and those abuse it who place it in rudeness and clownishness' (Matt. Henry). Dr C. H. Irwin points out that the whole transaction finds a parallel among the same peoples today. They negotiate through a third party (8); they make offers which it is understood will not be accepted (11); they settle the transaction at the gates, the place of public business (10); they state their price in a most gentlemanly way (13); they secure the attestation of reliable witnesses, without any deed of conveyance (18); and the terms of the purchase are given in detail (17). Though all the land was Abraham's by Divine grant, this alone passed into his hand during his lifetime (Heb. 11: 9–10).

MEDITATION:
'This sepulchre is said to be at the end of the field (9) for, whatever our possessions are, there is a sepulchre at the end of them.'

GOD-CENTRED MARRIAGE

Those who love God will never seek a love which is inconsistent with their supreme affection. This old-world story reminds us today that marriage is a sacred contract in the making of which God is consulted, which God approves and blesses, which none but God can break, and he only by death. A shallow view of marriage has become epidemic to our shrinking world. This is fostered by Satan who uses the natural corruptness of man's heart and the side-shows of Vanity Fair to spread false values in marriage. Society is so heavily conditioned by a mass media of vast and subtle persuasiveness that the Christian church suffers along with the community at large. Even the homes of professing Christians have drifted into dangerous complicity with this great evil. Here, in this long chapter, the Holy Spirit has given us a chaste and candid view of God-centred wedlock. We must admit that the love story of Isaac and Rebekah weighs western customs of love, courtship and marriage in a finely adjusted balance. Do we recognize how utterly self-centred and undisciplined our manners of courtship have grown; how uncourtly, uncouth and inconsiderate? Before we feel sorry for Isaac and Rebekah in what looks like an arranged marriage we need to ask the question out of our own climate of complete self-pleasing: Of what real significance is our freedom to choose a life partner if our freedom is conditioned by false standards of judgment, will brook no parental guidance, and asks no counsel of the Lord?

QUESTION:
What does it mean to marry 'only in the Lord'? (1 Cor. 7:39)

'MY MASTER'

Abraham's servant is doubtless the Eliezer of chapter 15. His favourite expression, 'my master', occurs eighteen times in this chapter. He calls himself by no lofty, high-sounding title, but simply Abraham's servant (34). He is wholly devoted to the business of his master (33), to the honour of his master (35), to the God of his master (42), and to the son of his master (48). In all of this he is a model of a Christian's devotion to his Lord (cp. I Cor. 4:2). In him, self is dead. 'The goods of his master are in his hand, the cause of his master is in his heart, the God of his master is above him, and he is perfectly content' (James Strachan). His testimony concerning his master's God-control-led life (40), and his own sense of God's minute guidance on this responsible errand (48), had a powerful influence upon the guardians of Rebekah (50). He represented this marriage as God's plan (48) and no mere accident of time and place and circumstance. He saw both duties and events as in the government of a holy and loving God. No Hebrew servant more fitly illustrates the dedication of Exodus 21: 5–6: 'I love my master; I will not go free . . . I will serve him for ever.'

MEDITATION:
> *How sweetly doth* my Master *sound!* my Master!
> *As ambergris leaves a rich scent*
> > *Unto the taster,*
> *So doth these words a sweet content,*
> *An oriental fragrancy,* my Master.
>
> > > (George Herbert)

LOVE

Far south on the edge of the desert near Kadesh, the heir of
Abraham, the quiet reflective Isaac, walked alone at the close of
the day. God filled his thoughts as the cavalcade bearing
Rebekah drew near. 'Isaac went out to meditate in the field at
the eventide' (63). Luther's Bible has 'Isaac went out to pray.'
The Hebrew word sustains both meanings. Here is a man of
moral and spiritual stature who had made it the habit of his life
to take time to be alone with God. It was precisely then that God
brought to Isaac the answer to his own and his father's prayers.
Many, like Isaac and the saintly Handley Moule of Durham,
have preferred to pray and meditate upon their feet as they
walked. This co-ordination of thought and action helps to
banish wandering thoughts, to elevate the affections, to
promote praise and to discourage doubt. And as Isaac, like
Enoch long before, walked with God, new worlds of wonder
and glory were unveiled to the eyes of his soul. Isaac's character
is shaped by his walk with God, and so is ours.

The closing scene is deftly painted into the golden light of an
eastern sunset. Rebekah is glad to see Isaac, and to see him all
alone, as if awaiting her (64). She alights from her camel and
glides into his life. Each was the complement of the other; and
each fulfilled defects in the other. Isaac will love Rebekah the
more purely and chivalrously because he already loves God so
well.

TO EXERCISE THOUGHT:
*The well La-hai-roi (62) is connected with another woman (16:14).
Contrast these dramas at 'the well of the living One who sees me.'*

ESAU

Esau breaks into the family story of the household of faith with fascinating abruptness, attractiveness and appeal. Oswald Chambers sees in him the type of the happy pagan who is often so much more interesting and more admirable than the housebound Jacobs. This very likeableness of the modern Esau, with his generosity, good-natured sportsmanship and dare-devil use of life and wealth and reputation, raises questions for us all. Christians can look very ordinary people in the presence of a Mr Universe or a Miss America. What can we say? Only what the Bible says: that from the same believing parents came these contrary sons; that Isaac felt about Esau as any father feels about his son with a great sporting reputation; that Rebekah's attachment to the crafty Jacob was rooted in the Lord's oracle (23); that the real miracle of conversion is to be seen in God's making a crooked Jacob into an Israel – a supplanter into a prince of God; that grace precedes the will (as Augustine put it) (cp. v.23 & Rom. 9: 10–13); that Jacob did not injure Esau half so much as Esau wronged himself, for it was not Jacob's plotting that was Esau's undoing, but his own passion (see Heb. 12: 16–17).

MEDITATION:
'A holy war is better than the peace of the devil's palace.' (Matt. Henry's comment on v.22)

ISAAC IN GERAR

'Tell him I'm out' was the manager's curt word to his new clerk.
The clerk hesitated, then said quietly, 'I'm sorry, sir, but I
cannot do that.' We cannot excuse Isaac's base action. But we
can note that environment makes such behaviour all too easy.
God had warned Isaac against repeating his father's mistake in
going down to Egypt (12:10). Gerar was in Philistine territory;
and although God sanctioned Isaac's sojourn there, he in no
way condoned his assimilation of Philistinism. In nature we call
this adaptation to environment protective colouring. We see it
in fish, birds, butterflies and countless little insects. But a man
of God is not a flounder or a chameleon. He can be recognized
by his integrity regardless of environment. You know how he
will act in any situation. This is character unfettered by the fear
of man (9).

The record does not linger over Isaac's sin, nor should we.
Restored to God's favour he enters into even greater blessing
and prosperity. He is the envy of his Philistine neighbours who
were better fighters than farmers. How could they prosper
when they spent time filling precious wells of water with earth
(15)? In this stupid way envy and ignorance pay the tribute of
spiteful ingratitude for a great man's labours.

QUESTION:
*Proverbs 29:25 says 'The fear of man bringeth a snare.' Show how
this fear snared Abraham (12:12; 20:2) and Peter (Mark 14: 66–
72). See also John 19:38 & 12: 42–43.*

[35]

BROAD ACRES

Today's portion is all about wells of water in a withered land. It reminds the writer of a question he asked a Pacific Islander about the ownership of village springs. 'God made them', was his prompt reply; 'they belong to everyone.' In face of the quarrelsome Philistine herdsmen Isaac seemed repeatedly to take a weak and losing part. But his conduct well illustrates the beatitude of our Lord, 'Blessed are the meek, for they shall inherit the earth' (Matt. 5:5, cp. Ps. 37:11). Although Isaac nicknamed each surrendered spring and well by such words as Contention (20) and Enmity (21) he carried none of these feelings with him to Broad Acres (Rehoboth v.22). He looked to the Lord to order his way and he had not long to wait. Underline 'the same night' (24) and 'the same day' (32). Interpret these providences in the light of Matthew 5:5. We do both ourselves and our witness injury when we allow our pride to make an issue of every insult of every churlish Philistine. The day will come when the tables will be turned (26–31).

In v.24 we have the first occurrence of the grand ascription, 'The God of Abraham'. This divine title flourished among the people of God in the Old Testament. It was on the lips of Christ, and of his holy apostles, and has rightly found its way into the praise and prayers of the Christian church. See, for example, Thomas Olivers' majestic hymn, 'The God of Abraham praise' set to the Hebrew melody Leoni. Every verse reflects the faith and testimony of Isaac.

SINAI

The Book of Exodus falls into two parts; the Redemption of the people of God (chapters 1–14) and the Consecration of the people of God (chapters 15–40). The Consecration is unfolded in three progressive sections: the approach to Sinai (chapters 15–18), the covenanting at Sinai (chapters 19–24), the tabernacle (chapters 25–40). Photographs of Mt. Sinai show a grand massif of rock of startling formation, rising sheer from the level plain to six thousand feet. An enclosed valley floor of one square mile is walled in by granite mountains. The silence of the desert combined with the majesty of the mountains to impose upon the nation the will to hear and obey. 'There is no spot on the face of the earth so well fitted for a nation's assembling on a business to be transacted by means of sight and sound' (George Rawlinson).

Here Israel was put to school under a curriculum which was God-centred, relevant to real life, and a training for eternity. Never were audio-visuals employed to better effect (16 ff.). Never were so many put to school under one Teacher. Never was it made more evident that in the things of God old and young can learn together.

But this was more than mere tuition. It is called a covenant (5). This implies two parties. God initiated the covenant ('my' 5) and stated the terms upon which he would make Israel his special people (3–6). Moses referred these terms to the elders of the people (7) who gave whole-hearted agreement (8), which Moses reported to God on the Mount (9). God then appointed the solemn day for the promulgation of the covenant and the giving of his holy law (10–15).

THE GOD OF SINAI

The stage is here set for the greatest drama of Israel's moral and religious history. Even Moses trembled (Heb. 12: 18–21). 'The law of the Lord is perfect, converting the soul' confesses the Psalmist, from deep personal meditation upon it (Ps. 19:7); the people of God today suffer from too low a view of Sinai, too distant an echoing of its thunders of awful majesty. We have forgotten what His lightning looks like. God here brings to bear upon the conscience of His covenanted people the strongest possible reasons for their loyalty and reverence. He surrounds His law with the sanctions and solemn warnings of His justice and His judgment. The thick cloud (9) represents the inaccessible majesty of God in His relation to all men always. The trumpet (16) will sound only once more like this (1 Thes. 4:16). The third morning (16) points to another and greater 'third day' (Lk. 24:21). Behind the repeated Divine warnings of verses 21–24 we detect first the restless curiosity of men in the presence of these signs and portents and, secondly, the sheer impossibility of men meeting familiarly with God. The solution is found only in God's provision of the Mediator, here typified in Moses and Aaron (24).

QUESTION:
What typical lesson do you take from the fact that this covenant was ratified by blood? (cp. Ex. 24:6 & Heb. 9: 19–20).

THE TEN COMMANDMENTS

The preface to the Ten Commandments (v.1–2) gives three reasons for God's right to command: he is their God, he has delivered them from exile, he has redeemed them from slavery. This preface should be read before each command, as it supplies the grounds for our obedience, as for Israel's. 'A natural order is observable. They present (1) Jehovah as the sole Object of worship (2) the mode of worship accordant with his spiritual nature (3) the intelligent reverence, and (4) the constant regularity required in worship. They then provide rules for social life, beginning with (5) its foundation in family relations, and forbidding any actions injurious to (6) the life (7) the personal purity (8) the property, and (9) the reputation of others; as well as (10) all selfish and irregular desires. Though most of these laws specify actions, the ninth refers to words, and the tenth extends to thoughts and desires of the heart' (Dr C. H. Irwin). Those who possess the *Westminster Larger Catechism* will find, at Question 99, the rules to be observed for the right understanding of the Ten Commandments.

QUESTION:
'The gospel does not abrogate God's Law but it makes men love it with all their hearts' (J. Gresham Machen). Can you point to New Testament scriptures which illustrate this?

'I LOVE MY MASTER'

Both Miss F. R. Havergal and Bishop H. C. G. Moule wrote hymns on the theme of the Hebrew servant who renounced his offered liberty because he loved his master (21:5). To Miss Havergal the incident spoke with beautiful simplicity of that moment in the believer's life when, tired of his false freedom, he renounces his own way to take the yoke of Christ. Then and there he desires that the holy hands of Jesus should lead him to the doorpost of the Lord's sanctuary and make him his for ever. The momentary pain as the sharp awl pierces his ear points to the undoubted cost of such a full and glad surrender. The giving away of our self-pleasing, the yielding of our stubborn will, is no easy response for the Christian. It may well be the deepest experience of his whole life. But it will issue in a measure of fruitfulness and effectiveness not known by him before, and it will, above all else, bring joy to the Master's heart to hear this declaration of one's love for him.

MEDITATION:

> *I love, I love my Master,*
> *I will not go out free,*
> *For he is my Redeemer,*
> *He paid the price for me.*
> *I would not leave his service,*
> *It is so sweet and blest;*
> *And in the weariest moments*
> *He gives the truest rest.*
> *(Frances Ridley Havergal)*

GOD'S JUSTICE

'Justice, justice shalt thou pursue.' These words, a literal rendering of Deuteronomy 16:20, ring through the whole of the Old Testament and are the keynote of the Sinai laws. 'Without justice what are kingdoms but great banditries?' said Augustine. Justice is the holy concern of God who presides as Chief Justice over the chosen nation and observes the rule of law (7). There must be strict justice in laying a charge (1a) as also in giving evidence (1b). The judge must be on his guard against two opposite forms of partiality, – the sentiment which makes him too lenient because the accused is poor (3), or the harshness which makes him too severe because the accused is poor (6). Out of court each private individual must let no personal feud interfere with public duty to others (4–5). Bribery is a subtle evil and goes to the root of all injustice (8). Young's Concordance shows a dozen Hebrew words for 'gift'. That which occurs in verse 8 has a tainted meaning. It means the sort of gift which will ingratiate a person or free him from punishment. If the gift looks as if it is wrongly 'making room' for anyone (Proverbs 18:16) then it must be declined.

A POINT TO BE NOTED:
The wrong use of a gift may be seen in 2 Kings 16:8; Proverbs 6:35; 17:8; Psalm 15:5; Psalm 26:10.

[41]

AN ANGEL

By 'an Angel' (20) is meant 'no common angel, but the chief of all angels, who has always been also the Head of the church' (Calvin). Though the Hebrew word means 'messenger', the Angel appears as God to *guard* his people from danger (20 'keep' A.V.), to *guide* his people to the promised inheritance, to *govern* his people by his holy law (21), to *go before* his people with the weapons of victory (23). 'My name is in Him' (21c) is the most solemn way of saying that this Angel of the Lord has all the attributes of Godhead; he can punish and he can pardon (21); he can speak as God's very self (22a). Two vivid illustrations of God's power occur: 'I will send my fear before thee, and will destroy all the people to whom thou shalt come' (27). Examples of this occur frequently in the Old Testament. See Joshua 2:11, 2 Samuel 5:24, 2 Kings 7:6. 'I will send hornets before thee . . .' (28). This reference is best taken quite literally, as Calvin does, adding, 'He does not threaten to send great and powerful warriors, but only insects . . . He would arm the smallest animals to destroy their enemies.'

QUESTION:
Compare the Angel of this passage and the eagle of Deuteronomy 32:11, and link up with 1 Corinthians 10: 4,9.

THE COVENANT SEALED

This chapter speaks of the solemn 'sealing' of the Sinai covenant between God and Israel in two stages: The sealing of the covenant (1–8), and the sequel to the covenant (9–18). Moses told the people the conditions they must fulfil under the covenant and they promptly gave their assent (3). But there can be no intercourse between God and man except through the shed blood. Hence the altar (4), the offerings (5), and the sprinkled blood (6). *Burnt* signifies consecration to God the Redeemer; and *peace*, communion with him in redeeming love. Now the cleansed and consecrated nation gives back its assent a second time (7). This sacrifice, constituting the covenant relationship, is the one sacrifice under the Old Testament which did not require to be repeated. It was the foundation of all, and is spoken of in Hebrews 9: 18–20. It typifies that second and greater sacrifice which constitutes the covenant of grace, by which the cleansing blood of Christ sprinkles us in the hour of our new birth and draws our redeemed hearts in loving obligation to obey the revealed will of God (1 Peter 1: 14–19).

INTERPRETATION OF VERSE 10:
'Saw' means without the veil of symbols, as the redeemed see God in heaven, 'face to face'.

THE ARK AND THE MERCY SEAT

During the forty days and forty nights (24:18) Moses received from God instructions concerning the tabernacle (chapters 25–31). 'Two chapters of Genesis are given to tell us how the world was created; there are sixteen to tell us how the tabernacle was constructed. For the world was made for the sake of the church, and the great object of creation is to glorify God in the redemption and sanctification of his people' (J. A. Bengel).

God allowed his tabernacle to grow from the freewill offerings of his people (1–9). Underline in verse 2 the various words which emphasize the glad alacrity which marked all their giving, and compare chapter 35: 20–29 for a moving account of their wholehearted response. Men and women of all classes made their gifts with a willing heart. Unless gifts come from the heart they are an offence to God (2 Cor. 9:7).

The first of the tabernacle furnishings God directed Moses to make was the ark (10–22). Its purpose was to be a container for 'the testimony' (16) i.e. the two tables of the law. The mercy seat (17) covered the law and symbolised God's merciful putting away of Israel's law-breaking through the shedding of blood on the annual day of Atonement (Lev. 16). The very word for the mercy seat has found its way into the New Testament as 'propitiation' (Rom. 3:25; Heb. 9:5).

PRAYER:

> *Approach, my soul, the mercy seat,*
> *Where Jesus answers prayer;*
> *There humbly fall before his feet,*
> *For none can perish there.*
> > *(John Newton)*

THE TABERNACLE

Here the Scripture is dealing with great exactness in measurements, ornamentation and other particulars of the tabernacle furnishings. If we are not to lose our way in these God-given particulars, and to become careless or even impatient in the reading of them, we should bear in mind the context. Chapters 25–31 give God's directions; chapters 32–34 give the episode of the golden calf; chapters 35–40 record the execution of the work and the erection of the tabernacle.

Immediately prior to all this the people were brought into their covenant relationship with Jehovah (chapters 19–24). That relationship gives the proper point of view for understanding the long chapters of the tabernacle history. The tabernacle is God's provision for his people's communion with him in unbroken fellowship, based upon the covenant. The tabernacle is the dwelling place of Jehovah among his people where, in his unspotted holiness, he meets his people as their Redeemer King. Thus it perpetuates, through symbols, that heaven on earth which Israel's nobles briefly enjoyed (24: 10–11) and prepares God's people of all ages for that time when they will no longer see through a glass darkly, but face to face (Rev. 5). As in the centre of heaven's worship his people see 'a Lamb as it had been slain', so at the heart of the Old Testament church stood the most holy place and within it the mercy seat.

QUESTION:
From what you have read of the tabernacle furnishings, illustrate the remark: 'Christ is an all-gold Saviour; there is no dross, no flaw, no blemish in him.'

[45]

Exodus 26: 30–37

THE VAIL

The vail which separated the holy place from the holy of holies is symbolic of the body of our Lord: 'the vail, that is to say, his flesh' (Heb. 10:20). In his earthly life he showed the beauty of holiness. The cherubim woven into the vail seem to point to our Lord's perfection of character. Throughout Israel's history the vail stood as a barrier against the intrusion of sin and the sinner. But now it has been 'rent in twain from the top to the bottom' (Matt. 27:51). The atoning death of the God-man, Immanuel, has given direct access into the holiest of all by this new and living way. 'Not from side to side, nor from the bottom to the top, which might have been man's doing, but from the top to the bottom, showing that the rending was not of man, but of God' (Horatius Bonar).

MEDITATION:

> *The sacrifice is o'er, the veil is rent in twain;*
> *The mercy-seat proclaims the spotless victim slain.*
> *Now none need stand without in fear,*
> *The blood of Christ invites us near.*

PRIESTLY ROBES

The ritual and colourful garments of the tabernacle worship are in striking contrast to the simplicity of New Testament worship. The holy garments 'for glory and for beauty', are now the property of our Lord as High Priest over the house of God, full of grace and truth. 'Such an High Priest became us, who is holy, harmless, undefiled, separate from sinners, and made higher than the heavens' (Heb. 7:26). Aaron, like the rest of Israel, was a sinner. Christ our High Priest 'knew no sin'. Aaron's holy garments proclaimed his personal unfitness and moral nakedness in the sight of God. They told what he was not. But they did more; they pointed to that Priest who was to come. He would need no gold and blue and purple and scarlet and fine linen. He would be all this in himself, in his moral perfections, in his tender compassion and in his royal priesthood. Aaron was the type, Jesus the reality to whom these long-vanished ritual garments pointed.

PRINCIPLE OF INTERPRETATION:
'Distinguish the times, and the Scriptures will agree' (Augustine). The Tabernacle ritual was God's audio-visual during the infancy of his people. It has gone for ever, swallowed up in the great Reality, Christ.

AARON'S GARMENTS

Aaron's garments are six in all (28.4). At his consecration (chapter 29) they were put on Aaron in this order:

The embroidered coat (39–40), worn next to the skin, made of fine linen, is a picture of the personal purity of our great High Priest, and of the righteousness with which we are clothed when we are 'in Christ'.

The girdle (39–40), held in place the embroidered coat, and girt the wearer for efficient service. It was only put on during ministration and points to our Lord's action in John 13: 4–5.

The robe of the ephod (31–32), was a long loose garment of blue, woven in one piece (John 19:23). Upon it the ephod was worn. Blue is the dominant colour in the tabernacle, a reflection of Heaven, a picture of the Divine character of Jesus Christ upon earth.

The ephod (6–12), was like a short smock over the other long garments. It was rich and costly, of the same materials as the vail, and was the great official garment of the high priest. The onyx-stones engraved with the names of the tribes were a reminder that Aaron carried all Israel with him into the Lord's presence (cp. Isa. 9:6).

The breastplate (15–29), was inseparable from the ephod, of the same materials and doubled, perhaps to form a bag for the Urim and Thummim (30). Each stone was different, yet all were alike precious, as we are to Christ.

The mitre and the 'holy crown' were for the head (29:6). Our High Priest is also our Saviour King who crowns us with royal gifts.

CONSECRATION

Chapter 29 is wholly occupied with the ritual for the consecration of Aaron and his sons. Today's reading is an appendix, giving directions to the ordinary priests for their daily service in the tabernacle. But, through the great promise at the close (45–46), this passage is connected with the original covenant and is a reminder of it. It also serves to safeguard the divine idea of priesthood as an office which requires an altar, points always to the altar, and has no standing apart from the altar. The daily sacrifices of lambs pointed forward to John the Baptist's cry (John 1:29). The central truth here is a life for a life; the substitution of the innocent lamb for the guilty nation. Seen in this central reality, the sacrifice of the Lamb of God can receive no further fulfilment in anything that we can do. But as a picture of entire surrender to the holy will of God, this is to be our daily example.

DEFINITION:
In the Bible 'consecration' is God's act and it is wrought upon us when we first believe. The results which flow from this divine act are self-surrender and whole-hearted devotion to Christ, which is what is incorrectly *called 'consecration' in our careless use of terms today.*

CHRIST IN THE TABERNACLE

Each of the furnishings of the tabernacle service points to the
Person and work of the Lord Jesus Christ. Those objects which
were outside the tent, in the courtyard, namely, the brazen altar
for sacrifices and the laver for ritual cleansing, seem to point
especially to Christ in his finished work of propitiation upon
earth. Those objects which were within the holy place and the
holy of holies seem to point to his present ministry in heaven
(Heb. 9:24). Notice the chosen materials for the altar of
incense. The tough desert acacia symbolizes our Lord's moral
strength; the gold which overlaid it, his divinity. The four
horns (2) point to the efficacy of Christ's prayers, and of His
people's prayers, offered in Christ's Name. The careful directions for the composition of the incense (34–36), and for its
exclusive use for the altar (37–38) point to the unique nature of
our prayers and praises when acceptable to the Father through
Christ's atonement. The words 'pure', 'perpetual', 'sweet' and
'most holy' are worth underlining. It is only through Jesus
Christ that we are able to offer 'spiritual sacrifices acceptable to
God' (1 Peter 2:5).

QUESTION:
*What hint can you find in this passage that our prayers need God's
forgiveness and are only acceptable through the sacrificial blood of
Christ?*

BEZALEEL AND AHOLIAB

Four verbs make crystal-clear the initiative of God in preparing Bezaleel and Aholiab for their tasks. 'I have called' (2), 'I have filled' (3), 'I have given' (6), 'I have put' (6). These link up with the clear New Testament teaching that 'if any of you lack wisdom' he may ask it of God (Jas. 1:5). The gift of the Holy Spirit at conversion renews progressively the whole personality. Part of this profound work is the renewal of the mind. Many have found that their minds woke up at conversion; others that new and exciting vistas were opened to their inquiry; others that old truths took on new depth and power. All of these familiar discoveries are to be traced to the work of the Holy Spirit (3) upon our intellect, as a result of the new birth. And, as James says in his homely Epistle, if any Christian worries about his lack of ability he has only to go to the Source of all wisdom for sustained and liberal aid. See also Romans 12:2, 'transformed by the renewing of your mind', and Colossians 3:10, 'renewed in knowledge after the image of him that created him'.

FIRST THINGS FIRST:
The quickened intellect pre-supposes (1) the changed heart, and (2) the surrendered life (Rom. 12: 1–2).

Exodus 32: 1–14

APOSTASY

The very presence of a man of God deters others from their sinful behaviour. But with Moses away Israel felt free to take all sorts of liberties. That very day they had gathered God's provision of the manna. Only a month earlier they had pledged their loyalty to Jehovah. At the sound of the voice of God they had trembled. But something more than fear and creature comforts is needed to incline our hearts to keep God's law. The word 'gods' translates the Hebrew *elohim*, commonly translated 'God'. It is Jehovah, 'the Lord' (5) whom they were invited to reverence in the calf. The practical question is not which of the Commandments – the 1st or 2nd – they intended to break. It is rather which of all the Commandments they did *not* break. They broke all the Commandments in breaking with the divine Commander, in rejecting his authority and his spirituality. Notice how false religious excitement leans towards indecency (6). 'To play' in this connection has a sinister meaning, as borne out by 1 Corinthians 10: 6–8. In fact the phrase 'to go a-whoring' emerges from this first moral and spiritual apostasy of the nation.

QUESTION:
Can you see any connection between this incident and the present-day trend to pop-music in religious worship?

Exodus 32: 15–35

THE GOLDEN CALF

The early church grew up like a white-petalled lotus out of the mire of a corrupt society. The revelry of the pagan festivals was recognized by the apostles as a source of dangerous seduction (Rom. 13: 12–14). In Egypt the people of God had lived among a people whose festivals were inducements to sin. At Sinai they broke through the new-built barriers of the Ten Commandments in the intoxication of a taste of the old life. How costly this proved! How tragic, having regard to the broken covenant, the violated vows, the fleeting pleasure, the desolated homes, 'for the end of those things is death'. But Sinai and the golden calf point to Calvary and the sinless Lamb who is not only Mediator of a new covenant but also Intercessor on our behalf at the right hand of God. Unlike Moses, Israel's intercessor, our Saviour need never say 'and if not –' (32).

INTERPRETATION:
The meaning of verse 25 is obscure. The word 'naked' means 'stripped', possibly of arms, thus exposing the reckless rabble to the contempt of their observant enemies, for example, the Amalekites (chapter 17, 8–16).

[53]

ISRAEL EXCOMMUNICATED

Israel's God and our God is a consuming fire. The flame burns vehemently in this incident (1–5) and provokes the first recorded act of national humiliation (4–6). Moses secedes from the people and by doing so virtually excommunicates them. The tent he erected 'without the camp' (7) was not the tabernacle of the holy place and the holy of holies. That had yet to be made (chapter 36). It was simply Moses' private tent. All the sacredness it had was from its divine Guest (9). What we see here is a judicial abandonment of Israel because of the nation's sin over the golden calf. They are now excluded from the fellowship of God. They stand awed into silent grief and contrition by the spectacle of God's presence removed from their midst. When they see Moses go and come (8–11) they have nothing that they can do or say. He and Joshua alone are left of all the nation to enjoy the favour of God's condescending grace. The nation now mourns its loss. God spoke with Moses face to face. And Moses prepared to plead again for the alienated and stiff-necked nation (34:9).

QUESTION:
What lessons can you learn here concerning the basis of our communion with God?

THE PRESENCE

As Moses is persevering in his fellowship with God so he is persevering in his yearning for the Lord's renewal of fellowship with his people. The promise of 'an angel' (2) is not enough, if this means that God will be far off. Hence Moses prays, 'Show me now thy way' (13). God then grants all that Moses desires: 'My presence shall go with thee, and I will give thee rest' (14). The 'presence' here is not simply the general omnipresence of God, but the indwelling personal Captaincy of Jehovah restored to the heart of the nation's life; the living, loving, redeeming God of the covenant back in that place of awful intimacy and irresistible majesty which was rightfully his. The 'rest' he promised was that of a daily abiding, comparable with the Christian's rest of heart as he abides obediently in Christ's will moment by moment (John 15). And this 'rest' looks to ultimate realities in the unveiled glory of heaven. Of this reality (8–23) the mysterious unveiling which Moses witnessed at Horeb, and again on the mount of transfiguration (Luke 9: 29–31) is the faint anticipation.

QUESTION:
God's action here is one of pure grace. Underline the words which reveal this fact and look up the New Testament verse which quotes verse 19 so emphatically.

WILLING

Four times we are told that these offerings came from willing hearts. Any other motive would make nonsense of the word 'offering'. The incident has given to the Lord's people the widely-used term 'a freewill offering'. But how casually and carelessly we offer to the Lord our offerings! 'Thy people shall be *willing* in the day of thy power' cries the Psalmist (110:3). Here 'willing' means 'freewill offerings'. Perhaps this helps to clinch the matter for us. There is no freewill offering without the cordial assent of the heart to the gift. There is no gift until the will that offers it is first sanctified by the new birth. The motives of the people of God at Sinai may have been those of gratitude for a great deliverance, or reverence for a great God, or acknowledgment of a great provision. 'Willing' implies some deep prompting of the heart; some deliberate purpose of the will, some adequate recognition of the Giver of every good and perfect gift. The sequel is worth looking up (36: 5–7).

Our prayer may be that of Charlotte Elliott for her friend Mrs S. C. Malan invalided from Calcutta to the Cape, with tuberculosis:

> Renew my will from day to day;
> Blend it with thine; and take away
> All that now makes it hard to say,
> 'Thy will be done!'

THE NAME

'The sermon on the Name' is how Luther describes this
revelation of the heart of God, where he speaks of himself not
as the Legislator of Sinai but as the Redeemer of the rebel race.
By receiving back his people Israel he has proved his title to
every Name which he here recites to every penitent sinner since
Adam. Select each jewel and thread it on the golden cord of
grace. Pause long enough over each word to ponder its length
and breadth, its height and depth. Let no familiarity dull its
lustre. Say each word over deliberately and aloud; each
attribute personified by the thrice-repeated Name. Notice how
grace triumphs over judgment; preceding it, overwhelming it
in the flow of its outpoured language, and transcending it. The
thousand generations (7) to which mercy is extended are here
put in contrast with the third and fourth generation upon which
iniquity is visited. These expressions of God's vindicatory
justice are reassuring to every sinner's conscience. The heart
will find no heaven in a love which is not holy.

CONSIDER:
*In verse 9 Moses prays to God, 'Take us for thine inheritance.'
Trace the later use of this term in the New Testament. This is its first
occurrence.*

THE SHINING FACE

God's glory upon his people
In chapter 33:18 Moses asked to be shown God's glory and God answered his request, in measure (33: 19–23). Shortly afterwards God again summoned him up into Sinai where the glory of God was partly unveiled to him (34: 5–8). The shining of Moses' face is used by the apostle Paul as a kind of Old Testament rehearsal for what should take place in the lives of believers when 'we all, with unveiled face, beholding as in a mirror the glory of the Lord, are transfigured into the same image, from one degree of glory to another, as by the Spirit of the Lord' (2 Cor. 3:18). Notice that the light on Moses' face was a *borrowed light* (34–35) received from God in face-to-face communion. It was also an *unconscious light*, for 'Moses wist not that the skin of his face shone' (29). And it was an *irresistible light*. The Hebrew for 'shone' (29) means 'beamed' as if sending forth convicting, heart-searching rays of light. This explains the fear of Aaron and Israel (30). There is in every Christian's deportment and appearance, even in repose, that which disturbs and even irritates, and this may partly explain the unprovoked dislike which some people have shown you as a Christian.

MEDITATION:
'*I am more than ever convinced that sanctification is carried on by the Spirit, by means of our direct looking on the face of Jesus, hour by hour.*' (*Andrew A. Bonar, in his Diary*)

[58]

Exodus 35: 30–35, 36: 1–7

WISDOM

Today's portion reminds us that God is the sole source of wisdom and knowledge. Since Christ is the fulness of God-head in bodily form (Col. 2:9), it is no surprise to read that in him 'are hid all the treasures of wisdom and knowledge' (Col. 2:3). The gradual overhaul of the Christian's life, as a result of the new birth, involves, among other profound effects, the renewal of the mind, the toning up of its powers of observation, perception, analysis, logical thought, concentration, memory and imagination. This work of grace is not confined to the New Testament. Here we see it in the vocation of Bezaleel and Aholiab. The Agent is always the Holy Spirit (unfortunately spelt with a small s in both AV & RV of verse 31). The range of his imparted skills is impressive: ability, intelligence, knowledge, craftsmanship (31); to design in a wide variety of materials (31–35); to give effect to these designs in expert workmanship (33); and to pass on these skills to others by tuition (34). That this wisdom 'from above is first pure' (Jas. 3:17) is evident in the honest way the craftsman refused all superfluous gifts (36: 5–7).

MEDITATION:
'Avoid intellectual pride when you grow older. I think it is by far the most vulgar thing in the world.' (Earl Stanley Baldwin in an address to pupils of Malvern College, 1939)

NEW YEAR'S DAY

From time immemorial New Year's Day has belonged to God. He has ratified his rights in three striking and successive events. (1) This was the day upon which Noah removed the hatch of the ark and looked out upon a clean new world (Gen. 8:13). (2) This was the first day of that 'beginning of months' (Ex. 12:1) wherein God redeemed Israel from the bondage of Egypt and ordained the passover feast for a memorial for ever. (3) This was the day which God appointed for the erection of the tabernacle (Ex. 40: 1–2). This New Year's Day was *God's day* for he prescribed its proper use on this occasion of the dedication of the sanctuary. It was *Moses' day*, for, as mediator of the old covenant, he executed with prompt obedience the command of his God (16). It was *Bezaleel's day*, because now his skill and workmanship are to be exhibited as every part of the pre-fabricated church is fitly framed together. It was the *nation's day*, for every weaver of fine-twined linen and every hewer of acacia wood and every worker in silver and gold and precious stones shared in the crowning joy of a visible sanctuary in whose building and furnishing he or she had had some part.

MEDITATION:
In the spiritual house of the new covenant Christians do not make the materials; they are the materials which the Lord employs (1 Peter 2:5, Eph. 2: 20–22).

'SO MOSES FINISHED THE WORK' (33)

Every board sat snug in its socket. Every curtain fell flush to the ground. Every article of furnishing was in its proper place. All was done 'as the Lord commanded Moses'. Underline the eight occurrences of this refrain. Why labour the point eight times? Why make this the refrain for New Year's Day? Surely because the Lord of the church knew how deep-seated is man's desire for independence and how prone he is to tinker with and 'improve' the plan given in the Mount – for the ordering of the Lord's house. Christians are not at liberty to be innovators in the house of God. 'Cloud' (34) translates a common Hebrew word first occurring in Genesis 9:13 ('I do set my bow in the cloud') and is consistently used in Exodus for the visible presence of the Lord (18 references in all). The cloud guided them (13:21); protected them from their enemies (14:20); warned them that their God is a consuming fire (19:16); shrouded the majesty of his person from the untried eyes of sinful Israel (19:21); assured them of mercy after judgment (34: 5–7); and verified for the youngest child the covenant faithfulness of Israel's God. The glowing pillar of fire by night would be an unforgettable memory for every infant who survived the wilderness wanderings. But our privilege is higher and therefore more solemn (Matt. 18:20).

QUESTION:
Exodus opened with Israel as slaves in Egypt, and closed with Israel redeemed but in a wilderness. Taking this as a type of the believer's experience, what blessings, afforded Israel in the wilderness, are now ours?

THE PICTORIAL GOSPEL OF
THE 'OLD TESTAMENT'

Dr Andrew Bonar, in his rich commentary on Leviticus, calls
this book 'the pictorial gospel of the Old Testament'. Let us
therefore approach the reading of it with eyes wide open for the
Saviour. William Cowper, to the same effect, sings thus in one
of his *Olney Hymns*:

> 'Israel, in ancient days,
>   Not only had a view
> Of Sinai in a blaze,
>   But learned the gospel too;
> The types and figures were a glass
> In which they saw a Saviour's face'

The Epistle to the Hebrews lays down the principles for the
interpretation of Leviticus. There are some forty new Testament references to this book. As Christ is the centre and soul of
all Scripture, so we shall look for the unveiling of his saving and
sanctifying work in the types and shadows of this third book of
Moses. Tyndale the Reformer, in his Prologue to this book,
insists that there is a 'starlight of Christ' in all the ceremonies,
and in some of them 'the light of broad day'.

The two main divisions are: chapters 1–16, the way of
approach to God, through the Mediator, culminating in the
great day of atonement (chapter 16): chapters 17–27, the way of
communion with God, with the emphasis upon the sanctified
life. Chapters 1–7 set forth the law of the offerings and teach us
that there is no access to God save through the blood of
atonement. They point forward to, and have their fulfilment in,
the death of our Lord Jesus Christ. See Hebrews 10:19 and
commit it to memory today.

TWO OFFERINGS

The burnt offering of Chapter 1 involved the shedding of blood and required first and foremost the confession of sin and its expiation (1:4). It also meant the offering up by fire of the entire sacrifice (except the hide, 7:8) thus symbolizing the full surrender of the offerer to God, body, mind, spirit – with everything he was or had or wished to be. Paul surely had this sacrifice in mind in Romans 12:1.

The meal offering of chapter 2 is called 'meat offering' in the Authorized Version because meal was the staple food of the people (cp. English usage: 'Grace before meat'). Here there was no blood and no thought of atonement for sin. When the offerer had, by the burnt offering, been reconciled to God through the shed blood, he came next to give up his whole substance to the Lord who had redeemed him. The moment we are pardoned, all we are and all we have become the property of Christ (1 Cor. 6:19). Until our sin and guilt are dealt with by the atoning sacrifice we cannot properly offer ourselves or our possessions to Christ. The Lord knows that the circumstances of his people differ greatly; hence the three varieties of meal offerings according to one's means (cp. the widow's mites, and our Lord's comment in Mark 12: 41–44).

QUESTION:
What light do the burnt offering and the meal offering shed upon the incident of Cain and Abel's sacrifices (Gen. 4)?

[63]

THE PEACE OFFERING

First turn your thoughts to Romans 5:1: 'Therefore being justified by faith, we have *peace* with God through our Lord Jesus Christ'. The connection with the two preceding offerings is this: when I am justified (burnt offering) and surrendered (meal offering), I delight in the rich benefits of a new-found peace and fellowship with God and with all who are his blood-bought children. The peace offering was a shared meal in which a portion was burnt (3–5) symbolizing the fact that our peace with God is the first concern and is sealed only in the atoning sacrifice of Christ. 'There is no peace, saith my God, to the wicked.'

But the new feature in this sacrifice is the fact that the residue of the flesh is to be a meal provided by God for the worshipper and his family, and for the priests (see 7: 11–21). Here we see symbolized the holy supper where he who is our sacrificial Lamb spreads the feast and provides the whole meal. This is no solitary feast, but a communion in his shed blood with all his people, a nourishing of his pilgrim church until he calls us home. As no believer can properly come to the Lord's table with unconfessed sin barring his access to God, so here, reconciliation with God precedes the privileges of the table and reconciliation with our brethren is implied.

For an illustration of how the holiest ordinances may be abused notice that the woman in Proverbs 7 had just made a peace offering and brought a portion home (7:14).

[64]

INADVERTENT SIN

It is a solemn fact that the Levitical sacrifices made no provision for deliberate acts of sin, done with a high hand. The sin-offering (chapter 4) and trespass-offering (chapter 5) are to meet the sins of ignorance of God's people (2) done 'unwittingly', or 'through ignorance'. Nothing is commoner today than to excuse such unconscious or unwitting transgressions. How low is our view of sin, and of God's holiness! Even sins of ignorance break the soul's communion with God and demand the fresh cleansing and expiation of the sacrificial blood. The requirements of the sin-offering were graded according to the responsible position of the transgressor (1) the anointed priest (i.e. the high priest) (3–12); (2) the whole congregation of Israel (13–21); (3) a ruler (22–26); (4) one of the common people (27–35). Clearly, guilt varies according to rank, though all are guilty. God's righteousness cannot overlook any sin, however trivial in our unfeeling view. Thank God, his love has made provision for those very sins. Our High Priest 'can have compassion on the ignorant' (Heb. 5:2).

PRAYER:

> *'Who can understand his errors?*
> *Cleanse thou me from secret faults'.*
>   *(Psa. 19:12)*

THE TRESPASS OFFERING

The difference between this and the sin-offering of chapter 4 is that in the sin-offering the main thought is that of *guilt*; hence the emphasis is upon expiation. In the trespass-offering the stress is upon the *injury* done to God (and man) and hence the emphasis is on satisfaction (including restitution). In all these sacrifices we have seen that the forgiveness of sin, and the reconciliation of God and the sinner, are possible only through the blood of atonement. How then can we explain the bloodless sacrifice of the poor man who cannot afford even the two birds (11–13)? His sin-offering of fine flour was burnt on the altar, 'upon the offerings of the Lord made by fire' (12 R.V.). The fine flour mingled with the fire offerings which were on the altar, and in this sense partook of the nature of a blood-sacrifice. 'In this way, what appears to be an exception to the principle that "without shedding of blood is no forgiveness of sins" (Heb. 9:22) . . . rather serves to illustrate the principle of vicarious substitution which it is the main object of the ritual of sacrifice to illustrate and enforce' (O. T. Allis in *The New Bible Commentary*).

QUESTION:
It is clear from verse 16 that restitution as directed must first be made before the slaying of the ram and the removal of the guilt. How does this illustrate Matthew 5: 23–24 and 1 Corinthians 11: 27–29?

THE CONSECRATION OF AARON
AND HIS SONS

Exodus closed with the account of the rearing of the tabernacle and its dedication (chapter 40). The furnishings are now all in order. But there is no consecrated priesthood to perform the divinely-planned services. Leviticus, chapters 1–7 are taken up with the law of the sacrifices. This precedes the consecration of Aaron and his sons, because the offering of sacrifices on their behalf was a pre-requisite of their own consecration to office. Chapters 8 to 10 now deal with their consecration and its consequences. What significance do you see in the role which Moses surprisingly fills as officiating priest (6, 10, 15, 18, 22 etc.)? He clearly acts for God as a kind of Melchizedek – prophet, priest and king (cp. Heb. 3: 2,5). The anointing oil was not sprinkled but was 'poured' upon Aaron's head (12), a picture of the Spirit poured without measure upon Jesus our High Priest. The sin-offering (14–17), the burnt-offering (18–21) and the consecration offering (22–29) were all accompanied by Aaron and his sons laying their hands upon the sacrificial victims. Verses 23–24 teach that their entire persons, with all their faculties and powers, are now consecrated to the Lord and to his service.

QUESTION:
'Ear – hand – foot' (23–24). In what ways do these symbolize the consecration of the entire life?

AARON'S BLESSING FOLLOWED
BY GOD'S JUDGMENT

The climax of these days of consecration of the nation's priests comes when Aaron blesses the great congregation assembled outside the tent. Perhaps he used the familiar words of the Aaronic benediction recorded in Numbers 6: 24–26. The fire of God consumed the sacrifices – the sacred fire which henceforth must not be allowed to go out. Then, as if to reveal the depths of sin in the hearts of the best of God's servants, there is recorded the act of sacrilege of Aaron's sons. Had they been drinking? Verses 9–11 give room for this conjecture and would explain the divine prohibition of verse 9. The searching aspect of their sin lies in the closing words of verse 1: 'which (God) commanded them not'. They offered worship, they were priests, they did this 'before the Lord'. Surely no blame should attach to such well-intentioned ministry! Yet swift judgment from God destroyed them both. There is no place in the worship of God for strange fire, for man-made novelties, for rank human pride and independence. 'Will-worship in any form is hateful to the Lord's holy nature' (A. A. Bonar).

QUESTION:
Are we right to interpret the words 'which he (God) commanded them not' as equivalent to 'which he expressly forbade'?

[68]

LEPROSY AND ITS LESSONS

Two long chapters are devoted to leprosy in Israel; how it is to be diagnosed (chapter 13) and how the symptom-free leper is to be restored to the fellowship of God and the society of his own people (chapter 14). 'Jehovah opens up sin under the figure of leprosy – sin, disgusting, diffusive, penetrating' (A. A. Bonar). But he does this, not only to confound us with its horror, but to point us to the remedy. The gospel is more than searching diagnosis; it is infallible treatment under the compassionate hand of the great Physician. The leper's sickness has placed him outside the camp. Thither the priest must go (3). If the leper is healed, a ritual is prescribed that covers seven days. The ritual with the two birds on the first day (4) is one of purification only, and not of sacrifice: the blood of the slain bird was not brought to the altar. The ritual of the eighth day is different in intention (10). The cleansed leper now offers three sacrifices – a trespass offering (12), a sin offering and a burnt offering (19). He has been brought to the very door of the sanctuary (11). The anointing with oil represents the consecration of the restored leper to the service of God. Cleansed lepers are as welcome to the blood and the oil as consecrated priests. The water (5) must have blood *in* it; the oil (17) must have blood *under* it.

[69]

THE DAY OF ATONEMENT

Having read today's graphic narrative of the solemn pageantry of the day of atonement in Israel, try to imagine the moral and spiritual impact of such an annual ceremony upon your town. All work has ceased (31); a solemn fast day prevails. The whole nation has been summoned in silence as awed and trembling observers, participating in this face-to-face encounter with God through their appointed representative (2) and in the appointed way (3–34). Provision has already been made for the expiation of every man's own sin in the sin-offering (chapter 4) and trespass-offering (chapter 5). The purpose of the sacrifices of the day of atonement is one comprehensive and all-inclusive act of total expiation of the sins of the whole nation, upon a stated day every year. Aaron first brings a sin-offering 'for himself and for his house' (6,17): In this priestly confession of personal sin Aaron differs from our High Priest (Heb. 7: 26–28). But the sacrifices brought to Aaron from 'the congregation' (5,17) properly typify the atoning death of Christ (cp. John 11: 49–53).

CONSIDER (7–10):
'The first goat had most to do with the glory of God; the second with the conscience of the sinner.'

THE MERCY SEAT

Aaron now offers the sacrifices for the nation's sins (15–19). The goat's blood is sprinkled eight times – once *upon* the mercy seat and seven times *before* the mercy seat. The mercy seat is the place of propitiation and has given its name to this word where it occurs in the New Testament (cp. Romans 3: 24–25; 1 John 2:2). There, and there alone, the holy God can enter into fellowship with redeemed sinners, and that, because of the atoning blood which satisfies heaven's justice and declares heaven's love. James Denney writes, 'It is in his blood that Christ is endued with propitiatory power; and there is no propitiatory power of blood known to Scripture unless the blood of sacrifice . . . An essential element in a propitiation is that it should vindicate the Divine righteousness. It should proclaim with unmistakable clearness that with sin God can hold no terms . . . In Christ's death it is made once for all apparent that God does not palter with sin; the doom of sin falls by his appointment on the Redeemer . . . It is the love of God which provides the propitiation by which God's righteousness is vindicated and the justification of the ungodly made possible'. (Commentary on Romans in Expositor's Greek Testament.) This was the heart of the Lord's message to his people on the annual Day of Atonement, and this is the heart of the gospel of God's grace in Jesus Christ.

THE BLOOD

'The life of the flesh is in the blood; . . . it is the blood that maketh an atonement for your souls' (11). All that has gone before (chapters 1–16), culminating in the blood sprinkled upon and before the mercy seat (16: 14–16), supplies the explanation of the two laws laid down in chapter 17. (1) *There were to be no private sacrifices* (1–9). Note the threefold requirement that every man's sacrifice (A.V. 'killeth', verse 3 has this meaning) must be brought 'unto the tabernacle . . . unto the priest . . . unto the Lord' (5). The tabernacle is the only place of sacrifice; the priest is the only mediator for the sinner; the Lord is the only one to whom sacrifice is to be offered. 'The open field' (5) is a symbol of freelance religion which shuns the atoning cross and assumes man's right to his Creator's indulgence. Hence the severity of the judgment pronounced by God in verses 4 and 9. 'Devils' (7 A.V.) is 'he-goats' in R.V. Another translation has 'false gods' and points to the worship of Pan which was widespread in the ancient world, and in Israel as a relic of their long sojourn in Egypt.

(2) *No blood was to be eaten* (10–16). God here gives a simple yet fundamental reason for this prohibition, which we first find in Genesis 9:4. The vital life of the animal is in the blood. When this is drained away, life is gone. God has made this blood the symbol of life, violently taken in sacrifice for sin, and offered in expiation upon his altar.

'THOU SHALT LOVE THY
NEIGHBOUR AS THYSELF'

The New Testament is bejewelled with this command (Matt. 22:39; Rom. 13:9; Gal. 5:14; Jas. 2:8), but a careless reading of the Sermon on the Mount at Matthew 5:43 has helped to foster a widespread suspicion of the Old Testament as if it stood in sharp contrast. The Mosaic law was God's law and in both Old Testament and New Testament it is the same Voice that we hear. Today's reading is a series of practical illustrations of how to love one's neighbour with robust realism. It begins with godly fear (1–4) and places filial love first after love for God (3). It studies the poor and the stranger in its legislation about gleaning (9–10). It searches out hidden vices like lying (11) talebearing (16) and nursing a grudge (17–18). It deals with the commonplace of casual work and daily wages (13). It knows and judges the nasty vice of mocking the cobbler for his black thumbs, and deriving amusement from the physical infirmities of others. Has the need for this legislation ceased? Has society outgrown these vices? Has the Christian triumphed over them?

Underline the 15 occurrences of 'I am the Lord (your God)' in Chapter 19. Account for this refrain.

SABBATH, SANCTUARY AND SOCIAL STANDARDS

These three stand or fall together. 'Take away the river that waters the roots of the tree and soon you will see the leaves wither and the sap dry up.' Andrew Bonar is here pointing to the intimate connection between the reverent observance of the Lord's Day, the faithful attendance at the Lord's house and the flourishing of healthy social standards in the nation. What is the remedy for the rising cults of black magic (31), the insolent disregard of age (32), the disappearance of the Good Samaritan from our highways (33–34), and the shoddy standards of the thirty-five hour week (35–36)? The remedy lies in the fearless and sustained preaching of the Word, the whole Word and nothing but the Word. This exalts God in his holiness, brings man's sins and violence to the bar of absolute justice, gives the arrogant wrongdoer no peace, leads to wide-spread conviction of sin issuing in Holy Ghost conversions and heaven-sent revival. This is the inseparable link between sabbath, sanctuary and social standards.

PRAYER:
'Wilt thou not revive us again; that thy people may rejoice in thee?'
(Psalm 85:6)

[74]

'THE NAME'

Shelomith's son (10–11) was doubtless as precious to her as any other growing lad to his mother. This execution was no rough desert justice but the revealed sentence of Heaven (12) carried out with careful precision and awful solemnity (14,23). 'The Name' (11 R.V.) means 'Jehovah'. The origin of the expression may be found in Exodus 3: 13–15. Almost certainly the apostle Paul applies the title to Christ in the words of Philippians 2:9; 'He hath given him a name which is above every name . . .' This incident led to a new law (15–16). The fact of the lad being the son of a Jewish mother and of an Egyptian father served to show that the law applied impartially to the Jew and to the stranger.

'Tooth for tooth.' The barbaric retaliatory spirit in the soul of man is here brought under divine restraint. Personal injuries are made the subject of proper laws (17–22). God is here speaking as Chief Justice of the nation. When he enjoins 'tooth for tooth, eye for eye,' it is not done as the scribes enjoined; it is not done by way of private vengeance (Matt. 5:38). On the contrary it is done judicially, upon the sound principle that, so far as possible, the punishment should fit the crime.

MEDITATION:
'The way to preserve the peace of the church is to preserve the purity of it.'

THE JUBILEE

We have nothing which answers even remotely to the Hebrew year of release. Our mortgages run on until we repay them; our alienated land is lost for good. Our school and church jubilees are mostly grateful festivals. The very word Jubilee is from the Hebrew 'Jobel' which seems to derive from the ram's horn trumpet which announced the nation's year of rest (9). This always began on the evening of the Day of Atonement, to show that salvation in Christ is the root and source of all national blessings. Property reverted to its original owners (13), debts were extinguished, those sold into servitude secured instant and final release. Business deals were regulated according to the nearness of the year of Jubilee (14–17). God promised enough food to meet the needs of the people in their Sabbatical and Jubilee years (21–22). These years of rest were to be spent in the study of the law of God (Deut. 31:10), a kind of all-age programme of religious education recurring every seventh year.

QUESTION:
Compare the command to work the land (3) and the command to rest the land (4) with these two aspects of the Fourth Commandment (Exod. 20: 9–10). Do you agree that it is neglect of the first aspect which easily leads to the breach of the second?

'IF . . . IF NOT'

Chapter 27 may be regarded as a kind of appendix on vows and tithes. Chapter 26 is the fitting climax of the Book of Leviticus and compares in tone and solemnity with Deuteronomy 29–30. The 'if' of verse 3 introduces the *promised blessings* of God upon an obedient Israel (3–13). These are vivid, homely, heartening word-pictures, closing upon the note of God's right to command because he has redeemed his people. 'Was it not I . . . that . . . struck the chains from your necks, and gave you the upright carriage of free men?' (13). The 'if not' of verse 14 introduces the *threatened penalties* upon Israel's disobedience (14–39). 'The curses, or judgments, that follow are the effects of despising the blessing [15, 'despise . . . abhor'] . . . They illustrate that misery which arises from rejecting the offers of grace. Israel needed to be warned of this danger in special, for it was to characterize their history. The judgments mentioned here did not fall on heathen nations (A. A. Bonar). It is a terrible thing to be taught of God and then to despise his Word to our soul (Heb. 10: 28–29).

QUESTION:
Why is more space given to the evils which are threatened than to the blessings which are promised?

'I WILL REMEMBER'

As God 'remembered Noah' (Gen. 8:1) after the deluge had done its premeditated work, so God promises to 'remember' Israel upon their confessing their iniquity (40). This remembering is another word for God's grace, his active mercy, his cleansing love. Not for nothing does it occur three times in verse 42, finding its explanation in the word 'covenant' and its roots in Genesis 12. This covenant conveyed a grant of the land. Israel's repentance and Israel's restoration to her estates go together. The passage is prophetic and has in view the captivity in Babylon and the gracious return of the remnant. The return will bring blessing to the nation; it will also bring blessing to the land – 'I will remember the land' (42). These words were spoken at the foot of Sinai. Jehovah sees the end from the beginning. He knew their hearts. He did not choose them for their worthiness. He chose them to show forth the meaning of his grace.

MEDITATION:
'When I look to my guiltiness I see that my salvation is one of my Saviour's greatest miracles, either in heaven or earth'. (Samuel Rutherford)

THE SECOND LAW

Every generation needs to be reborn. In this sense the church is always only one generation away from extinction. If left to man, that would be its fate. But Deuteronomy begins and ends with God, and all the way through he keeps reminding Israel of this fact. 'The Lord's portion is his people. Jacob is the lot of his inheritance. He found him in a desert land and in the waste howling wilderness; he led him about, he instructed him, he kept him as the apple of his eye' (32: 9,10).

The old rebellious Israel who heard the first Law at Sinai is all but extinct (2:14). In the 38 years of wandering a new generation has grown up, uncircumcised, illiterate, the children of murmurers and complainers (12). They sorely need the ministry of the plains of Moab and the disciplinary refresher course of Deuteronomy, the Second Law. In verse 5 the Hebrew word for 'declare' seems to be connected with the reducing of the Law to writing. It would seem that, at this juncture, Moses, shortly before his death, put the laws and the history in permanent form. No doubt he had the same strong motive as a New Testament writer, the Apostle Peter: 'Moreover, I will endeavour that ye may be able after my decease to have these things always in remembrance' (2 Pet. 1:15).

PISGAH

It is a minister's duty to read the Obituary columns. Some time ago, as I glanced down the back page of the New Zealand Herald, I noticed half a column in fine type entitled 'The End of the Pilgrim Journey'. It had been contributed by Dr W. H. Pettit, one of the 'fathers' of the Scripture Union in New Zealand, as a testimony to the way a Christian faces death, for his wife had recently gone to be with Christ. Here is the opening sentence: 'The note of triumph which gilds with ineffable glory the sudden home call of the Christian to be for ever with the Lord is inimitably portrayed in the closing words of Bunyan's *Pilgrim's Progress*.' In the long and moving account which Bunyan gives of Christian's entry to the Celestial City is this extract: 'Then I saw in my dream that the Shining Ones bid them call at the gate: the which, when they did, some from above looked over the gate, to wit, Enoch, Moses, Elijah etc. . .' We cannot hope to enter into the longing in the soul of this grand old man of the pilgrimage as he besought the Lord, 'Let me go over and see the good land that is beyond Jordan' (25). God granted him his request in a far more glorious way than he desired. Before Joshua had led Israel across the Jordan Moses had crossed his Jordan to 'see the King in his beauty and to behold the land that is very far off'.

NOTE:
The Lord's, 'Let it suffice thee' (26) is a sharp reproof and also a hint that far more than Moses asks for is in store for him.

GOD'S STATUTE BOOK

Pigs are an important factor in the social life of the South Sea islanders. The festivals associated with the acceptance of a new chief, or with marriage, involve the slaughter of great numbers of pigs. The animals are kept in an extensive yard on the fringe of the bush. They are hedged in, either by a stone wall, or by a palisade of fence posts erected side by side. A wily old pig may sometimes be seen working his way along the palisade testing each picket with his snout. When he finds a weak or rotting post he worries away at it until he has made an opening. Then out he struggles to the freedom of the bush, the rest of the pig-yard squealing and jostling their way out after him. The human heart is like that, for ever seeking a way to breach the palisade of God's laws. Hence the warnings which preface the Second Law in today's reading. God sees our proneness to tinker with his statute book (2), to sit lightly by his laws (6), to forget them (9), and to neglect to teach them to our family (9). Here are four common evasions of God's commandments. The first evasion is a crime against God, and is frequently referred to in Scripture. See Deuteronomy 12:32, Proverbs 30:6, Revelation 22: 18,19; and note carefully our Lord's exposure of this crime in Matthew 15: 3–9.

QUESTION:
Which of these four tendencies do you find most frequently in your own heart? Have you ever found yourself saying, 'But that's in the Old *Testament!' Christ's attitude to the* Old *Testament should be decisive for the Christian: see Matthew 5: 17–20.*

PREACHING THE TEN COMMANDMENTS

Over quite a number of years spent in the same parish the writer
of these notes preached a course of sermons on the Ten
Commandments thrice. Each time he was impressed by the
eagerness of the congregation not to miss any of the addresses.
He was also impressed by their long memories for these
sermons. Why is this? One reason is that our hearts, if honest,
tell us that we need the constant repetition of the law to sensitize
us against the hardening influences of our daily life. The law
gets our conscience functioning normally towards God. This in
turn leads us to a higher sense of God's purity and holiness. And
that serves to deepen our own healthy sense of spiritual and
moral failure and shortcoming. Thus the law is spiritual, as
Paul confessed (Rom. 7:14), and points the sinner to the only
fountain opened for sin and for uncleanness (Zech. 13:1). The
law does this for the believer also, and saves him from seductive
spiritual pride or from an easy-going complacency. 'Sanctification grafts the law upon the soul' (Kupyer). 'Only the grace of
God can enable man to keep the commandments. But it is
exactly in order that man should keep them that grace is given'
(G. T. Manley).

WHY WE NEED THE TEN COMMANDMENTS:
*'The doctrine of the law remains, through Christ, inviolable, which
by tuition, admonition, reproof and correction, forms and prepares
us for every good work' (Calvin).*

THE KERNEL AND THE HUSK

The Ten Commandments are the kernel of the law of God and hence are given first in this comprehensive address by Moses. This is the meaning of the words 'and he added no more' (22). The rest of the legislation is in the nature of subordinate regulations which derive their significance from the covenant entered into by God with Israel at Sinai. We may compare them with the regulations made under Authority of an Act of Parliament. Both Act and regulations proceed from the same source, and have the same authority, but the Act is the kernel and the regulations are the husk of the covenant legislation. Moses recalls the original solemn setting and circumstances (22,23); and shows that the Ten Commandments were not invented by him, but delivered to him by God (22). Had they been written by the finger of God on baked clay men might, with some show of justice, have argued for their transience. But the finger of God wrote them on tables of stone to point to their permanence. 'They are a law of life both to the regenerate and to the degenerate' (Lecerf). The nation signified its acceptance of God's conditions when the elders said, 'We will hear it, and do it' (27). And God signified his heart's delight with this acceptance when he added 'They have well said all that they have spoken' (28). Try to memorise verse 29.

THE MEDIATOR:
Moses is here seen as mediator between God and the nation ('stand thou here by me' (31)). In this respect he is a type of Christ (Gal. 3:19).

[83]

THE HEBREW CREED

Verses 4 and 5 are singled out by our Lord as 'the first and great commandment' (Mk. 12: 29,30). Embedded in them is a doctrinal fact – the unity of God. The unity of Jehovah is the key-note of the Jewish faith. It was not a discovery of the Hebrew people, but a revelation of Israel's God. The nation was surrounded in Egypt by many gods. In Canaan they would again find many gods. The living and true God is one. The Hebrew word for 'one' in verse 4 is significant, viewed in the light of the fuller revelation of the New Testament. It stands not for absolute unity, but for compound unity, and is thus consistent with both of the names of God employed in this verse. *Jehovah* ('Lord') emphasizes his oneness. *Elohim* ('God') emphasizes the three divine Persons. The revelation of God as Triune, though seen in the Old Testament in these veiled ways, was explicitly revealed when the Father sent the Son to be the Saviour of the world; and the Father and Son sent the Holy Spirit to represent Them in the church:
'Long before the Christian church fixed its faith in certain binding formulas, this very faith had been sung or confessed in the liturgy. In the worship of the church the Trinitarian formula was present long before it was fixed in the Trinitarian dogma' (Klaas Runia, *I Believe in God*).

THE ELECTION OF ISRAEL

There never was a time when the people of God stood in greater need of this bracing doctrine of the election of Israel. The seven nations which Israel was asked to dispossess (1) have since swarmed over the face of the earth. They threaten the life of the Israel of God. There are those who counsel God's church to come to terms with them. Unable to beat them we must join them! But this is not God's idea of election. Election commits God's Israel to warfare, not diplomacy or sloth (2); to uncompromising puritanism (3,5), not to endless experiments in the secularisation of the church (3,4). Every trace of alien gods and alien worship must be removed (5). Only after these obligations have been laid upon Israel does God confide in them the miracle and mystery of his electing love (6–8). Notice particularly the word 'love'; underline it in verses 7, 8 & 9. What are the other key words in God's vocabulary of election? Thread these jewels on the golden necklace of grace: holy, chosen, special, oath, redeemed, faithful, covenant, mercy. Is there any statement in verses 6–9 which you doubt or disown? Is there any ingredient in the New Testament doctrine of election which is missing from these verses?

NOTE:
'a special people' *(6). The same word occurs as 'peculiar treasure' (Exod. 19:5); 'jewels' (Mal. 3:17); and to describe King David's private property in 1 Chronicles 29:3.*

'REMEMBER'

Underline the two occurrences of 'remember' in verses 2 and 18. The first is a call to gratitude for God's guidance in the *past*. And what a past! Forty years of multiplied miracle and mercy (2–6); and the greatest miracle of all, the fact that God chastened Israel as a son, instead of rejecting him as a worthless ne'er-do-well (5). The second 'remember' (18) is a call to loyal obedience in the *future* based upon heart attachment to Jehovah and fidelity to his commandments.

'*Forget*'. Now underline the three occurrences of 'forget' in verses 11, 14 and 19. These all occur in the context of the pleasant life in the goodly land into which God is about to bring them. It is so easy to forget when we have eaten and are full (10–12) and when our silver and gold are multiplied (13–14). How long does it take a Christian to forget the Lord's mercy? Paul asks the Galatians 'Where is the blessedness ye spake of?' (Gal. 4:15). In the prosperous conditions of our day it is fatally easy to forget the Lord our God (19), to apologize to ourselves for our early zeal; to soak up luxury and comfort; and to forget that man does not live by bread alone (3).

ALL OF GRACE

The theme of Moses' message at this point is the grace of God. His grace is lavished upon his people Israel in spite of what they were and are. The victories which will make possible their entrance into Canaan are God's victories. Their dispossessing the sons of Anak will be God's work (2). Three times in verse 3 the emphatic Hebrew pronoun is used for God's decisive initiative – 'He . . . He . . . He'. These promises are not given to free Israel from strenuous fighting. 'He will destroy if Israel drives them out. We must do our endeavour in dependence upon God's grace; and we shall have that grace if we do our endeavour' (Matthew Henry). Verses 4–8 most vividly set forth the crimson emblems of grace. Grace is not merited by any supposed superiority of goodness in Israel, or in us. The record of the wilderness years shows that Israel was a stiff-necked people (7–8). The record of our pilgrimage since first we sought the Saviour is no better. Not because of Israel's goodness, but because of the Canaanites' badness, God is granting these dramatic victories (4). The whole point of God's grace is this, that all whom he rejects are rejected for their own wickedness; but none of those whom he accepts are accepted for their own righteousness. *A distinction.* The *calling* of Israel is unconditional, sovereign and irrevocable. The *blessings* are conditional upon obedience (chapter 28). The *calling* vests the promise in Abraham's 'seed' which is Christ (Gal. 3:16) and to all who are 'in Christ' (G. T. Manley).

PREVAILING PRAYER

It is best to read verses 18 and 25 as referring to the same period of forty days and forty nights which immediately followed upon the second occasion on which Moses was with the Lord on Mt. Sinai. This latter period terminated with the incident of the golden calf, God's declared purpose to destroy the people, and Moses' descent and deliberate shattering of the covenanted law in the face of the rebellious nation (17). Then ensued Moses' agony of prayer (18ff.) which kept him fasting and prostrate before God for forty days and forty nights. Notice *the marks of Moses' prevailing intercession*: He was burdened for their sin, the most terrible condition of the human race (18). He knew the fearful *fate* which awaited Israel if God gave them their deserts (19). He pleaded God's covenant made with their fathers (27). He reminded God of his own honour which was inseparably tied to his people's future (28). He persevered in what seemed a forlorn hope for forty days and forty nights (25). He renounced all self-interest in his prayers (14b). He was concerned for the individual as well as for the nation (20). He prayed on until he had assurance: 'The Lord hearkened unto me at that time' (19).

MEDITATION:
Moses had learned to say 'thy' not 'my'. Underline the significant pronouns in his prayer (26–29), and seek to apply this lesson as a corrective to self-centred prayer.

RECONCILIATION

Chapter 9 was a searching reminder of Irael's sin. Chapter 10 is
a reassuring reminder of God's mercy. Both chapters should be
taken together as illustrating two chief inducements to obedience. God now gave Israel *four pledges of his reconciliation to
them*: he wrote out afresh the shattered Law of the covenant as
the firm and enduring evidence of his favour and their fealty
(1–5); he led them on toward Canaan (7–8); he gave them a
settled ministry (8–9); he accepted Moses as mediator and
intercessor for the erring nation (10–11). In the second part of
the reading we hear *Moses' appeal to the nation* (12–22). First
Moses stresses *their duty to God* (12–15). They are to adore his
majesty, acknowledge his authority, revere his Person, and fear
his wrath. Then Moses stresses *their duty to themselves* (16–17),
to rid themselves of all corrupt thoughts, words and deeds, and
to live their lives in the full blaze of God's holiness. Finally
Moses stresses *their duty to others* (18–22). The hard-up Israelite
had the backing of his family and clan, but the 'stranger' was
absolutely alone and helpless. Hence the repeated directions
about helping the 'stranger'. They are to '*love*' . . . the stranger'
and are reminded that in doing so they are but imitating God
(18). 'I am more and more impressed by the command to be
hospitable and to entertain strangers' (Oswald Chambers in his
diary).

FOURSQUARE OBEDIENCE:
'*To fear . . . to walk . . . to love . . . to serve*' (*12*).

[89]

HOLY GROUND

All the passion and pathos of Mrs Hemans' *Pilgrim Fathers*
wells up in the opening verses of today's reading. Israel's quest
is 'freedom to worship God'. The ageing Moses is filled with the
eloquence of a God-centred appeal which loses none of its lilt
and light by reason of his approaching death. He will not drink
of these perennial streams, nor eat the produce of its fertile
fields. But he speaks as one who knows he understates the
blessings in store for those who wholly follow the Lord. It was
the height of summer when I saw the Holy Land. Water melons
were piled beside the country roads. Crops of sunflowers
drooped their heads, heavy with succulent seeds. Across the
Jordan in Amman the cultivated fields had just been shorn of
golden crops and lay bristly with sharp stubble. There is every
reason to believe that the rape of the soil has been especially
savage in Palestine. But despite it all we see, through the haze of
history, 'a land which the Lord . . . careth for. The eyes of the
Lord are always upon it, from the beginning of the year even
unto the end of the year' (12). With this chapter Moses closes on
a solemn note his eloquent preface to Deuteronomy. The
blessing and the curse of verses 26–28 will be repeated with
even greater solemnity and detail in chapter 28.

NOTE ON VERSE 20:
*'In the houses of orthodox Jews today there may be seen in the porch
a small box containing a copy of Deuteronomy 6: 4–9' (G. T.
Manley).*

THE POOR (7–11)

A life insurance man told me that he has many business friends among the Jews of Auckland city. Spontaneously he added 'and they know how to look after one another.' He instanced cases of poverty, misfortune and death in which immediate relief had been provided by fellow Jews. The Jews are notable for the care they take of their poor. Where did they learn this? From the Torah, the directions of this and other passages of the Old Testament. Widespread prosperity does not make people generous. Rather the reverse, as any collector for Bible Societies will agree. Verses 9 & 10 are a little sermon to Christians on how to give as God would have us give.

Slavery (12–18). These laws would apply to those who had sold themselves as servants, or had been sold by their parents through extreme poverty (2 Kings 4:1), or as punishment for some crime. Jot down the humane provisions of verses 12–18. It is almost as if a parent were liberally loading his son or daughter with gifts in anticipation of marriage!

John Newton (1725–1807) before his conversion spent years in the African slave-trade. In his study, as a minister of the gospel, he had hanging the text of verse 15 (beneath Isaiah 43:4).

NEGLECT OF DUTY IS SIN:
For examples, see verse 9, and compare 23:21 & 24:15. What are the duties here mentioned? How do they crop up in present-day life?

THREE FESTIVALS

This chapter deals with the three great feasts (festivals) of the Jewish calendar – the Passover, the Feast of weeks, and the Feast of tabernacles.

The Passover (1–8) was primarily a festival of remembrance (3) and points to the Lord's Supper which we observe in remembrance of him (1 Cor. 11: 24–25). But note that it was immediately followed by the Festival of unleavened bread (3) which finds its anti-type in our putting away of the leaven of malice and wickedness (1 Cor. 5: 7,8). The Passover offering had to be a lamb or kid (Exod. 12:5). The following day the Feast of unleavened bread was ushered in with the sacrifice of bullocks (Num. 28:19). The final day of the Feast of unleavened bread was to be a day of humiliation and fasting as the word 'solemn' (lit. 'restraint') implies.

The Feast of weeks (Pentecost, 9–12). The Passover celebrates the deliverance from Egypt: Pentecost marks the entry into the land of promise. Here, in New Testament language, we pass from Easter to Pentecost. Note that the time lapse of seven weeks was to be counted from the day after the sabbath (Exod. 23:16). Thus God marvellously crowned these Old Testament festivals with profound fulfilment in the death and resurrection of Christ and then, fifty days later, in the sending of the Holy Spirit and the first-fruits of the Spirit.

'HARVEST HOME'

It will be hard for the family which buys everything at a
supermarket to sense the hilarity of this event. The Feast of
tabernacles was to be the climax of the year for Israel as an
agricultural nation in Canaan. The spirit of Henry Alford's
harvest hymn must have pervaded this week-long festival:

> Come, ye thankful people, come,
> Raise the song of harvest home:
> All is safely gathered in,
> Ere the winter storms begin;
> God, our Maker, doth provide
> For our wants to be supplied:
> Come to God's own temple, come,
> Raise the song of harvest-home.

Joy and gratitude were to be the theme as the whole nation
celebrated God's goodness in the matter of daily bread. 'Thou
shalt be altogether joyful' (15 R.V.). Nor was their gratitude to
be a matter of mere words: 'No one shall present himself before
the Lord empty-handed' (16). This festival is the type of the
final harvest when God's angels will put in the sickle and the
elect will be gathered in, and the tares burned (Matt. 13: 37–
43).

'Justice, justice shalt thou follow' (18–20). This refrain, which
translates quite literally the opening clause of verse 20, may be
taken as one of the grand axioms of Israel's moral and social
structure. 'Justice' here anticipates Magna Carta, the Bill of
Rights and the Habeas Corpus Act by two and a half
millenniums. And it means more than a square deal for small
and great alike. Justice and righteousness are almost synonyms.

THE KING AND THE CONSTITUTION

Israel already had a King and a constitution. Jehovah was the nation's King. Hence Israel is called, not a democracy but a theocracy – a nation governed by God. Into this theocracy God now *permits* the introduction of a viceroy 'whom the Lord thy God shall choose' (15). He is to make the God-given constitution his constant study, personally transcribing a copy for his own use (19). He is subject to the constitution, not above it. The King must be 'one from among thy brethren', a qualification beautifully realized in David, and most eminently in David's greater Son (Heb. 2: 11–12). The natural tendency to 'trust in chariots' must yield to dependence upon the mighty God, whose chariots are twenty thousand (Psa. 68:17). Egypt was the source of both chariots and horses. It was also the source of idolatrous contamination in Israel. Therefore Egypt must be renounced with all its works, a picture of the old life which dominated our thoughts before our conversion (16). It was in the breach of verses 16 and 17 that Solomon took the first fatal steps which led Israel into apostasy and ultimate collapse.

OUR CONFIDENCE:
'Some trust in chariots, and some in horses: but we will remember the name of the Lord our God' (Psa. 20:7).

GOD OR A GHOST (9–14)

Those who know the abiding fellowship of a personal Saviour do not need the auguries of the people who read teacups. The good old-fashioned doctrine of God's particular care for every one of his large family takes the tension out of our anxieties about the future. We do not need to consult specialists in lock-picking. We are content to leave both our past and our future in his hands.

The One Mediator (15–20). The connection between these verses and the preceding section is brought out in Isaiah 8:19: 'When they shall say unto you, seek unto them that have familiar spirits . . . : should not a people seek unto their God?' The Prophet of verse 15 is Christ. He is so identified by Peter in his sermon in Acts 3: 22–26, and by Stephen in his defence in Acts 7:37. He has 'the keys of hell and of death' and knows all their secrets. The Lord Jesus, our Advocate in heaven, and the Holy Spirit our Comforter on earth are enough for all our daily need. What we cannot learn from them it is better not to know. And to seek to know what God has been pleased to leave hidden is not faith but the clumsiest evidence of unbelief. Our faith should be simple and secure enough to cry:

> God holds the key of all unknown,
>   And I am glad;
> If other hands should hold the key,
> Or if he trusted it to me,
>   I might be sad.

'A SYRIAN, READY TO PERISH, WAS MY FATHER'

There was no room for haughty thoughts in this confession (5). The grateful Hebrew, farming his little holding in the promised land, was taught to memorize this formula. The words of the formula run from verse 5 to 10a. The Syrian was Jacob and the references in verse 5 seem to be to his early life. His mother was from Syria. Thither Jacob fled after his treachery against Esau. There he made his home and was in turn imposed upon by his father-in-law Laban. Returning to Canaan he faced a life-and-death crisis when in danger from Esau and his armed men. And even when finally settled in Canaan he knew famine and trouble. The formula continues to celebrate God's mercy to His people in multiplying Jacob's descendants (5), in delivering them from the oppression of Egypt (6–8) and giving them possession of 'a land that floweth with milk and honey' (9). 'They owed it to God that they were not now bringing a tally of bricks, but a basket of first fruits' (Matthew Henry). This practice still continued among the New Hebrides people where the writer served as a missionary. They had learned this lesson in their pre-Christian culture. They recognized the high God and knew that in the use of the land they were tenants-at-will of the high God. If an islander failed to bring his first fruits to God, the village chief would warn him that he would have to forfeit his land. The right to farm the land was considered to be bound up with the obligation to acknowledge that the land is the Lord's, and man uses it by gracious permission, and not by right of purchase, conquest or prescription.

QUESTION:
What land does the Lord still own? Has modern man forfeited his right to use it? In what ways has man abused his tenancy? How will God finally assert his absolute ownership over the land?

'HE IS THY LIFE'

'He' is emphatic and points to Jehovah their God (20). 'Life' is a curious idiom and translates a Hebrew plural noun which occurs some 135 times in the Old Testament and is almost always translated by our singular noun 'life'. It first occurs in Genesis 2:7 where 'the Lord God . . . breathed into his nostrils *the breath of life*'; and again in Genesis 2:9, 'Out of the ground made the Lord God to grow . . . *the tree of life*'. The same word occurs four times in today's reading. At verse 15 it is used as the ideal sum of all spiritual and temporal blessings. In this comprehensive sense it stands contrasted with 'death and evil'. In verse 19 this 'life' is made the subject of every man's personal and responsible choice. Hence we infer something of the spiritual significance of 'life' in this chapter. It is much more than normal blood-pressure and a good digestion. And when 'life' is starkly contrasted with 'death' (19a) it is so used to remind us that there is a death which men choose for themselves. Most remarkable of all is the use of this theme in Romans 10: 6–9 for the soul's choice of Christ as Saviour. Here the word 'life' is in full bloom and speaks of the righteousness which comes to us by faith in Jesus.

QUESTION:
'His divine power hath given to us all things that pertain unto life and godliness' (2 Peter 1:3). Jot down some of the 'all things', commencing with the references in Genesis 2: 7 & 9.

READ THIS LAW

Moses did not organize buzz-groups to discuss the law of the Lord and to bring down their findings for editing by a steering committee. He treated God's Law with the reverence and finality that it deserved. 'Thou shalt read this law before all Israel in their hearing'. It is a fact that many a lad does not know the law until he finds himself under arrest for breaking it. That could not happen in the ideal Israel envisaged here by Moses. Already the parents have been charged with the duty of the diligent teaching of their children at home (6:7). And the word 'diligently' means what it says. It comes from a Latin root which means 'to love', 'to take delight in'. When family worship is led in this way God blesses it to all the household. Under the direction of verses 10–13 the whole nation was called to school every seventh year for a refresher course in the law of the Lord. Thus the children grew up to know, and strangers to acknowledge, the law under which they must live their lives towards God and their neighbour.

MEDITATION:
'The Spirit of God maketh the reading, but especially the preaching of the Word, an effectual means of convincing and converting sinners, and of building them up in holiness and comfort, through faith, unto salvation' (Westminster Shorter Catechism: 89).

THE ORATORIO OF THE FIRST PILGRIM FATHERS

The dictionary describes an oratorio as a semi-dramatic musical composition on a sacred theme performed by soloists, chorus and orchestra, without action, scenery or costume. The reference in Revelation 15: 3–4 to the song of Moses, the servant of God, should not be overlooked. Nor should the earlier song of Moses which celebrated Israel's triumph at the Red Sea (Exod. 15). The sacred theme is consistently the same: 'Ascribe ye greatness unto our God' (3), 'The Lord's portion is his people' (9), 'They provoked him to jealousy with strange gods' (16), 'The Lord shall judge his people' (36), '(He) will be merciful unto his land, and to his people' (43). The symbolism is vivid and magnificent. Jeshurun (15) is a poetic name for Israel, a term of divine endearment. It occurs four times in the Old Testament: Deuteronomy 32:15; 33:5, 26; Isaiah 44:2. The root is probably the word for 'upright' and hence may be used here both as a reminder of what God wanted his people to be, and a reproach upon them for what they have become as stated in verse 15a, 'A people so well-loved! And now, pampered, they would throw off the yoke'.

NOTE ON VERSE 4:
'No such combination of all the words for uprightness, sincerity, equity *and* reliability *is to be found elsewhere in all Scripture. This is the character of* the Rock . . . *The Septuagint, in this song and in many other places, does not translate 'Rock' at all, but gives it as* God *(Theos). In other places the word* pétra *(never* petros) *is employed. This fact convinces me that the* petra *of Matthew 16:18 could only have been understood by Jews as denoting Deity; and that it not only referred to Christ, but to* Christ as God'. *(C. H. Waller in* Ellicot's Commentary)

PROPHECY SET TO MUSIC

The blessing of Moses is too grand for prose. The writer speaks his heart in poetry. It is a sustained prophecy, in mingled prayer and praise, about the future of the tribes. Only Simeon is left out (6) and it is difficult to suggest why, unless it is due to the fact that the tribe of Simeon was gradually absorbed into that of Judah. Since it is poetry, and enshrines both prophecy and history, no doubt it was preserved as the spoken blessing of Moses and written down after the death of Moses (1). The expression 'Moses the man of God' suggests that the recorder is not Moses himself and verse 4 seems to confirm this. But the theme and the words are his, darting shafts of light from Sinai (2), piercing the veil and revealing the angel hosts of God (2), pointing to their heavenly King (5) and possibly to the Messiah himself (3). The order of the tribes first follows that of Rachel's and of Leah's children. Levi was Moses' own tribe (Exod. 2: 1–2). He sees Levi in this divine role as the custodian of the Word of God, and this fact no doubt explains the four verses devoted to the blessing (8–11).

PRAYER:
'Bless, Lord, his substance' (11a). Levi had no land. Levi's substance was Israel's tithe. This petition was therefore a prayer for God's blessing upon the land of all the tribes.

THE EVERLASTING ARMS

It is my practice in hospital visiting to write a 'prescription' in the form of an appropriate text upon a plain envelope. One tries to fit the text to the patient's need. I remember one such visit to an old saint of God. She and her husband had lost their farm in the depression of the 1930's. They had battled on undaunted. When I arrived in my parish she immediately impressed me because she walked six miles to church regardless of the weather, along rough country roads. Now she was near the end of life's journey and her mind was confused. I repeated the words of verse 27: 'The eternal God is thy refuge, and underneath are the everlasting arms'. A tired voice called from behind a screen 'Would you please speak with me too?' I found a young woman recovering from a breakdown. 'Those were *beautiful* words', she said at once, 'who spoke them?' 'They are God's words', I replied, 'and they were spoken to people who had been for years in the wilderness'. 'I am in the wilderness now; my whole life has been a wilderness', she confessed. I wrote out the verse and handed it to her. She said it over to herself slowly, measuring every word. Then I prayed. I never saw her again. I did not need to. She had grasped Deuteronomy 33:27, and was able to go home.

QUESTION:
Today the wilderness is sprinkled with the groping lives of unnumbered people. What Old Testament passages have you memorized for them? Here are three which I constantly use: Isaiah 54:10; Jeremiah 31:3; Deuteronomy 33:27.

SUNSET

Moses died, as he had lived, by one simple motto: 'As the Lord commanded'. Verse 5, 'According to the word of the Lord', is literally 'upon the mouth of the Lord'; hence the Jewish suggestion that he died by the kiss of God. It was one last act of obedience to go up from the plains of Moab to the top of Pisgah. What he saw can still be seen from the craggy ridge of Jebal Osha on a clear day, from snow-capped Hermon in the north to the shimmering silver of the Dead Sea in the west. It is extraordinary how wholly self is cast aside. His reticence is absolute, and his calm silence is sublime. He died in the company of Jehovah and found the deepest meaning of his own confession of faith: 'Underneath are the everlasting arms'. Verse 6 tells us that God buried him. The Son of God, incarnate, was buried by believers. Moses had the honour of burial by Jehovah.

INTERPRETATION OF JUDE VERSE 9:
'I have always believed that the contention between Michael and the devil about the body of Moses was, in fact, a struggle for his body – *that Moses was to be raised from the dead, and that Satan resisted his resurrection.* When *the contest took place we cannot say. Moses, who died and was buried, and Elijah who was translated,* 'appeared in glory' *on the holy mount, and the New Testament gives no hint of difference between them'* (C. H. Waller in Ellicot's Commentary).

GOOD NEWS FROM GOD

The man who wrote this letter had a threefold qualification: he was the slave of Jesus Christ, the apostle of Jesus Christ, the separated man (1). He never tired of telling how this happened (Acts 9,22,26, Gal. 1). When he wrote this letter from Corinth to Rome in 58 A.D. there were Christian congregations right round the Mediterranean. What was the secret?

The secret lay in the Person he wrote about: promised in the Old Testament (2), truly man (3) and no less truly God (4). The resurrection of Jesus was God's way of serving notice on humanity that Christ is God, a sympathetic Saviour and a mighty King. Hence his coronation title, Jesus Christ our Lord (4).

Paul's parish is the world (5). John Wesley said the same, and John Williams, the apostle to the Pacific, protested, 'I could never content myself with the confines of a single reef'.

The called of God (6) are all who embrace the Lord Jesus as their Saviour and devote themselves to 'the obedience of faith'. But we cannot have the benefits without the burdens; to be beloved of God is also to be called to be saints (7). What double dignity! What superb vocation!

THE CHURCH TO WHICH PAUL WROTE

Ever since Aquila and Paul enlivened their tent-making in
Corinth with stories of the seed plot of Christ in mighty Rome,
Paul had hungered and thirsted for their fellowship. From time
to time that emotion surged through his eager soul like a silent
ground swell. He soon knew the men and women of chapter 16
as if they were his own kith and kin; and he loved them with a
more than human love. *He prayed for them* (9). While nimble
fingers wove the coarse hair of the Cilician goats he gave thanks
for Nereus, and Julia and the household of Narcissus. 'Whenever I call a fellow by his first name I make it my business to
pray for him', wrote Forbes Robinson in one of his intimate
'Letters to his friends'. Paul boldly called God to witness that he
makes this prayer-covenant upon oath (9). 'I long to see you', he
confessed (10), and used a Greek word full of ardent expectancy. He wanted to help them in their Christian growth (11).
What he had to give was *spiritual*. He desired to receive as well
as to impart. This is the insignia of true nobility of soul (12). He
comes to them as debtor, not as patron; as their servant not their
superior (14).

The Christian manifesto is recorded in verse 16 in the language
of the heart, in verse 17 in the language of the mind, in verse 16
in the language of Christian experience, in verse 17 in the
language of Christian doctrine.

THE GOOD NEWS BEGINS
WITH BAD NEWS

Today's reading unveils the progressive steps in the reign of sin. *Sin began in the soul* (18). The sinner's soul is the seat of ungodliness and unrighteousness. This is sin's nerve-centre. *Sin reaches out to the intellect* (21–23). 'They became futile in their thinking, and night settled down on their soul' (21). 'While they kept chattering about their cleverness, they became plain morons' (Greek). Moron minds breed moron morals; hence the logic of sin's next conquest. *Sin masters the body* (24– 27). Only a few years ago we would have read these terrible verses and wondered where such depravity could be found. Today we no longer wonder. Bold perversion struts across the stage with leering insolence. We are paying the price for our progressive retreat from the clear incisive teaching of God's holy Word. But more is to come. *Sin finally dominates man's social life* (29–31). Parent and child, husband and wife, master and servant, friend and friend – all these fundamental relationships of a wholesome social order are invaded by divisiveness, corruption and frustration. Is this all some savage accident? No, it is the moral logic of Satan's reign in a man's and woman's life. Hence the threefold verdict, 'God gave them up' (24,26,28). This is God's first word to sinners. Bad as it sounds we do well to receive it as the beginning of the Good News.

THE JUSTICE OF GOD

Chapter 2 opens in the atmosphere of the law court. Constantly recurring are the words 'judge', 'judgment', 'justice'. You can feel the hush in the courtroom as the Judge takes his seat on the bench. Here are the facts which stand out as we watch the drama.

God's justice is wedded to absolute truth (1,2). We, as guilty sinners, have good cause to be thankful that we are being tried before a tribunal whose judgments never err and from which there is no provision for appeal. Look up Bildad's rhetorical question in Job 8:3, Moses' verdict as the Chief Justice of a nation in Deuteronomy 32:4, and the Psalmist's tribute in Psalm 89:14. 'Shall not the Judge of all the earth do right?'

God's judgments are hidden behind his merciful delays (3–5). Milton represents Satan as saying to Eve, in Eden, 'God cannot hurt you, and be just.' (*Paradise Lost* IX. 700) How many have fooled themselves with the serpent's smooth theology! These verses show us how, as sinners, we trade upon God's delays. There is a clearly announced terminal point to God's day of grace – the day of wrath! (5).

God's judgments are plain in their principle (6–10). God judges us 'according to our works' (6). On the face of things this should suit modern man very well. But by 'works' God means more than cups of cold water. Verse 16 points to judgment of the hidden secrets of the heart.

God's judgments are based on a known standard of duty (11–16). For the Jews this was found in the Old Testament. For us it is found in the entire Scriptures. For the heathen it is found written deep in his moral conscience. None shall plead ignorance at the bar of God.

'RELIGION' IS NO DEFENCE

Several times in Romans Paul pauses to address himself directly to Jews (cp. 3:1; 4; and 9–11). He now does so in order to show them that their religion – or any religion for that matter – does not exempt people from the responsibility of answering to God for their sin, and of looking to Christ alone as their Saviour.

These Jews made a high religious profession (17–20). The five verbs in verses 17 and 18 are a convincing proof of their religion's sincerity and earnestness amidst the blind bewildered multitudes without the Book (19,20). They believed that such privileges and such religious scrupulousness meant that in God's eyes they were on board an unsinkable ship. Paul has now to show them *their shameful shortcomings* (21–23). It is Vinet who says that you could construct the most exalted ethic from what people expect of others, and the most degraded ethic from their own lives. This is glaringly true of these verses. Yet these devoted Jews had never seen themselves in God's light. Have we? *The effect on the Gentile outsider* (24). Listen to him as he blames God for the inconsistencies of God's people. *Religious rites can degenerate into mere excuses* (25–29). God will not be put off with a well-worn communion card, or with a public ceremony of baptism.

INTERPRETATION:
In verses 25–29 read 'baptism' for 'circumcision' in order to get an up-to-date version of Paul's argument.

WEEDS

Docks, fat-hen, twitch, convolvulus – these are the weeds I
have had to fight for years in my modest manse garden. When I
sow, there is no sign of them. Before the seeds are up the weeds
appear. Only the persevering use of the hoe keeps the plot
clean. How did the weeds get into the soul of man? Are the
weeds in the human heart as numerous and varied as those in
my lettuce plot? The answers are given in today's portion which
Calvin describes as 'nothing but a description of original sin'.
Here our heart is x-rayed, not the good heart which God
created, but the bad heart which sin has corrupted. In the
running verbal duel of verses 1–9 the unseen heckler is a
religious person, a devout Jew. He feels that what is said in
chapter 2 applies to the pagan play-boy, but not to himself. At
verse 9 the Judge announces that every defence has failed.
Before he pronounces sentence of death he reads the death-
dealing quotations from the Jews' own statute-book (10–18).
Then, this infallible Judge, whose Name is mercy and truth,
pronounces all the world guilty before God (19). The prisoner is
asked if he has anything to say. He puts his hand over his
mouth, bows his head and is hurried to the condemned cell.
Thus the Good News begins with bad news. Every way of
escape is barred. We are shut up to God's way alone (20–31).

*List the sources of the Old Testament quotations in verses 10–18.
What inferences do you draw from Paul's 'it is written' of verse 10
and Jesus' 'it is written' of Matthew 4: 4,5,10?*

ROYAL PARDON

The dramatic arrival of a pardon on the very steps of the scaffold is heralded with the abrupt words, 'But now . . .' How this Royal Pardon was effected is the subject of verses 20–31. It was certainly not a verdict of 'not guilty' (20,23). The whole court-hearing of chapters 1–3:19 has made that clear. So it is pardon on other grounds than those of personal merit (21a). Nor is this a mere fancy of Royalty (21b). Pardon is God's prerogative, clearly announced in the Law book by both law and prophets (21c). Nor is it a mere pardon, but infinitely more. It is a quashing of the sentence of condemnation (8:1), a public announcement of acquittal (5:1), the banishment of all guilt and guiltiness in the justified sinner (8: 33,34), and the clothing of the saved sinner with the garment of Christ's righteousness. The pardon avails nothing unless it is embraced by the sinner as sinner (22,23) and is seen to be his ex-gratia, by Royal favour (24). Five key words sum up this supreme act of God in Christ: redemption, propitiation, blood, justified, grace (24,25).

PROPITIATION:
'Christ a propitiation is the inmost soul of the gospel for sinful men . . . It meets the requirements, at the same time, of the righteousness of God and of the sin of man' (James Denney).

THE FAITH CHAPTER

The most fool-proof parachute will not open until you pull the rip-cord. God has made a perfect and complete way for our salvation. But it is not automatic. It requires my response. This is faith, five times mentioned in the verses which closed chapter 3 (22–28). 'The just shall live *by faith*' is no discovery of Paul's religious mind. It is thrice quoted from the Old Testament prophet Habakkuk (Hab. 2:4; see Rom. 1:17, Gal. 3:11, Heb. 10:38). Paul now demonstrates it at length from the life and experience of Abraham. Today's reading touches three aspects. (a) *What principles does Abraham's faith set forth* (1–5)? He is the Archimedes of the Old Testament; the verb 'found' in verse 1 is the same as 'Eureka'! 'Justified' in verse 2 is used in a popular, not a doctrinal, sense: 'If Abraham has proved himself a splendid man by his behaviour, that is fine, but it in no way makes him righteous in God's sight'. Only faith in God his Saviour could do that (3, quoting Genesis 15:6). Faith acknowledges its need ('ungodly' verse 5) and pleads no personal merit. (b) *David's experience exactly corresponds with Abraham's* (6–8). In Psalm 32:1, 2 it was God who declared righteous the rejoicing Psalmist, and he in turn defined the grounds of his new-found blessedness. (c) *How does Abraham's circumcision bear upon the faith question* (9–12)? Abraham was declared righteous *before* he was circumcised (9, 10). The true beneficiaries of God's covenant with Abraham (Gen. 17) are his *spiritual* descendants (11,12 and see Gal. 3: 26–29).

THE NECESSITY OF FAITH

Paul, with his eye on his Jewish readers, now removes another big obstacle in the way of their acceptance of salvation by *faith*. The orthodox Jew, like the average citizen today, asked in a puzzled tone, 'Then where does behaviour come into God's reckoning? What about our Law?' Paul answered this in verses 13–16, by showing that God made no mention of the Law to Abraham in Genesis 15 and 17 (13). Such a set-up would have killed the promise of God, and with it the inheritance (14), because the broken Law leads straight to the lock-up (15). The inheritance would have lapsed long ago for want of a perfect man, had Law decided the matter. Hence God settled the inheritance on *believers*, and it has never lapsed, and never will, since God in his electing grace will raise up his own benefic- iaries. Verse 16 clinches these truths. In verse 17 we see in startling clarity the initiative of God's grace (he both 'quickens' and 'calls'), and the impotence of the sinner (he is 'dead', and even the best of sinners, in the literal Greek of 17b, are 'non- entities'). Thus God kills human pride and self-merit and makes room for the exercise of saving faith. Verses 18–21 now show us *faith's audacity*; and verses 22–25 *faith's consequences*. The resurrection of Christ stands guardian over these unchang- ing facts of personal salvation (24, 25).

MEDITATION:
'Faith is the hand of the soul which lays hold of the Cross' (*Luther*).

THE FRUITS OF FAITH

At chapter 5 verse 1 we turn a sharp corner in the Epistle, marked by the key word 'justified'. The long judicial trial is over. It has ended in our acquittal on the ground of faith in Another's life and death and resurrection. Chapters 5 to 8 now unfold the fruits of faith, or the outworking of Christlikeness in the life of the newborn child of God. We can expect a strong subjective strain here, with our own inner experience verifying in daily life those new and thrilling discoveries which the Apostle tells us are to be ours.

Peace at last (1–5); and first, *Godward* (1). This arises from our new status (justified, acquitted, sons of God); and from our new privileges (access verse 2). Secondly, we have peace *manward* (3–5). This arises from a new poise amid troubles, the fruit of the Holy Spirit who has come to live in our hearts (5). He counters the old familiar reactions of bitterness and retaliation with the spring-tide of divine love (5). *Seeing Christ with new eyes* (6–11), and first, as to the miracle of his past love in redeeming us (6–8); secondly, as to the miracle of his present love on our behalf (9–11), assuring us of security from judgment (9), and of daily grace for the life of Christian obedience (10). These facts are a fountain of perennial joy in the souls of the redeemed (11) who have made the astonishing discovery that 'this hope never lets you down' (5a).

MEDITATION ON VERSE 5:
'You cannot have the hyacinth of love without the bulb of faith' (*Spurgeon*).

THE REIGN OF SIN AND
THE REIGN OF GRACE

As you have worked your way through the many contrasted ideas in today's reading, one impression should have stood out – the majestic sweep of God's plan of redemption. Read the passage again as follows: read verse 12 and then verses 18, 19 to get the sense of the passage. Take verses 13–17 as a parenthesis, explaining the 'how' of verse 12. Adam and Christ are both seen as real persons, the federal heads of lost and redeemed humanity. Compare 1 Corinthians 15: 21, 22, 45 and consider J. H. Newman's hymn on this exalted theme, 'Praise to the Holiest in the height'. The climax in verses 20, 21 exalts triumphant grace. (a) *The reign of sin* (12–14). 'Death reigned as king' (14 Weymouth). This is a brute fact of history (12) of personal experience (12) and of universal experience (14). 'Man is not only dead, but lying in the midst of death, ever sinking more deeply into death, until eternal death stands revealed' (Kuyper). (b) *The reign of grace* (15–21). 'But' halts the deadly entail of sin and guilt and damnation. 'Many be dead' (15) is an aorist verb and should read 'many have died' (R.V.). We are all included in the 'many'. 'Much more' (15, 17) is exultant and means 'infinitely greater'. Grace has both hands wide open in verse 15. Grace flows freely from the wounds of Christ, the one Man who 'to the fight and to the rescue came'. The climax (21) sees grace on the throne and death's tyranny at an end.

EXERCISE:
In parallel columns list what is said of Adam and Christ. This will sharpen your sense of the contrasted truths in the passage.

CHRIST OUR SANCTIFICATION

At chapter 5 we stepped out of the shadows into the light in hearing the declaration from the throne of God, 'we are justified by faith'. I am free! But how am I going to use this new-found freedom? That is the theme of chapter 6. In God's sight the saved sinner is a saint because he has put on him the righteousness of Christ. But other folk find us far from saints. Ask the family! Saints in name and status, God now wants us to be saints in very truth. He has a recipe for saint-making, for personal holiness; it centres wholly upon Christ. 'Christ comes to us with a blessing in each hand; forgiveness in one, and holiness in the other. He never gives either to anyone who will not take both' (Alexander Whyte).

The burning question (1). 'Shall we continue in sin . . . ?' 'God will always forgive me', says the antinomian (lawless) Christian. 'But I didn't know it was wrong!' protests the ignorant Christian. 'Look, other Christians do it!' retorts the easy-going Christian. These three tendencies dog the gospel, and are frankly faced in this chapter.

The blunt reply (2–10). *First* an exclamation (2a) – 'Unthinkable!' (A.V. 'God forbid'). *Then* a rhetorical question which gives the keyword for the ensuing discussion – 'dead' (13 times in 11 verses). *Then* the personal argument centring on the fact of my crucifixion (6), death (8) and burial (4). The consequence for 'the body of sin' is that it can bully me no longer (6). Further, I possess Christ's risen life as the pattern (4) and power (9) for my new life 'in Christ'. *The practical outworking* (11). We are to navigate by 'dead reckoning'!

A PRACTICAL GUIDE TO A HOLY LIFE

Resist (12)! Sin (sing.) here stands for the deposed bully, the sin-principle, whose 'tentacles' (A.V. lusts) are always reaching out to master us. Constant vigilance and counter-attack are necessary.

Surrender (13,14)! 'Yield' occurs first in the present tense and then in the aorist. 'Don't feebly surrender the guns of Man's soul one by one to your persistent Enemy, but get a resounding victory by once-and-for-all surrendering your whole redeemed self to your victorious Lord, and by putting all your guns at his disposal (cp. verse 19 and chapter 12: 1, 2).

Remember (15–23)! A second blunt question jolts the conscience (15) and draws the same retort as the first (1). Two vivid words, 'slave' and 'free', provide the theme for Paul's argument (16–22). The passage is firmly rooted in the Roman Christians' own experience of the Saviour (17, 21). Their *past* life was a slavery to sin (16–18) with death staring them in the face (16, 23). Its memory makes them blush (21). Their *present* life began with a decisive step of total submission (17: aorist). This liberated them from the handcuffs of sin (18: aorist) and made them slaves of a nobler sort (18).

'Now' (22, emphatic), at long last, they are in a position to serve God unencumbered by the shackles of sin and to bear fruit in the direction of a sanctified life (a process is implied). Their sunset will be golden with the glory of eternal life.

THE CHRISTIAN'S RELATION TO THE LAW OF GOD

In 6:14 Paul had declared, 'for ye are not under the law, but under grace'. Few statements in Romans have been more misunderstood. Paul now goes on to explain what he means by this (1–6). The key verse is 4. Death dissolves all legal obligations. The believer was crucified with Christ (Gal. 2:20) and in his new resurrected life is already married to Christ. The fruit of this holy union is our total life of Christian obedience (4). Contrast the fruit of our old life, provoked by the accusing law, and expressing itself through the 'motions of sin' (R.V. 'sinful passions'). 'But now' (6) is emphatic and applies to the new enjoyment of our 'death' and 'discharge' (R.V.) from the law.

Does this mean that the law of God is a bad thing (7–12)? In this section Paul is speaking autobiographically. He gives us a glimpse into his own struggles as a Christian. In verses 7–13 he tells us of his past experience; in verses 14–25 of his present experience. 'Before the law x-rayed me and showed me what I was and what I looked like to God, I thought I was doing fine (7)'. The wickedness of our heart is comparatively inactive and its virulence unsuspected until stung into protest by the law's 'Thou shalt' . . . and 'Thou shalt not'. Hence verse 12 recognizes that 'the law is *holy* in nature, *just* in its claims and sanctions, and *good* in its tendency' (C. H. Irwin).

[116]

CIVIL WAR

Civil war implies a conflict of opposing forces within the very soul of the nation. It is the most distressing of all forms of warfare. And this is the daily experience of the Christian. The conflict is between our 'old man' (the sinful nature we receive by birth as children of Adam) and the 'new man' (the new nature we receive at our new birth). Look up John 3: 5–8 and Romans 8:4. The apostle calls them the 'flesh' and the 'Spirit'. This civil war is a matter of painful experience to every single-hearted believer. 'God's child remains the old man's gravedigger until the hour of his departure'. Paul is here looking at the facts of his own daily experience: *First experience* (15) I want to do good, but I do evil. Three inferences follow: (a) I consent to the law, that it is good (16); (b) it is not my new nature but the sin-principle which drags me down (17); (c) I have to face the hard fact that in my old self there is nothing particularly lovely (18). *Second experience* (18–24). This reveals the 'double self' of the Christian who all the while prizes the law of God and loves the will of God (22), but is reduced to agonies of humiliation and shame by the re-asserted sin-impulses (24). There is no justification for placing verse 25b after verse 23 as Moffatt and C. H. Dodd do. This arbitrary action arises from their mistaken view that verse 25a is the moment of Paul's conversion.

QUESTION:
What light does chapter 7 shed upon the couplet:

> *'And they who fain would serve thee best*
> *Are conscious most of wrong within'?*

'NO CONDEMNATION!' –
OUR CHIEF GROUND OF ASSURANCE

Last among the fruits of faith (chapters 6–8) is *Christian assurance*. Paul's chief concern in chapter 8 is that every believer should be sure. Here is a reality which has almost disappeared from the Christian church. The Council of Trent condemned such a doctrine as a 'vain and ungodly confidence'. The cults have no doctrine of assurance. A 'faith' based upon works fights the gospel teaching about assurance and regards it as the height of presumption that a Christian should say 'I know'. Yet the New Testament is full of it. 'These things have I written . . . that ye may *know* that ye have eternal life' (1 John 5:13). If you are among the multitude who do not *know*, but only hope for the best, then make much of this important chapter and ask the Holy Spirit to direct your heart and conscience to rest in its bracing truths. Assurance is a river fed by five streams. The first of these is the Word (1–8); the second, the Holy Spirit (9–17); the third, suffering for Christ's sake (18–25); the fourth, a Spirit-controlled prayer-life (26–27); the fifth, the fact of our predestination in Christ (28–30). The Hallelujah Chorus of verse 31–39 is the fitting climax to such glorious realities.

THOUGHT:
'I possess assurance of faith only so long as I see these two things simultaneously – all of my sinfulness, and all of God's grace' (O. *Hallesby*).

[118]

ASSURANCE AND THE HOLY SPIRIT

The gift of the Holy Spirit is God's engagement ring, and there are no broken engagements with God. This is the meaning of the word 'earnest' in Eph. 1:14 and the word 'first fruits' in 8:23, as illustrated by Samuel Rutherford's saying, 'Our Lord will not lose his earnest, or go back or repent him of his bargain'.

(a) *The Spirit lives in every believer* (9–11). This is the greatest statement on the Holy Spirit's relation to the Christian that Scripture makes. Not an 'influence' from the Spirit, but The Spirit himself; not a part of himself, but his entire being; not for a while but for ever (11: 29; cf. John 14: 16, 17).

(b) *The Spirit cripples sin's power in the believer* (12–13). 'Mortify' means to do to death. The Spirit takes up the quarrel against our old self and its unstable moods and longings. And he shows us that the lifelong struggle is now going in our favour.

(c) *The Spirit guides the believer* (14). A Christian is one who can see the golden milestones of God's guidance right from childhood, through all the restless, turbulent years of the far country, and the secret agonies of dread and hope and despair. This guidance is more evident to us the further we travel the road with Christ.

(d) *The Spirit's inner witness* (15–17). This verifies our Divine sonship (15) and corroborates the testimony of our own redeemed consciousness (16). Since the sonship is certain, so is the inheritance (17).

ASSURANCE AND SUFFERING
FOR CHRIST'S SAKE

Assurance is all very well in good times, but what about the
Christian's *sufferings and troubles*? This word (17,18) now gives
Paul his opportunity to show that assurance thrives best in
adversity. Note the language of suffering in these verses and
watch for the vocabulary of assurance right alongside: sufferings (18), *glory*; waiteth (19), *revealing*; vanity (20), *hope*;
bondage (21), *liberty*; groan (23), *redemption*. The Reformation
gave us the resilient motto – *sub pondere cresco* (I grow under my
burdens). Suffering belongs only to the Christian's present, and
is not worth comparing with the 'glory which shall be revealed'
(18), a glory which is mere 'pie in the sky' to the sinner glutted
at the stalls of Vanity Fair. The 'glory' includes (a) our open
recognition as sons of God (19, 23); (b) the emancipation of the
whole creation of God from the down-drag of the Fall (20–22);
(c) the redemption of our body (23) – we are only partly
redeemed till then, hence our groaning. Then, and only then,
'*hope*' (5 times in 2 verses) passes into open sight (24, 25).
Profoundly moving is Paul's picture of the cosmic aspect of
man's sin, involving the entire creation (A.V. 'creature' 20) in
marred energies and frustrated purpose, which verse 21 calls
'the bondage of corruption'. With this is contrasted the coming
day of liberation (21b) for which all Nature is vividly pictured as
gazing eagerly on the tiptoe of expectancy (19).

ASSURANCE AND PREDESTINATION

Whatever your feelings about this hard word, 'predestination', remember that Paul's purpose in stressing it here is too good to miss. Folk often quote verse 28 without its first two words – '*We know*'. The Forty-two Articles of the Church of England (1553) affirmed: 'The godly consideration of predestination, and our election in Christ, is full of sweet, pleasant and unspeakable comfort to godly persons . . . as well because it doth greatly establish and confirm their faith of eternal salvation to be enjoyed through Christ, as because it doth fervently kindle their love towards God . . .' The operations of grace (30) are riveted together like the links of a chain, so that even the Christian's glorification is spoken of as already settled (all aorist verbs). In the light of such certainty the 'all things' (28) cover the whole range of the Christian's sufferings (18–22), yearnings (23–25) and accusations of conscience (31–34). The mood changes at verse 31 and Paul is back in the law court (remember chapter 2 and the black cap). Now Heaven is on his side (31). One by one every accusing voice is stilled, within the Christian (31–34) and without (35–37), and Paul reaches a solemn affirmation of absolute certainty in the 'I am persuaded' of verse 38. The chapter which opened with 'no condemnation' closes with no separation. And the meaning of the plural 'us' is surely this, that, as there can be no separation from God, so there can be no separation from God's redeemed people.

GOD IS SOVEREIGN:
I AM SAVED BECAUSE HE CHOSE ME

So far as the average believer in Rome was concerned, chapter 8 closed the doctrinal part of the Epistle. But many of the Christians were converted Jews. In the Old Testament they had a unique standing before God. In the gospel which Paul preached they seemed to be no different from anyone else. Does this gospel fit in with the long-standing promises of God to Israel? Does it square with God's consistent character? Has he deceived them? These were some of the questions Paul was constantly hearing from Jewish listeners. So he now devoted chapters 9–11 to answering them. He shows that God is sovereign (chapter 9) and man is free and responsible (chapter 10). Chapter 11 is the synthesis and application of these truths.

Chapter 9: God is sovereign: Note the eight advantages which made Jews think that they were on board an unsinkable ship (4, 5). Note the fact of the *two* Israels (6–8) and compare Galatians 3:29 and 4:28. In 6–13 God's election is stated and illustrated in its sharpest form in relation to Jacob and Esau (11–13). This provoked reaction, and still does. But, instead of accommodating the ways of God to man's idea of fair play, Paul states the fact more provocatively in words which make the unbeliever furious and the believer humble (14–18).

APPLICATION:
Paul's agony of concern for his unsaved kinsmen (1–3) rebukes my easy unconcern for my unsaved relatives and friends.

QUESTION:
What does the promise of verse 8 refer to, and what bearing has it on our salvation?

FINDING FAULT WITH GOD

Then, as now, the truth of God's sovereign grace, expressed in
the teaching of predestination, brought forth protests (14,19),
for example, 'God hasn't given man a chance!' Paul's answer is a
further vindication of the rights of the living and true God over
his human rival – the clay-god (20–21), and a marriage of the
concepts of wrath and mercy (22,23) which the unsanctified
heart cannot fathom. These protests are next answered from the
Jews' own statute-book (25–33) and Paul shows how the same
predestination operated in Israel's history. Sovereign *mercy* is
seen in the quotations from Hosea (25, 26), sovereign *justice* in
the quotations from Isaiah (27–29). The consequences of God's
dealings for both Jews and Gentiles are given in 30–33, and the
explanation, on the human side, is shown to be the absence (32)
or presence (33) of saving faith. This gently prepares us for
chapter 10 with its emphasis on 'the word of faith' (10:8). The
'stone of stumbling' (32) points back to Isaiah 8:14 and 28:16,
and forward to 1 Peter 2: 6–7. By the time of Justin Martyr – he
died in 165 A.D. – 'The Stone' (Gk 'lithos') was virtually a
proper name for Christ.

MEDITATION:
*Consider the alternatives for every soul, that Christ is either a stone
of stumbling, or a chief corner stone, elect and precious.*

'WHOSOEVER'

This is the 'whosoever will' chapter, following hard upon the heels of the 'predestination' chapter. Should this strike us as strange? It should not do so if we remember Charles Simeon's helpful suggestion that *both* statements belong to God's truth. There is a common idea that the teaching of chapter 9 on predestination makes nonsense of the free offer of the gospel and cripples evangelism. But Paul makes no apology for what he is saying and attempts no simple harmonising of these two chapters, which really belong together. There *are* views which frustrate the gospel, and Paul now mentions three of them (2–7): *Sincerity* is not enough (2); *trying hard* is not enough (3–5); *spectacular proof* is not enough (6, 7). The very idea of demanding another Bethlehem (6)! Another Empty Tomb (7)! Saving truth is with me *here* and *now*: 'The word is nigh thee,' just waiting to do its mighty work (8). The conditions? Believing and confessing (9,10). When the believing is from the *heart*, there will be no difficulty about the confessing with the *mouth*. The 'whosoeverness' of 11–13 is underscored in verse 13 with a heavy pen: 'everyone without exception . . .' (Weymouth). Every reader of this generous offer of Heaven can be saved. God has put his Son within arm's length of your deepest need. What condescension was his! What solemn responsibility is ours!

QUESTION:
Consider the different meanings of 'confess' in 1 John 1:9; Romans 10:9; Matthew 10: 32, 33 and James 5:16.

WHAT ABOUT THOSE WHO
HAVE NEVER HEARD?

The Bible never theorizes. Christians are now called upon to listen to the Good News with a map of the world on the wall of their lounge and a globe on the communion table of their church. Paul answers the theoretical questioning about the state of the heathen by the practical necessity of obeying the Great Commission. To the academic question Paul poses a four-fold rhetorical question: How? How? How? How? (14, 15). Turn the sequence round and work back from verse 15 and this is what the Holy Spirit is saying:

> Our duty is to *send* (15)
> Those sent are to *preach* (14c)
> Those hearing are to *believe* (14b)
> Those believing will be *saved* (14a)

So the Bible's answer to the question of the spiritual state of those who have never heard the gospel is 'What are *you* doing about it?'

How to be lost (16–21). '*But*' (16) introduces a sombre fact of experience – of Isaiah's experience, of Paul's experience, of every missionary's experience. The way to be lost is to do nothing about it (16–17); to resent the conversion of others (18–20); and to go on resisting 'all the day long' (21).

QUESTION:
Provoking to jealousy (19) is a standard divine procedure. It was used by the Lord Jesus (Lk. 4: 23–30), and Paul (Acts 13: 41, 46). When may we rightly employ it?

THE REMNANT

To the casual observer the Christian church is a lost cause. Wherever you go, in the college lecture room, on the football field, or merely mingling with the busy folk at the supermarket, you have the feeling that Christians are in a pretty small minority. This is no new discovery. Elijah knew what this felt like (3). But, well-informed and truthful as he was, he miscalculated the real situation. Where Elijah counted one man, God counted 7000 (4). And the lesson of verses 1–6 is that God has always had his faithful remnant (5) and always will, because his sovereign grace guarantees the survival of his church (6). There is probably another Christian where you work, but how can you find one another until you witness?

In verses 7–10 we read that the rest of Israel were hardened. List the words in verses 7–10 which describe this hardening. Look up in a concordance other New Testament references to hardening. Note the consistently passive form of the verb. What does this suggest (a) as to God's part and (b) as to the terrible consequences of sin? 'Seeing then that this imprecation remains for all the adversaries of Christ – that their meat should be converted into poison (as we see that the gospel is to be the savour of death unto death) – let us embrace with humility and trembling the grace of God' (Calvin, quoted by Moule).

'*Blinded*' (*7 A.V.*) is from the Greek *poroo* (to harden) which Hippocrates used for the formation of a stone in the bladder.

THE TWO OLIVE TREES

When you look at the ageing olive trees on the plain of
Bethlehem or in the Garden of Gethsemane you are looking at
an enigma. How can these gnarled trunks, rough and unsightly
and ready for the axe, possibly go on bearing fruit? This is the
enigma of the people of God. Paul here speaks about two olive
trees – Israel (the good olive) and the Gentiles (the wild olive).
'The fruit of the wild olive is small and worthless. It is made
plentiful and valuable by grafting in scions from a good stock.'
Notice the points Paul now makes: *The two trees are quite
different.* The wild can never bear good fruit; the good olive is
the only tree through which salvation comes to the world. The
hardening of part of Israel has robbed the true olive of many
branches (Jer. 11: 16, 17). But the tree's fruitfulness is not at an
end. By a miracle of God the Husbandman, the marred olive is
restored to symmetry and fruitfulness by the grafting in of wild
olive shoots (the Gentiles). This is 'contrary to nature' (24) and
incensed the Jews (Luke 4: 23–30; Acts 13: 41, 46). Now both
wild and good olive branches are growing side by side from the
same ancient stock. These Gentile grafts will forfeit their
privileged position if they cease to abide in Christ (22b). The
severed branches of the good olive can be grafted in again when
they (the Jews) turn from unbelief to Christ. Note the emphatic
'thou' in verses 17, 18, 20, 22 and 24; emphatically we Gentiles
are the privileged ones.

THOUGHT:
God's miracles of grace transcend the laws of nature (24).

'AND SO ALL ISRAEL SHALL BE SAVED'

The central question in this chapter seems to be the spiritual status of the Jews; and the key verse is 26, '*All Israel*'! Here we face a problem which has been answered in different ways:
'All Israel' means (1) the actual Israel of history (Sanday and Headlam); (2) substantially the whole nation (Charles Hodge); (3) the 'spiritual' Israel, comprising all who are saved through faith in Christ – whether Jews or Gentiles (Augustine, Calvin). Readers of these notes will have differing convictions at this point. The writer of the notes is concerned to point out that the Israel of God spoken of in Galatians 6:16 is a larger Israel than the nation of Israel, as the tree is bigger than the root from which its life sprang. See also Galatians 3: 26–29.

This crescendo of electing grace, which can take up the old Israel into the new Israel, and can make Christ's cross central to both dispensations, is the reason for Paul's doxology in verses 33–36. When logic is too frail an earthen vessel for so vast a revelation of the heart of God, Paul always bursts into song (cp. 8: 31–39). He sets his remaining questions to music and in this doxology all trivial doubts and questionings melt away like mist.

CAN YOU READ?
Read verse 36 again, placing the emphasis where it belongs – upon the pronoun 'him' (God).

FULL SURRENDER

We now enter upon the final portion of the Epistle for which chapters 1–11 have been the necessary preparation. Chapters 12–16 speak about the kind of life we should live as Christians in the world. Chapter 12 tells us that we first need to surrender our whole selves to God (1–5). Only then are we in a position to use to the full the spiritual gifts entrusted to us by Christ (6–8). These are our preparations for a life of service which then reaches out through church (9–13), community (14–21) and state (13: 1–7). 'Therefore' (1) assumes that we have passed through the phases of experience in chapters 1–11. Reflect on these for a moment. The *motive* for surrender is 'the mercies of God' (1). Note down these mercies as you have come to experience them. The *method* of surrender is a definite act of unreserved committal (the verb 'present' means 'hand over once and for all'). This often involves a sharp crisis, a conflict in the soul. It is doubtful if true surrender can ever be easy. The *scope* of surrender is our body (1), our mind (2), our self-life (3), and our so-called 'rights' (4,5). *God's gifts for service* follow (6–8). But how can he trust such gifts to the cheap uses of a self-centred life? They are only entrusted to the yielded life.

QUESTION:
Seven spiritual gifts are mentioned in verses 6–8. Write them down and, if you are able, check the meaning of each word from modern translations.

SATISFYING CHRISTIAN SERVICE

The Christian stands at the centre of three concentric circles –
his church, his community and his nation. In each of these three
environments his light must shine unmistakably and his
testimony must be above reproach.

(1) *I must serve Christ in my church* (9–13). The keynote here is
love, for which three different words are given (9, 10). The
dangers of bossiness in the church, and of a love which
degenerates into mere chattiness are ever present. 'Put *affection*
into your love for the brotherhood' (10a); yes, and such
practical ingredients as hospitality (13) and help for the
impoverished.

(2) *I must serve Christ in my community* (14–21). In this section
we can feel the prickles of an unfriendly paganism. The greatest
circumspection is needed. The persecution of verse 14 is not
organized; but the 'turning on the heat' which many a Christian
experiences at his job. There must be no snobs and no snobbery
(16), and we are to watch our window-display (17). And when
all else fails and we are face to face with ugly hostility, we must
abstain from provocation, retaliation and resentment.

EXPLANATION:
'*Heap coals of fire on his head*' (20) *means, you will 'make him feel a
burning sense of shame*' (Moffatt, following Augustine).

I MUST SERVE CHRIST IN MY NATION

Nations have personality as well as people. For Paul, the nation he had to deal with was pagan Rome. Nero Caesar was the emperor when Paul wrote these words. He begins with basic principles in verses 1 and 2 and goes on to details about taxation in verses 6 and 7. This whole passage needs to be read in the context of Mark 12: 13–17; 1 Timothy 2: 1–3 and 1 Peter 2: 13–17. Here rulers, including tax-inspectors, are called deacons (diakonoi) and ministers (leitourgoi) of God (4, 6). The 'tribute' of verse 7 was the Roman war-tax paid by subject peoples. Christians then, as now, were in danger of relaxing their loyalty to Caesar because of their new-found loyalty to Christ's kingdom.

A goad for the sluggish servant (8–14). Paul first refers to love as the inward motive to a life of holy and obedient service (8–10); and then to the Way of the Lord as the outward motive (11–14). The tense of the verbs in verse 8 means, 'you go on fulfilling the law of God as you go on loving the people of God'. The expectation of the Lord's return, so far from unnerving the Christian, girds him to energetic obedience (11), reflected in the 'putting off' and 'putting on' of verses 12–14.

BIOGRAPHY:
Augustine's memorable experience of these verses (11–14) is recorded in his Confessions Book VIII, chapter XII. *The next Book opens with the words of Psalm 116: 16, 17: 'O Lord, truly I am thy servant . . . Thou hast loosed my bonds'.*

IS IT RIGHT OR WRONG?

In chapter 14 we move into a new area of Christian behaviour, the realm of 'doubtful' things. This chapter faces the regrettable but obvious fact that earnest Christians often differ in their views of certain matters of conduct. For the Christians of Paul's day such vexed questions were: should a Christian (a convert from paganism) eat the meat of animals offered in heathen sacrifice and later sold by the butchers (2, 3)? Should we be tied to the Jewish Sabbath and the festival days of the Old Testament church (5,6)? Should a Christian touch liquor (21)? These vexed questions were doubly difficult because they tended to affect the terms and warmth of church fellowship (1,15:7).

Paul lays down no detailed rules, but refers every Christian to the guidance of the Holy Spirit, speaking in his conscience (22, 23). Here are his five principles which we believe are of permanent value and of the highest importance: (1) we are not to criticize other Christians who differ from us on these 'doubtful' things (1–9); (2) God alone is Lord of the conscience and to him alone are we answerable (10–12); (3) a word to the 'strong' Christians: always reflect on the effect of your actions upon the 'weak' (13–21); (4) a word to the 'weak': when in doubt, don't! (22, 23); (5) learn the supreme lesson of Christ's own example (chapter 15: 1–7).

QUESTION:
Think of difficult questions of behaviour of today upon which sincere Christians are divided. Apply the above five principles to them. Does this shed new light upon your duty?

THE USE AND ABUSE OF
CHRISTIAN LIBERTY

Anybody can criticize, and Christians find this habit hard to unlearn. The keynote in today's passage is patient and generous consideration of the feelings and prejudices of others whose judgments differ from our own. Especially is this true of those whom shallow people call 'narrow'. Paul is speaking to the 'strong' and urging them to renounce their 'right' to take a drink etc., where such conduct disconcerts the weaker Christians. Everyman's conscience is a strange world of individual hopes and fears, strengths and weaknesses. We must face this fact and not ride roughshod over weak consciences (15), becoming young Apollyons in the process (Greek: apollumi, I destroy). The same verb occurs in 1 Cor. 8:11 and there, as here, the resultant spiritual casualty is viewed as certain – a very sobering fact for the flamboyant Christian to ponder. Hence verse 16 seems to mean, 'So don't turn the good gift of Christian liberty into an occasion for others to charge you with hurtful licence'. Surely Christ has given you more to think about than food and drink (17)! Keep your spiritual outlook positive (17), practical (18) and peaceable (19). Not another drink if I am hurting a single fellow-Christian (20, 21)!

The doubt which is sin (22, 23). 'When in doubt, don't.' 'All conduct not based on faith is sinful' (Weymouth).

[133]

THE DECISIVE EXAMPLE OF CHRIST

Paul concludes the section on the strong and the weak by
bringing to bear upon the strong the highest possible motive for
consideration of the weak – the Lord's own example (1–7).
Here he clearly associates himself with the strong ('we', 1) and
uses a verb which means to bear the cross and has become a
symbol of cross-bearing in later Christian literature. The
discussion broadens out into the simple realities of Christian
fellowship with its mutual obligations (1–3), and leads on to the
wider spiritual consolations of patience and comfort (4, 5).
Only thus is it possible for Christians to reach the 'one mind'
and 'one mouth' of verse 6.

Christ, Scripture and the human soul (8–13). Paul is writing to
Christians in a city where aliens had every reason to chafe
against their disabilities. By the use of four quotations he ranges
the entire Old Testament against the bigot who is tempted to
revert to caste as a test of Christian fellowship. Jew and Gentile
are one, and this unity must be striven for in the fellowship of
the congregation in Rome. Verse 7 'receive': the tenses mean,
'You are to go on giving a welcome (present tense), because
Christ has once and for all welcomed you (aorist tense).

MEDITATION:
*'Even Christ pleased not himself' (3). Illustrate from the Gospels,
first in his relation to the Father, secondly in his relation to the
disciples.*

PAUL'S POSTSCRIPTS

The ever-broadening stream of the Epistle's doctrinal and ethical teaching has reached the ocean. At verse 14 Paul is consciously drawing his letter to a close. We share a few of his personal reflections as he thinks gratefully of the Christians in Rome (14), as he speaks out frankly about his special calling to be a missionary to the Gentiles (15, 16), as he recalls his missionary achievements (17–21), outlines his plans for the future (22–29), and makes his appeal for their prayers (30–32).

(1) *Paul's high view of the Christians in Rome* (14,15a). What three facts about them does he mention?

(2) *His sacred calling* (15b, 16). Paul here speaks of himself as a sacrificing priest, of the converts as a sacrificial offering, and of the gospel as a sacred liturgy. For a similar use of this bold metaphor, see Philippians 2:17.

(3) *His boasting* (17,18). This was centred upon Christ – not Paul; and it gave full credit to the work done by others in the same field.

(4) *His missionary achievement* (19–21). Three Greek words in verse 20 sum up New Testament missionary practice – 'preach' (evangelize), 'foundation' (the work of teaching the new converts), 'build' (the work of organizing a strong congregation).

AMBITION:
'Striven' (20) translates a word which means 'I make it my ambition'. It occurs also in 2 Corinthians 5–9, 'labour' and in 1 Thessalonians 4, 11, 'study'. How do my ambitions square with Paul's?

PAUL'S PLANS

Hindrances (22) test the mettle of the man of God. To lesser folk
like ourselves it is a help to know that Paul's plans suffered
endless delays and frustrations. But these hindrances had not
crippled either his vision or his effectiveness and in verse 23 he
tells of the astonishing results in the area of Roman Europe East
of the Adriatic. The time span was probably ten years, to 57
A.D.

   Distractions (25–28) also test our mettle. Paul did not see
anything amiss in his devoting so much time and thought to the
collection for the saints in Jerusalem. He pursued this task with
the greatest earnestness, as witness the passages in 1 Corinthians 16: 1–4 and 2 Corinthians 8, 9.

   Spain (24, 28) 'We take it for certain that St. Paul, some time
after the spring or summer of A.D. 62, and probably before the
spring of A.D. 66, visited Spain' (Moule).

   Prayer-partners (30–32) Prayer is wrestling (A.V. strive, Gk.
agonize). Prayer-partners are those who know this costly aspect
of prayer and are prepared to become co-wrestlers with Paul.
Three reasons are given in verses 31, 32 which give definiteness
to Paul's prayer requests. Jot them down. If Paul, the mighty
apostle, so felt his need of prayer-warriors, what do you suggest
are the prayer needs of your own congregation?

QUESTION:
*Note the three benedictions in verses 5, 13 and 33. What facet does
each contribute to our knowledge of God? What reflection does each
create in the life of the Christian?*

'ALL ONE IN CHRIST JESUS'

This artless last chapter, full of lowly folk made immortal by Paul's mention of their names and graces, is the best possible proof of the message he set out to deliver. Here is the true flowering of chapter 1: 16, 17, the transcription into real life of Galatians 3:28 just one generation after Calvary.

The three great chasms in Roman society were race, class and sex. In the 27 names in verses 1–16 we see the gospel's silent answer to the unbridged rifts in the pagan world of the first century.

Race: Latins (Ampliatus and Urbanus), Jews (six in all), and Greeks (the great majority of those here named) make up this modest list. They are now 'all one in Christ Jesus'.

Class: The majority named here are from the lower classes – slaves and freed slaves. Those belonging to the households of Aristobulus (10) and Narcissus (11) were doubtless household slaves in wealthy Roman homes.

Sex: Roman Law imposed disabilities upon women, who were considered not legally grown up. But Paul begins this list with Phebe the deaconess and next mentions Prisca (R.V.) in terms of high tribute. Both were active workers. There are six or seven other women in the Honours List.

Application: Contrast the degradation of sex which we saw in chapter 1 with the chaste nobility of this unadorned record. Who has made all the difference? Count the frequency of the Lord's holy Name in verses 1–16. Can you find any suggestion here of Paul's message being accommodated to the prevailing pagan view of sex? What has this passage to say to us for our day?

FINAL WARNING

Trouble-makers are no new feature of Christian assemblies.
They have shadowed the church from its inception. What four
marks identify them (17, 18)? 'Good words' and 'fair speeches'
(18) draw attention to the apparent *earnestness* and the apparent
rightness of what they were saying. The professional con-
troversialist is depicted here, and he is assured of a gullible
following (18b). What is our double responsibility when we
detect such trouble-makers (17)? Who is behind them promoting their evil business (20)?

The God of peace (20) sets himself against the demon of
discord and our confidence is in his final triumph.

Greetings from Corinth (21–24). A handful of Christians were
about Paul in Corinth when he 'signed off'. Tertius was Paul's
penman (see Galatians 6:11). Erastus (23), the city treasurer,
'stands almost alone in the apostolic history as a convert from
the dignified ranks' (Moule).

The Doxology (25–27): Thus far the penman wrote. Perhaps
at verse 25 Paul grasped the stylus in his own hand and added
these glorious words which lift our eyes from Paul the apostle to
Christ the Lord of glory.

QUESTION:
*From the doxology of verses 25–27 select the familiar words which
gather up the entire thought of the Epistle into this ascription, and try
to relate them to the unfolding of Paul's message in Romans.*

THE DIVINE CHOICE OF DAVID

As we turn from our New Testament readings in Romans to an Old Testament series on the early life of David, we shall see the truth of Augustine's axiom for the interpretation of Holy Scripture, 'The New is in the Old concealed; the Old is in the New revealed'. Romans 9 showed us that God is sovereign in his dealings with his creatures; Romans 10 showed us the complementary truth that man is free and responsible. No real attempt is made to harmonize these two parallel truths of revelation and Christian experience. But time and again they are vividly illustrated in the lives of Old Testament characters. This is so in today's reading which shows us the initiative of God in four aspects:

God rejects (1). The reason is given in 1 Samuel 15: 16–23. Saul had abused his holy office. He went on wearing his crown years after God had dismissed him from his service.

God selects (2–5). The rejection of Saul and the selection of David are stated in the same verse (1), to show us that God's total plan is no makeshift. The selection is particular and personal.

God directs (4–12). If this holy man Samuel had been left to his own shrewd judgment he would have blundered (6). God had to tell Samuel, 'This is *he*' (12).

God equips (13). To David's fine natural endowments God added the supernatural gift of the Holy Spirit.

QUESTION:
Who alone has the right to tell us that we have been called into full-time service?

'HERE GOD ONCE DWELT'

King Saul appears before us as the Judas Iscariot of the Old Testament. The departure of the Holy Spirit from his life left him an apostate. The presence of an evil spirit from the Lord agitated his soul with new terrors. Intense moods of depression and frustration were followed by violent exhibitions of flaming resentment and hatred. These enemies within the soul made the last state of that man worse than the first, and they finally destroyed him. Who was King Saul's most trusted privy councillor? Samuel! Yet we learn from verse 2 that Samuel dreads the consequences of Saul hearing that another has been anointed king. Here in the desolated sanctuary of Saul's inner life we read the diagnosis of modern man in search of a soul.

Into the sick king's life his advisers now pour the drugs of human palliatives (16). When George Fox felt his need of a clean heart and consulted one whom he thought most fitted to help him, he was roundly told 'to drink more beer and dance with the girls'. The harp is the symbol of all those novelties which, for a time, take the tension and fretting out of the soul, only to leave its deepest needs unmet. The electric guitar, world travel, change of work, marriage – these are a few of the prescriptions given to the unsettled soul to still its restlessness.

DEFIANCE

Goliath the giant shouts his defiance at the armies of Israel, and Saul and all Israel are 'dismayed and greatly afraid'. It is a pitiful and tragic spectacle exactly reflecting the disdain of the world for the church, the contempt of confident pagans for the servant of God. And Israel's army looked the part. There was sarcasm in the Philistine's voice as he demanded 'a man'. But none stirred himself with holy indignation. Arthritis held them to their tents, and they heard without shame the daily reproach upon themselves, upon their nation and, by implication, upon their God. Is this the courageous Saul, whose bold intervention had earlier saved the men of Gibeah from the barbaric demands of 'Snake' the king of Ammon (chapter 11)? Is this the man whose holy zeal called forth the proverb: 'Is Saul also among the prophets?' What then has happened to transform this hero into a coward; this bold opportunist into a procrastinating weakling? Two things have happened. The Holy Spirit has deserted Saul and the affronts of evil men no longer stir and rouse his soul with ardour for his God. The springs of moral courage, robbed of their mysterious source in God the Holy Spirit, have dried up. The hero stands unmanned. The giant boasts and carries on to his heart's content while all the paralysed people of God hope for somebody else to fight their battle.

QUESTION:
From the lives of recent martyrs, what would you suggest gave them their moral courage?

INDIGNATION TRUE AND FALSE

David's indignation was of the right quality (26), spontaneous, agitating his youthful soul, so that his face flushed and his hands were clenched and he could not get his eyes off Goliath. It was not an act, a show of adolescent recklessness. It was the inner man himself, the deep, authentic David, selfless, God-regarding, patriotic, a true moral response. All over the world the religious press is reporting the decay of civilized man's moral sense; the loss of man's sense of righteous indignation. If this betrayal continues God will raise up a new race of striplings to challenge the Goliaths which defy God and his laws and play havoc with the weak and helpless.

Eliab's indignation was unreal and affected (28). He was touchy because his stripling brother had shown up his cowardice, and innocently unveiled his own pure indignation. Unreal indignation like Eliab's is easily detected for its bluff and bluster, its tendency to fix on personalities and make smart remarks to buy a laugh from the coward-circle of its own ilk. Eliab gave himself away when he sneered at his brother: 'With whom hast thou left those few sheep in the wilderness?' (28). David showed himself a man when he 'turned from him (Eliab) toward another' (30). The event will soon declare the calibre of the man.

QUESTION:
Why is indignation of the right kind so rare? What nourishes it? What silences it? What is its greatest peril?

[142]

FIVE SMOOTH STONES

With a pious 'God bless you' King Saul accedes to David's request (37) and leads the barefooted shepherd boy to where his royal armour hangs awaiting a worthy tenant. The weight of the armour about the agile youth made him feel that he was already in his coffin. He hastily extricated himself and, lithe and free as an antelope, bounded to the dry creek-bed and selected with practised eye five stones fit for his sling. This weapon was more than a device for stunning birds. It was the ancient shepherd's rifle for dealing with prowlers at a distance. The tough acacia staff served the same purpose in close encounter. Some have asked 'Why *five*, when the first stone did its deadly work?' He is a wise personal worker who masters as many texts as he can handle. The *first* text does not always meet the seeker's need. And, besides, David has an eye on Goliath's armour-bearer. It is too late to look for more smooth stones when the battle is joined. The older I grow the more thankful I am for parents who expected their seven children to memorise key chapters of the Bible. The smooth stones are always at hand in the bag and it brings no small comfort to finger them in an hour of danger or desperate need and reflect to oneself, 'That stone will be just right'.

FOR SELF-EXAMINATION:
Can I tell one sling-stone from another? David's victory turned on an instructive selection of the right stone from the bag.

THE WEAPONS OF OUR WARFARE

The odds were all against David. Goliath had already won the battle for the mind. Israel's silent army was demoralized. Saul allowed David to enter the fight with the confident Philistine more to sustain honour than to achieve victory. But David's indignation was of God and took its energy from holy inspiration. His own life did not matter, but God's honour did. The giant's sword and spear and javelin (A.V. shield) were so many playthings to be cut in pieces and cast into the Almighty's bonfire (Psa. 46). The one thing that mattered to the shepherd boy, as he fingered the thongs of his sling, was the vindication of the God of Israel. And that God, David reflected, could well care for his people. There was *courage* in David's utterance; but there was something more, there was inspired *prophecy*. This alone can account for the precision of David's utterance (46a). This explains the God-centred testimony and the absence of bravado in David's words. David as a man of God saw Goliath's weapons. But Goliath, a heavy-fisted man of the world, could not see David's. He saw the staff and laughed at it (43). He did not notice the sling – and died by it. The New Testament reminds us that the weapons of our warfare are not carnal, but are mighty through God (2 Cor. 10:4). The Old Testament amply illustrates this principle of the Christian's campaign for Christ.

QUESTION:
Can you suggest what weapons the Apostle Paul had in mind in 2 Cor. 10:4?

[144]

'TO HATE IS TO KILL'

(1) *The friendship of Jonathan and David.* This seems to have sprung from Jonathan's instant recognition of the nobility of David's mature young manhood. Jonathan had won his spurs at Michmash (14: 1–2) and knew what valour was. It takes a noble soul to see nobility in others. This friendship had a spiritual basis. The 'covenant' of verse 3 was a solemn pledge of mutual loyalty and devotion. It involved the sacrifice of an animal in which the parties to the covenant called upon God to witness their solemn pledge. Twice later in circumstances of deepening tragedy they will ratify their covenant (20:16 and 23: 16–13). The pledges which Jonathan gave to David as the mark of his respect for him were something more than generous presents. The robe, the sword, the bow and the girdle were symbols of Jonathan's princely status as the heir apparent to the throne of Israel. Jonathan therefore acts with majestic humility, spurning all temptation to rivalry and jealousy. This action showed that he was trampling these beastly tyrants under his feet; a mark of rare and God-inspired greatness. But he also acted with prophetic insight, declaring by this stripping off of robe and sword and the giving of them to David that he acknowledged David as the divinely appointed heir to the throne.

(2) *The hatred of Saul for David.* Note the downward steps in Saul's new attitude to David, underlining the key words, and noting the key verse (12).

QUESTION:
'To hate is to kill' *(Vinet). Check with the words of Jesus in Matthew 6: 21–26.*

'THE LORD'S BATTLES'

It is no evidence of our spiritual health that we continue to use the words 'the Lord'. Here is Saul with a javelin in his hand and murder in his soul talking to David in his best religious idiom of 'the Lord's battles'. We are altogether blameworthy when we cheaply invoke the Divine Name. Our Puritan forebears were much less free and familiar. How little warrant there was for Saul's degrading use of the divine Name is evident in the vindictiveness with which he now plots the young hero's death, and weaves a web of love-entanglements about his ardent soul. We can only guess how many savage skirmishes were fought and won by David and his gallant men before Saul faithlessly broke up the 'engagement' of David and Merab and married her off to another (19). There is a hint of anxiety in David's shy reply, 'Seemeth it a light thing to be a king's son in law?' (23). The bargaining manner of Saul, over his second daughter Michal, must have profoundly shaken David's whole concept of the dignity of human love and may well have sowed seeds of trouble in David's soul from which the noble youth was later to reap 'flowers of rank odour upon thorny lands'.

Beware of the creeping evil of attaching the Name of 'the Lord' to private opinions, pig-headed prejudice and improper emotions.

JONATHAN THE MEDIATOR

Jonathan, and Joseph, were men of like passions with the rest of us, but they appear before us in Scripture as men of singular excellence, faint and shadowy types of Christ. Yesterday we saw Jonathan as the royal son who divested himself of his glory in favour of the gallant youth David. Today we see him as the mediator. (1) He was vexed by the rift between his father Saul and the popular national hero David. (2) He was willing to do something to heal this breach. (3) He confided in David. (4) He delighted in David. (5) He spoke good of David. (6) He interceded for David's life. (7) His mediation was successful and brought about a reconciliation. While Saul could never be a type of our heavenly Father, we believe that we see here in Jonathan's mediation a setting forth of the work of the great Mediator: (1) in his love for us in our sin and peril; (2) in his willingness to be our Saviour; (3) in his unveiling of his heart to us; (4) in his setting his love upon us; (5) in his speaking for us to the Father through the merit of his own dignity as the royal Son; (6) in his bringing us to the Father.

This type breaks down, however, when we remember the morose and fickle spirit of king Saul and his renewed attempts upon the life of David.

QUESTION:
David composed an ode on Saul and Jonathan (2 Sam. 1) but no poem on his wife. Can you suggest from the little we learn of Michal, why there is this omission?

HONOUR THY FATHER

Yes, even when he is undeserving of that honour! The fifth commandment will not budge. Jonathan, under many aggravations, never gave way to the kind of rejection of his parents that is common enough today. His loyalty to his new friend David in no way weakened his loyalty to his fickle father Saul. He faced the dark realities of his father's violent hatred and murderous purpose and did all he could to frustrate their accomplishment. But he did not abuse his father's name, nor ridicule his father's loss of dignity, nor feed his friendship with David on the husks of gossip and contempt. The Westminster Larger Catechism has a searching answer. 'The honour which inferiors owe to their superiors is all due reverence in heart, word and behaviour; prayer and thanksgiving for them; imitation of their virtues and graces; willing obedience to their lawful commands and counsels; due submission to their corrections; fidelity to, defence, and maintenance of their persons and authority, according to their several ranks, and the nature of their places; bearing with their infirmities, and covering them in love, that so they may be an honour to them and to their government' (Answer 127 on the fifth commandment).

FOR SELF-EXAMINATION:
'. . . *bearing with their infirmities, and covering them in love.*' *Do these words describe my attitude to my parents, children, life partner?*

[148]

'THOU SHALT BE MISSED'

In old Israel the time of new moon was celebrated as one of the festivals of a religious nature which afforded also an opportunity of social fellowship. King Saul, as the Lord's anointed, would acknowledge his obligations by solemnly observing the festival. David, as a member of the royal household, would be expected to be present. He confided to Jonathan 'I should not fail to sit with the king at meat'. Let us pause to reflect upon the fact that, on the festival of the Lord's day, we, who are members of his household by saving faith, 'should not fail to sit with _our_ King at meat'. This is a privilege and a duty arising from our sonship. Our King will be looking for us in his house and at his holy table. It is his day. How is it to be observed?

Jonathan, in verse 18, is very much concerned that David is not to be present at the festival in Saul's house. 'Thou shalt be missed, because thy seat will be empty.' Jonathan, his closest friend will miss him, and will feel impoverished by his absence. The royal household will miss him, as we would miss a leading deacon or elder whose seat appears empty. But the most serious aspect of David's absence is that _the king_ will miss him. And this is the most solemn aspect of our not being in our place at the house of God. Whoever else will notice our absence, _the King_ will miss us 'because our seat will be empty' (18).

RIGHT OR WRONG?
'I did not go to church this morning; I decided to have a quiet hour alone with the Lord.'

[149]

WHITE LIES

Let us face the unpleasant fact that 'white' lies are as old as human nature and in one way or another we can easily be involved in telling them. We can lie by our failure to speak, by our speaking the truth with a slight twist of emphasis, or by our repeating, at the direction of another, what we know to be false. This last was the form in which Jonathan lied to Saul (28, 29). Jonathan knew that David was hiding not far from Saul's village (5). He repeated only the words which David had told him to repeat (28, 29). But he knew the statement to be false. He no doubt reasoned that David's life was at stake, that one little lie was a lesser evil than the king's murdering of David. This 'cunning bosom sin', to use George Herbert's phrase, is to become a habit with David and is to hurt him more than he yet realizes. It crops up again in chapter 21 when David seeks to give plausible reasons to Ahimelech the priest for his sudden appearance and his urgent demands. We have often heard it said that in time of war the first casualty is *truth*. And war, with its vast organized propaganda and espionage, seems to make lying a science and deception a pre-requisite for survival. Let us make all possible allowance for this aspect of David's duplicity. The terrible fact remains that when David's *need* to use deception had long since passed, he resorted instinctively to this 'cunning bosom sin' to obliterate the incriminating evidence of his greatest sin (2 Sam. 11).

MEMORISE:
'Lying lips are abomination to the Lord; but they that deal truly are his delight' (Proverbs 12: 22).

AHIMELECH

Ahimelech enters the vendetta between Saul and David innocently, and everywhere he conducts himself as a man of the highest integrity. Though he sensed trouble when David arrived, a solitary fugitive from no-where, he gave immediate credence to David's false story and in no way acted dishonourably towards his God or his king. His exceptional action in breaking the ritual requirement regarding the 'hallowed bread' (4) i.e. the 'shewbread' of God's Sinai directions (Lev. 24: 5, 6), showed him to be a spiritual man who recognized that the second table of the law was plainly summarised in the words 'thou shalt love thy neighbour as thyself'. This New Testament epitome of the commandments ruled this priest of the old order and governed his decision to give David five of the twelve holy loaves. The only requirement he insisted upon was one of ritual cleanliness of life (4b, cp. Exod. 25: 30). This requirement points forward to the necessity of daily purification by the appropriated cleansing of the blood of Christ (1 John 1: 7).

It is a tragic paradox that David, by misrepresentation and fraud, should have secured hallowed bread from a 'pure table before the Lord' (Lev. 24: 6). But before we turn in dismay from David's action we need to recollect our own ambiguous testimony both before and after we have taken the broken bread and the cup and remembered the Lord's death. Ahimelech and his family are to forfeit their lives for David's crime and for Ahimelech's act of mercy. Christ died, the Just for the unjust, to bring us to God. We eat this Living Bread from off 'the pure table before the Lord'. But how unworthy we are to do so!

A SAFE STRONGHOLD

David's falsehoods and folly did not mean that he had forfeited
God's protection. Nor do the daily shortcomings of a Christian
rob him of the present reality of the promise 'I will never leave
thee, nor forsake thee'. This is one of the mysteries of God's
grace. The cave Adullam (1) has become a byword for
disaffected Christians who come together with their several
grievances against their church, minister, assembly or deno-
mination. David showed his mettle in welding such a rabble
into a commando force whose morale and loyalty were soon to
be apparent (chapter 23). The refugee David became anxious
about his parents who might at any time become the objects of
Saul's vengeance. In taking them to the king of Moab we
assume that David was invoking that blood relationship which
was rooted in the marriage of Ruth of Moab to Jesse's
grandfather, Boaz (Ruth 4: 21, 22). The prophet Gad (5) was to
play a significant part in the life of David. See 2 Sam. 24. It is
clear that the prophet's command was a real test of David's
obedience, for to return to Judah was to forsake the safety of the
wild country between there and the Dead Sea. And the record
here shows that God brought David, in this way, back into the
arena of harsh events and testing circumstances where he
seemed to stare death in the face. It is to circumstances such as
these that we owe the mingled light and shadow of the Book of
Psalms. See especially Psalms 57 and 142.

PRAYER:

> '*My soul trusteth in thee;*
> *Yea, in the shadow of thy wings will I make my refuge,*
> *Until these calamities be overpast'.*
> *(Ps. 57: 1)*

HIDE-AND-SEEK

The underdog has few friends. David never knew whom he could trust. While Saul continued to rule, and to be influenced by suspicion and jealousy, it was unsafe for any Israelite to show the least interest in the outlawed David. The game of hide-and-seek went on in deadly earnest. The arrival of Abiathar as sole survivor of the savage massacre of priests smote David with a deep sense of accountability (22: 22). Very nobly does the young priest subordinate family considerations to those of the people of God (22: 21); and with equal sensitivity David speaks sympathetically of 'all the persons of thy father's house' (22: 22). Abiathar brought with him the ephod of the priest. He was to prove a faithful friend to David amidst all the upheavals of his later reign, and to be high priest until the king's death. By means of the ephod David and his men were delivered from Keilah before Saul could spring the trap on the outlaw band. It is interesting to reflect how shabbily the men of Keilah rewarded David's timely intervention on behalf of the city (23: 12). We are not to expect recognition for our exploits on behalf of others. We are to do our duty without regard to praise or blame. David will wear the crown all the more nobly because of the long discipline of the wilderness. And so shall we.

QUESTION:
With David's wilderness years compare those of Moses and John the Baptist.

SUNDERING ROCK

This is how the long name in verse 28 may be translated. David's plight was desperate, and he had 'lost hope of slipping through Saul's hands, now that Saul's men had encircled his, ready to cut them off' (v.26). Just at the last moment God intervened and drew off the pursuers to deal with their chronic enemy the Philistines. If David had given up hope, Jonathan had not. His last visit to David is full of tenderness and prophetic truth. He knew the daily temptation confronting David, the temptation to despair of ever winning through to liberty and a quiet, ordered life. Therefore he repeated his prophetic words, all of which were to be fulfilled save the beautiful and self-denying sentence 'and I shall be next unto thee'. He has long since renounced all claim to the throne and is happy now to reaffirm the vow in a freshly-sealed covenant with David. But Jonathan will not live to be David's deputy. Loyal to the end, he will perish with his father in the defeat of Israel on Mount Gilboa. Amidst the brushwood and the badlands, among the crags and caves which frown down upon the Dead Sea, David and his men were pursued and hunted; but the God of Sundering Rock presided over the destiny of his anointed and no weapon formed against him was to prosper.

QUESTION:
The rocks of the Old Testament form a fascinating study. Starting from 'Sundering Rock', find five more and the way in which they became significant (e.g. Gen. 28: 22; 31: 45–49; Jos. 24: 26).

'THE LORD AVENGE ME OF THEE' (12)

Right through the Bible runs the golden thread, 'If thine enemy hunger, feed him; if he thirst, give him drink' (Prov. 25: 21, 22 cited in Romans 12: 20); and closely twined with this is a crimson thread, 'Vengeance is mine; I will repay, saith the Lord' (Deut. 32: 35 cited in Romans 12: 19). David had many and good reasons to follow the urging of his motley band and to kill Saul while he was within their grasp. David and his men were hunted outlaws and prudence argued that sooner or later they would walk into an ambush and be killed without mercy. In addition to this prudential motive David's men had worked out a rough and ready theology to justify the taking of Saul's life (4). Their quotation of what the Lord is alleged to have said is nowhere to be found in the earlier narrative, and reminds us of Satan's handling of Scripture texts in his temptation of David's greater son (Matt. 4: 6). David did something impulsively which he immediately regretted (5), but it stopped him from doing something worse (6,7). How great a misfortune it is to lack friends! But how much greater a misfortune to be the victim of the opinions of our friends! David corrected the bad theology of his well-meaning band when he closed his manly appeal to Saul with the words of verse 15.

Can you remember to keep a promise after 20 years?
Compare verses 21, 22 with 2 Sam. 9.

NABAL LIVES UP TO HIS NAME

Nabal means fool. Fool in name he was also fool in nature. 'A churlish fellow and wicked and spiteful in all his dealings' (3). The story dwells upon the contrasting character and graces of his wife Abigail for whose feminine gifts and resourcefulness the churlish Nabal provides the foil. *He was a rich fool* (2) – whose riches may well have been the fruit of tight-fisted individualism. There are go-getter farmers who never help a neighbour and never ask for help and they become a byword in their district and often earn an apt nickname. *He was an ungrateful fool* (10) – dismissing with a shrug his debt to David, and refusing to take any notice of the good offices of David's men when sheep and shepherds alike were afforded their protection (15,16; cp. 21). *He was an insolent fool* (10), taunting David with being a mere nobody and mocking David's men with a barbed reference to their shady past. *He was a short-sighted fool* (11), who failed completely to sense the implications of his churlish refusal of food, and of his insulting words about David and his hungry band.

MODERN VERSION:
A Christian hospital sister can sometimes mar her testimony by using harsh language to her staff. A Christian school teacher can become a humourless purveyor of sarcasm to all and sundry in his charge.

[156]

AN ANONYMOUS FARM LAD

An anonymous farm lad now introduces a warm realism into the
threatening events of this chapter. He had learned in his job to
go to the boss's wife and let her reason with the boss. From
painful experience the lad had to confess concerning his boss,
'He is so cross-grained a man that there is no reasoning with
him' (17). It is proverbial that no man's biography should be
written by his private secretary. He knows him too well – his
foibles, trivialities, vanities and inconsistencies. The unknown
farm lad spoke out in plain honesty to the boss's wife and she
knew he spoke the truth. His canny good sense, his artless
candour, his practical concern all produced an immediate effect
upon Abigail. She sprang into action and was only just in time
to avert the reprisal which David and his men planned to inflict.
It was the initiative of this nameless farm lad which lay behind
the deliverance of Nabal and his household. Examples of a
similar kind are to be found in 2 Kings 5: 2, 3 and Acts 23: 16–
22. Can you think of other such examples?

THE MORAL ISSUE:
*Verse 21 clearly shows that David made a lawful claim upon
Nabal; only when Nabal refused to honour this obligation did
David resort to force – a step which he soon regretted (33).*

MARRIAGE

A broken engagement (18: 19) and a violently ruptured marriage (25: 44), both at the instance of Saul, had left David solitary (though it is possible that he had already married Ahinoam). There is no doubt that Abigail impressed him as a woman of exceptional tact, charm and spirituality. The encounter, as these two remarkable people met at the bottom of the valley, would give large scope to artist or poet. The man's thoughts were swimming in the blood of contemplated carnage. He was taken aback by the presence of a woman who placed herself directly in his way and thus checked his angry course. Her acceptance of all blame (the 'me' in verse 24 is emphatic), her honesty about her husband, her confidence that David would not proceed with his reprisal, her liberal gift, said to be the quickest way to a man's heart, her obvious interest in the destiny of David and in the integrity of his bearing during his life as an outlaw, her spoken conviction that he would certainly be king, and, supremely, her referring all to the sovereign hand and heart of God – all this in Abigail quite conquered David. And when, later, the invitation came to become his wife she, for her part, could scarcely demur, for had she not already said, 'Remember thine handmaid' (31).

NOTE:
A son was born to them (2 Sam. 3: 3) whose name Chileab means 'daddy's pride', a name which, unlike most of David's other sons, he seems to have lived up to.

[158]

SAUL AND DAVID –
THE LAST ENCOUNTER

Saul's earlier remorse and assurances have spent themselves (chapter 24). He grows restless again at the intelligence from the men of Ziph. How could he act otherwise? The loss of the arbitrating and stabilizing Holy Spirit from his soul has left him the weak victim of his fears and of the opinions of his people. What David owed, in his later generalship, to the tough apprenticeship of these outlaw years we can easily imagine. With the instinct of a fine soldier he took great personal risks (5) and held the respect of his pocket-sized army. Abishai, who was to prove himself another fine soldier, penetrated the enemy lines and urged his chief David to allow him to kill the king with his own spear. Was this the javelin Saul had twice hurled at David? Was it true that the Lord had planned this opportunity of a lifetime to rid themselves of a capricious enemy, and Israel of an apostate king? The man of God in David battled against the subtle suggestions of the flesh. The nobility of David's reply showed that the Holy Spirit in David had triumphed over the flesh. It is so easy to give a push to the hands on God's clock, to meddle in his slow-moving purposes. David, for all his faults (which the record nowhere camouflages), was unshakeable in his conviction that God would ultimately deliver him out of all tribulation, as tomorrow's reading (verse 24) assures us.

A LONG FAREWELL

Pleased with their exploit and planted at a safe distance from the camp of Saul, David disturbed the sleeping king with his unusual reveille (14–16). He also concentrated his ironic remarks on Abner, Saul's chief of staff, who deserved all that he got and took a long time to forget it (see 2 Sam. 3: 20, 21). With the king, David is respectful and earnest. The meaning of verse 19a seems to be, 'If an evil spirit from the Lord is at the root of your inveterate hatred of me your remedy is a spiritual one, – you must go to God with a peace-offering and God will surely accept you'. Saul's spontaneous 'I have sinned' (21) is a confession, but we see and hear nothing of the sacrifice, of the peace-offering. To confess our sins to God, and our faults to others may ease our feelings but cannot reconcile us to God. Reconciliation is possible only through the blood of sacrifice and all true confession is made to God in the Name and claiming the merit of the 'one true, pure, immortal sacrifice' of our Lord Jesus Christ (1 John 1: 7–9). There is something pathetic and deeply moving in the words which the remorseful king spoke to David: 'My folly, I see it now; my long blindness, I see it now' (21). Here their ways parted never to meet again, and across the valley rang the prophetic blessing of the unhappy king.

PRAYER:
From all secret grieving of the Spirit, from all sinful refusal of his still small voice, preserve me, O God of all grace, for Jesus' sake. Amen.

CLAY FEET

At every point in this chapter we see the clay feet of a man of God and we are ashamed as we read the record of his slaughter, perjury and deceit. The first lesson seems obvious. When we begin to doubt God's power to take care of us (1) we are necessarily cast upon our own resources. The cunning and calculation of our sinful nature take over the reins of our life and we are driven at a dangerous speed further and further from the will of God. A man of God who begins to practise deception quenches the Spirit. Yet this is by no means uncommon. We speak about the need for prayer, and neglect our own trust with God. We find fault with conduct in others which we somehow excuse in ourselves. We are all a bundle of contradictions and fundamentally much closer to David in this chapter than we may care to confess. Another mark of waning spirituality is insensitivity and callousness where others' lives are concerned. The heartless slaughter of men and women for the sake of plunder and perhaps of policy has its mental parallel in our day. With unfeeling hearts we hear and read of famines and disasters, then turn off our TV set and drop into bed grateful for an electric blanket.

HISTORY BOOK:
Every great revival has seen an awakening of Christian compassion. Illustrate from Wesley's societies, and General Booth's Salvation Army?

THE WITCH OF ENDOR

We live in a day when the resurgent nations of Africa and Asia are renouncing witchcraft, while the wrinkled nations of Europe and America are learning the black arts again. Behind the Old Testament warnings and prohibitions against traffic with the dead and other occult practices (Deut. 18: 9–15) lay a Divine reason which is only partly revealed. All such trafficking is a spurning of the true God (15) and an embracing of Satan's kingdom of darkness. To new converts from animism, 'darkness' is alive with hostile spirits. The deliverance which Christ has wrought for them, and in them, has invoked the mighty authority of Christ who triumphed over Satan and all his demonic legions. These realities are not poetic extravagances nor myth-accretions to be stripped from the Gospels. They are denied and neglected at our peril. But no man or woman who has put on Christ need fear these demonic powers. Saul is now a self-confessed sepulchre. The lights have all gone out in his soul. He invokes the only supernatural power that is left to him, though forbidden to do so by his own official decree (3b). There is no hint that the woman-medium is deceiving Saul or that the spirit of Samuel is not really present. This is the clearest example in the Bible of forbidden spiritism and the strongest possible warning against meddling in it.

LITERATURE:
Rudyard Kipling's poem, 'The Road to Endor' is worth reading as a serious commentary upon spiritism.

THE DEPARTURE OF GOD (15)

The great sin which destroys a man's reputation is not the first of its kind, but the last. These are Henry Drummond's words, written from a different context, but they focus accurately the chain of fatal events in Saul's life. Think back to the glorious days of his unspoiled manhood when he stood head and shoulders above the people and won the loyalty of the tribes to whom he brought national unity and new hope. Think of the humility and fervour of his early service of God. Then remember the first hints of pride and self-will which issued in stubborn rebellion over the matter of Amalek (18). The rending of Samuel's garment still sounds in Saul's ears and with it the doleful sentence 'the Lord hath rent the kingdom out of thine hand and given it to thy neighbour, even to David' (17). When 'the Spirit of the Lord departed from Saul' (1 Sam. 16: 14), all the wide-winged bats of hell flew into the silent cloisters of his soul. Jealousy, hatred, cunning, murder, revenge, all these hideous things ruled his life and robbed it of its warm humanity. Prostrate upon the floor, limp with apprehension of death and utter darkness, this man, once glorious in God's strength, now crumples up, an apostate on the verge of eternity.

THOUGHT:
'A little swerving and the way is lost' (Dante).

LAST-MINUTE DELIVERANCE

Within a few hours of the apostle Peter's appointed time of execution God sent his angel to the prison cell, liberated Peter, answered the prayers of the Jerusalem church, and baulked Herod's savage purpose (Acts 12). Today we read of a similar eleventh-hour intervention of God. The fateful battle of Gilboa is at hand. Achish of Gath, one of the federation of Philistine cities, has brought David and his commandos to strengthen the militia which Gath contributed to the Philistine army. There has already been some playful banter between Achish and David about this (28: 1–3). But behind the light-hearted rejoinder of David there lay an unwelcome necessity. The last thing he wanted was to have to join the Philistine ranks in the clash against Israel, against the Lord's anointed, and against Jonathan. Miraculously a hitch occurs. The commanders of the other Philistine units object to David and his men, fearing treachery (4). Achish tries to defend his action and David pretends the part of a slighted ally, but the outcome was Divinely ordered. David and his men were discharged and, on returning to Ziklag, found that other urgent work awaited their weapons of war.

CONSIDER:
If God tested the praying band in Acts 12 and the warrior band in 1 Sam. 29 with delays until the eleventh hour, may he not have good reason for doing this with us? What real benefits accrue to those who are kept in suspense?

FORCED MARCH FROM ZIKLAG

We can understand the sheer exhaustion of the 200 troops who were left at the ravine Besor (10). They had been on forced marches for at least six days and were now involved in a most agonizing crisis. Their jangled nerves and spent reserves of discipline are evident in the insubordination which seized upon the 600, and almost cost David his life. We only know a great man when we see him in a mortal crisis. 'David encouraged himself in the Lord his God' (6). The first and immediate result was Divine guidance. Although all seemed lost, David was led to call for Abiathar and inquire of the Lord. No thunderbolts or hailstones fell from heaven on the victorious freebooters as they headed south to their desert hide-out. The necessity of bold action fell squarely upon David's weary and demoralized men. The pronoun 'he' in verse 9 is emphatic. David saw with the instinct of a military leader that he must *lead*. When he did, not a man refused to follow. Not a man pleaded exemption. There is almost certain success for that Christian taskforce – whether in church or commando evangelism – where the leader leads and does not merely direct.

LOCAL ILLUSTRATION:
A minister was keen to gather a team for visitation evangelism within his parish. Discouraged by no response to his urging from the pulpit he announced one Sunday that 'the visitation began last Thursday night with a team of two', the minister and his wife.

FIGHTING IN THE BATTLE . . .
OR TARRYING BY THE STUFF (24)

The 400 warriors who grimly pursued and overwhelmed the predatory Amalekites deserved their share of the plunder. And no exception was taken to David's laying claim to the flocks and herds which the Amalekites had thieved from the Philistines. He did so for a purpose, and doubtless the 400 were privy to that purpose. His friends in Judah to whom he sent these beasts as presents (26–31) were those squatters who, unlike Nabal, had often helped David out when he was foraging for food as a hunted out-law. The detail that interests us in today's reading is the dignity given to those who tarried by the stuff (9, 10). David refused to regard them as second-class soldiers, and silenced the protests among the 400 who grudged their comrades an equal share. 'The man that stays behind with the baggage has the same rights as the man who went into battle; all must share alike' (24). William Carey taught the principle that 'ropeholders' are essential to every outreach in Christian missions. They are not second-class Christian workers but are sharing vitally in the maintenance of the campaign which began on the Day of Pentecost and will continue until the day of the Lord's second advent. However urgent the need for full-time workers in the church and in the world, let us not forget the essential equality of the reward in the day when God makes up his jewels (John 4: 36–38), 'All must share alike'.

THE PRICE OF DEFEAT

The late Professor A. M. Renwick deals helpfully in the New
Bible Commentary with the difficulties and apparent discrep-
ancies which make the harmonising of the three accounts of
Saul's death an apparent problem (cp. 2 Sam. 1 and 1 Chron.
10). The crux of the problem is resolved if we see in the
Amalekite of 2 Samuel 1 a cunning opportunist out to ingratiate
himself with David, and a barefaced liar. David was evidently
suspicious of the story. He deferred any action until the
evening. In David's view the coronet and the golden bracelet
were taken in plunder. David listened to the uncorroborated
story of the Amalekite and accepted it as ground for his
summary execution.

The humiliations to which defeated kings were subjected are
commonplace themes on the monuments which archaeology
has brought to us. It was such barbarities as these which Saul
dreaded (4a). His head and armour were paraded in triumph
from place to place, and in the temple of their Philistine gods
Israel's God became the object of mirth and derision. So does
the collapse of an eminent servant of God give the Lord's
enemies occasion to blaspheme.

The writer lingers in closing, over the one bright shaft of light
in this unrelieved gloom. The passage of the years (nearly forty)
since Saul saved the men of Jabesh Gilead has not robbed them
of a sense of gratitude and love. Then Saul was valiant on their
behalf; now they are valiant in their reverence for the dead.

THOUGHT:
When a forest giant is felled many saplings are crushed in its fall.

INTRODUCTION TO 2 SAMUEL

Many readers of these Notes will have seen the two-volume life of Hudson Taylor. The first is called *The Growth of a Soul* and the second *Hudson Taylor and the China Inland Mission*. The First and Second Books of Samuel stand related in much the same way. 1 Samuel deals with the growth of a soul, against the background of opposition and severe trials. This was God's way of training David for kingship. 2 Samuel deals with David's forty years' reign, immediately following upon the death of King Saul. In twenty-four chapters we see etched vividly the memorable events of his reign. The ground is partly covered again in 1 Chronicles.

This is a real life story, full of surprises and with some disappointments. Nobility in David seems strangely mixed with folly. In this he is a man of like passions with ourselves. No small part of the benefit of our daily readings in 2 Samuel will come from that disposition which cries in the face of his mistakes, 'Lord, is it I?', and in the face of his triumphs 'Consider how great this man was!' In his royal office he is a type of Christ the King of kings. In his prophetic office he frequently points to the One who was to come (see the cluster of quotations in Heb. 1 and 2, including the quotation of 2 Samuel 7: 8 at Heb. 1: 5). In his personal relationship to God he knew himself to be a sinner saved by faith in Christ (Psalm 32: 1, 2 quoted in Romans 4: 7, 8).

A SIMPLE OUTLINE OF 2 SAMUEL:

David becomes King	*Ch. 1– 5*
David's victories	*Ch. 6–10*
David's great sin	*Ch. 11–13*
David and Absalom	*Ch. 14–18*
David's closing years	*Ch. 19–24*

AN AMALEKITE

As the tree is bent, so it will grow. Something stronger than dreamy wishes is needed to deliver life from the rut of conformity. More than twenty years earlier King Saul had failed to obey God in the matter of the destruction of the Amalekites (1 Samuel 15). The terrible irony of this chapter is the claim of an Amalekite that he killed Saul (8). We are not convinced that this camp-follower was telling the truth. No witness was present to corroborate his story. David, though profoundly shocked by the report of Saul's and Jonathan's death, and of the disaster to Israel, nevertheless seemed sceptical of the facile story of this talkative opportunist. Be that as it may, there is drama in the man's report that the last words the tormented Saul heard before life was stricken from him were 'I (emphatic pronoun) am an Amalekite' (8). David had just returned from a raid against Amalek (1) and the word Amalekite would sound oddly in his ears. He checked the fact again in the evening after the first wave of mourning and was again told 'I (emphatic) am the son of a stranger, an Amalekite.' (13). The vagrant died at the command of David upon his own testimony that he had slain King Saul. The Amalekite symbolises what George Herbert calls the 'cunning bosom sin' which resists all argument, defies all resolves and refuses to die. Let William Cowper have the last word:

> 'I am no preacher; let this hint suffice –
> The cross, once seen, is death to ev'ry vice:
> Else he that hung there suffered all his pain,
> Bled, groaned, and agonized and died, in vain!'
> (*The Progress of Error*)

THE SONG OF THE BOW

In the hands of a master the violin can speak. To a man of war the bow made music too. It was the sensitive weapon with which the skilled warrior won his victories. Through its quivering strength he expressed himself. The bow and the bowman made an harmonious pair. They understood each other. They were pliant in each other's grasp. In this exquisite poem the music of death sounds softly in our ears. The bow with its taut string plays sadly, slowly, resonantly.

Jonathan's bows (22) are in David's mind: the bow that fell from his hand on Gilboa; the bow that he gave to David as the pledge of his covenanted loyalty (1 Samuel 18: 4); and the bow that turned not back from the pursuit of the mighty (22). David sees the heroic prince in all his nobility of soul as the master bowman, and around this metaphor he builds the theme of his folk-song.

The Philistine bows (1 Samuel 31: 3) are in David's mind; the bows that were powerless against the God-fearing Saul; the bows that were mighty against the demoralized Saul.

The finest of our modern folk-songs are plaintive like this song of the bow. The song was simply called 'The Bow', and verse 18 should be understood as an instruction to Israel to keep green the memory of these her mighty men by the inclusion of this elegy among the patriotic songs of the young and struggling nation.

DAVID KING OVER JUDAH

One cannot read the grim record of cold-blooded carnage in this chapter without a deep feeling of revulsion. Life was cheap. It always is where rivals fight their way to power. Saul's death did not lead at once to the choice and coronation of David. Saul's general Abner had his own ideas and was in no mind to come to terms with David. He still smarted under the reproach which David had thrown at him during his outlaw years (1 Samuel 26: 14–16). Saul's son Ish-bosheth (8–10) had Abner's support, but, behind the puppet king, Abner would rule as virtual dictator. Such a man resented this Robin Hood who had now left the greenwood for the throne. It appears that Abner took the initiative in the civil war which flared up from the tournament at the pool of Gibeon (13–15). The victory for David's general served notice on the ambitious Abner that he had miscalculated. But the tragic civil strife continued and blood flowed freely in the tiny nation until a circumstance arose which angered Abner and drove him over to the side of David (3: 7–12). The history of these fateful years of strife is summed up in the first verse of chapter 3.

ANALOGY:
In the Christian life there is also 'long war' between two contending forces. What are they, and which deserves to win? Look up chapter 5 in the Epistle to the Galatians.

GETTING UP BY THE GUTTER (8)

The writer of these notes remembers as a boy pulling himself up
the wall of the Sunday School hall in his father's country parish
in New Zealand to look for starlings' eggs in the gable. The only
way up was by clinging to the downpipes and guttering. This
proved to be the way to David's capture of the ancient fortress
of Zion. Visitors to Jerusalem are shown the Virgin's Spring
with its lavish gushing supply of cool fresh artesian water. The
discovery was made some years ago of a vertical shaft forty feet
deep and a horizontal tunnel over sixty feet long. This had
apparently been hewn by the Jebusites to secure a water supply
during siege. The capture of the fortress, in spite of the
confident taunts of the defending forces (6, 9) was by means of
this water conduit. The attackers secretly entered the city and
overpowered the unsuspecting soldiers. David was exasperated
by the taunts of the populace whose cat-calls became a kind of
proverb for just such a situation. The modern visitor to the
Virgin's Spring and the Pool of Siloam hardly suspects that so
much critical history has hinged upon the possession of the
spring and its secret passage-way (cp. 2 Chronicles 32: 30).

QUESTION:
*To whom did David attribute his powerful position? Why had this
authority been entrusted to him?*

UZZAH AND THE NEW CART

It was God who commanded Moses to make the Ark of the Covenant (Exod. 25: 10–22). He gave detailed directions regarding its dimensions, materials, purpose, position, and contents. The Ark stood at the centre of Israel's life of union and communion with the living God. The blood sprinkled upon the mercy seat was a vivid foreview of the Cross. When Israel turned this proper use into a superstitious ritual, God promptly let them learn how silly God's Ark looks as a ritual relic (1 Samuel 4: 3–6). Once among the Philistines God again clothed the Ark with his wonder-working power (1 Samuel 5). Now the hour has come to put matters right. King David's motives are good. But we can, in our ignorance and in our wilfulness, do the right thing in the wrong way and thereby bring down upon us and our work God's swift disfavour. *The new cart* was man's way of improving upon God's way. God had already laid down the procedure for the removal of the Ark from place to place. This was to be done by bearers, who were priests and Levites (Numbers 4: 15). Such a humble procession may have looked ignoble; but it was God's appointed way. The new cart was a man-made intrusion into God's order for his church. A long cavalcade of new carts trundles across the broken landscape of church history. Let us beware of this passion for sleek new carts in the work and worship of God. Uzzah's act was not the breaking of an ancient taboo, but the climax of an intolerable affront to God and his word.

DAVID REALIZED HIS ERROR:
See verse 10, 'carried', and verse 13.

ASPIRATION (1–3)

Aspiration (1–3). David, by the grace of God, King of all Israel, now lived in a house of cedar. It was a strange contrast to the cave of Adullam and the wilderness of Engedi. He felt this contrast acutely. It was time to act. He shared his aspirations with the saintliest man he knew (2). He would build a temple for his God where the Ark of the Covenant would find its proper rest. The prophet Nathan applauded David's purpose. The saintly man spoke out of his turn. No human advice is infallible. We are to make no man our master.

Disappointment (4–5). If David felt God's veto he did not show it. He had long since learned to spell 'disappointment' with a capital 'H'. And yet we find no No! in all the succeeding verses. Instead we find two emphatic pronouns which tell the Divine purpose; – 'thou' in verse 5 and 'he' in verse 13. What father would not thrill to the fact that his son was to be so favoured by God, and so concerned for God's glory? Later God confided more fully in the king the reason for his veto. See 1 Chronicles 22: 5–11. The blood-stained hand cannot raise the temple of the God of Peace, in the city of Peace. Only the son of Peace may do that.

Discipline (14–17). When David is gone God will prove a Father to his gifted son; and the pronouns again invite notice: 'I (emphatic) will be his Father, and he (emphatic) shall be my son' (14).

MEDITATION:

> *O Will, that willest good alone,*
> *Lead Thou the way, Thou guidest best.*
> *A little child, I follow on,*
> *And, trusting, lean upon Thy breast.*
>   *(Tersteegen)*

DAVID'S GRATEFUL SUBMISSION TO GOD'S PURPOSE

God's answer to David's deep desire came immediately; and the 'No' was concealed in the greatness of God's promises concerning David's house. When God says 'No' it is in order to a greater good; our desire is denied us in order that his larger blessings may be ours. It is the recognition of this profound fact, which any Christian should be able to confirm from his own experience, that leads David to the tent of God. In spite of the denial his heart is overflowing with wonder, love and praise.

Wonder: 'Thou, Lord God, knowest thy servant' (20). In these words David acknowledges the wisdom of God's overruling. *God knows us.* God knows us better than we know ourselves. He knows our tendency to vanity and self-praise; to egotism and flattery. What God has determined is therefore in every way best for David's own soul.

Love: Our love is a fragrant flower springing from the bulb of faith in the Redeemer. David reads redemption into all God's dealings with Israel (23). He reads redemption in the record all the way back to Egypt, and all the way forward, 'for ever' (24).

Praise: 'Thou hast spoken of thy servant's house for a great while to come' (19). David's vision, as he shades his straining eyes, can see across the centuries. The New Testament tells us that he saw more than we realize. He saw great David's greater Son. He saw the kingdom which cannot be moved. And this awe-inspiring foreview of the purposes of God through David's house gives the quality of eternal reality to his praise.

MEDITATION:

> *Thy wonderful, grand will, my God,*
> *With triumph now I make it mine;*
> *And faith shall cry a joyous 'Yes'*
> *To every dear command of Thine.*
> *(Tersteegen)*

[175]

MEPHIBOSHETH – AND THE KING'S GRACE

The king, at the height of his greatness, leaves off the cares of state, the affairs of his subjects, and the direction of his armies to show the meaning of grace to an obscure and frightened cripple.

A man deformed by a fall (2–5). How he became lame in both his feet is recorded in 2 Samuel 4: 4. We too suffer from a fall and are moral cripples who cannot, unaided, walk with God (Romans 3: 10). His deformity gave him a new name, 'Ugly' – for he was, at birth, named Merib-baal (I Chron. 8: 34), meaning 'the utterance of the Lord', and ugly is what our moral deformities make us in the sight of God.

A King constrained by a Covenant. More than twenty years had passed since David and Jonathan entered into a Covenant. The formality of the Covenant involved the cutting in two of the sacrificial beast. It was sealed in blood, (1 Samuel 18: 23 and 20: 14, 15, 23, 42). The word 'kindness' in verses 1 and 3 translates the Hebrew word for 'grace'. It is the 'grace of God' which David is consciously displaying (3), a grace of which he himself was soon to stand in deep need (chapter 11).

A grace which shows forth Christ. The king gives the cripple a royal audience (6); speaks to him with royal kindness; confides in him the terms of the royal Covenant; restores to him his forfeited inheritance; and pledges a lifelong provision and an enduring fellowship (7). And none could see those crippled feet beneath the royal table.

MEMORISE:
The cripple's anthem of praise in Isaiah 44: 23.

DAVID'S GREAT SIN

The film 'David and Bathsheba' had been running as a serial on T.V. There was a Christian fellow at the factory. His mates were quick to remind him of what they had been viewing. 'Queer birds you Christians have in your Bible. Take this David who wrote those Psalms; we don't go much on him.' The Christian fellow was silent. David's sin is indefensible. But it is not inexplicable. He asked his workmates whether they were any different from David. Why had they soaked up the film so avidly? Why had they remembered it so clearly? Would they have acted any differently in the same circumstances, assuming they had the freedom and power of an eastern monarch?

The detailed exposure of David's baseness in this story is a clear lead as to its purpose. God the Holy Spirit is not talking about one man and one woman, but about every man and every woman, whether believer or unbeliever. He is showing us how little we know our own deceitful hearts; that unsuspected springs of iniquity flow close to the surface of the most consecrated life. He is asking us to take to heart the warning of this man's moral collapse. In a society which is today as lenient as it was in that far off day we are to 'consider ourselves lest we also be tempted'. The lines of the Christian's behaviour are clear in the Bible, but blurred in the confusion of our day. Hence the greater cause for continuous self-examination. Am I drifting in my thought life, in what I read, in my easy attitude to women or men?

PRAYER:
'Keep back thy servant from presumptuous sins; let them not have dominion over me.'

[177]

AWKWARD QUESTIONS

The consequences of sin are like pond-weed, which spreads rapidly from bank to bank. Pull a bunch of the weed with a crooked stick and the entire mass begins to move. David's secret sin is secret no longer, though he seems to think that he can cover up the consequences. The unspeakable baseness of his calculated dealings with his loyal and single-hearted officer, Uriah, fills us with horror. There must have been some persistent questions in Uriah's mind as he hastened back to the battle with the death-letter in his hand. But sudden slaughter sealed his lips for ever. And there were questions in Joab's mind too, which Joab's crafty and ruthless nature was hardly likely to dismiss until he had an explanation. By virtue of this explanation, which soon came to light (27), David placed himself, crown and all, under the moral ascendancy of Joab. The final humiliation for David was to see Joab siding with Adonijah in the rebellion which hastened the coronation of Solomon (1 Kings 2: 28, 29). The royal household whispered its misgivings about the hasty marriage, and soon Jerusalem and Judah were gossiping the story abroad. We may be sure that the story would grow more grievous in the telling until the entire people of God were numb with shame and astonishment. David would find pardon, but he could never regain the place he had come to hold in their hearts.

Try to tell the story from the lips of the unknown messenger (*19*), *expressing his natural questionings, doubts and final dismay when he learned the true facts.*

HIDING A SICK SOUL BEHIND
A STRAIGHT FACE

The Bible urges instant confession of known sin (1 John 2: 1–2). But for a variety of reasons we delay this duty and make repentance more difficult.

God's initiative (1–4). Uriah has been dead for months. The babe had arrived. David was pleased with his camouflage. Yet his sin was the gossip of the nation. He has carefully separated public and private morality. Every passing day finds him more secure in his dangerous casuistry. It is for God to act, as he did less directly with Abraham (Genesis 12: 17; 20: 3). How grateful we should be for the divine kindness which brings our secret sins into the light!

David's straight face (5, 6). As Chief Justice of the nation David's sense of right and wrong was at once outraged. From the bench he gave the instant verdict; he pronounced the death sentence – upon himself. You could construct the most exalted ethic from every man's standards for his neighbour; and the most degraded ethic from every man's own conduct. The history of moral philosophy and modern theology does not lack illustrations of this assertion of Vinet.

God's judgment (7–12). Though pardoned (13), sin always leaves its mark on the servant of God. People have long memories. We can never forgive ourselves. To these consequences God judicially decreed others (10–12) of terrible import. It is the unfolding of these calamities which now clouds this great man's reign.

Psalm 51 should now be read on one's knees.

THE CHILD DIES

A New Hebrides child, born out of wedlock, is called a 'child of the road'. It is inevitable that some stigma should attach to illegitimacy. There is a popular shifting of blame from the parents to the child. But we need to see that the child, like every child, is a particular creation of God (Psalm 127: 3). David's child was not stricken because it was conceived out of wedlock but because here, at the most sensitive relationship of life, God began to implement the calamitous judgment pronounced against David's family. The anguish of the king (16–19) is in striking contrast to his callous treatment of Uriah. Penitence arrests hardening arteries and plants the flowers of gentleness and meekness in the soul. Little can be inferred of the character of Bathsheba, but her second son – if it be even partly true that sons are like their mothers – appears as a man of singular promise and high destiny. On him she lavished the love due to two sons and over his future she watched with jealous solicitude (see 1 Kings 1: 15f).

Joab now begins to show the arrogant ascendancy which slowly planted its boot in the door of David's kingdom (26–31). He knows too much. And David knows he knows. Here is another facet of the price of sin, though forgiven. Joab has within his knowledge the facts for blackmailing his king, and he plans to build skilfully upon this delicate circumstance (cp. 14: 19).

THOUGHT:
The only way to escape blackmail is to renounce sin.

[180]

BAD SONS WITH GOOD NAMES

The Covenant which God made with David led him to hold high hopes for his family. So he called the eldest Faithful (Amnon); the next Father of Peace (Absalom) and the next Jehovah is my Lord (Adonijah). They proved the very opposite of their names. Amnon was unfaithful; Absalom carried the hot embers of murder and revolt in his bosom; Adonijah's rebellion nearly succeeded (1 Kings 1). Chapter 13 records the tragic swiftness with which God's judgments fell upon the house of David. The sins of Amnon and of Absalom were identical with the sins of David in relation to Bathsheba and Uriah. We are meant to see in the character of Amnon's and Absalom's sins the visitation of exactly-weighed justice. David was silent. How could he condemn Amnon and Absalom to the death which their crimes merited when their offences were vivid post-mortems upon his own iniquity? This probably explains the apparent weakness of the king in dealing with his sons. He grieved, he was angry, he knew his duty; but his hands were tied. This is what wilful sin does in robbing us of moral freedom, liberty of speech and testimony. Joab's action (14: 1–3) is hard to fathom. Was he sorry for Absalom? For David? Was he secretly scheming to ally himself with Absalom? His later support of Adonijah at least hints at a treacherous motive. And how otherwise can we read the shrewd intuition of David, 'Is not the hand of Joab with thee in all this?' (19).

THINK IT OVER:
'Christian' is a good name, with a Bible history (Acts 11: 26). Who has the right to bear it?

[181]

SINISTER TURN OF EVENTS

Joab is not the sort of general to grovel on the ground for nothing (22). The wise woman of Tekoah has confessed to Joab's motives. Joab is in a delicate situation. He subdues the arrogance of his growing ascendancy over David and humbles himself in gratitude for the granting of his heart's wish. This looks like the beginning of a plot. Why did Joab go in person to Geshur? What did he and Absalom talk about on the long road back to Jerusalem? The two years of restricted movement cramped Absalom's style and kept Joab powerless to help him (28). Absalom's repeated requests were too risky for Joab to comply with (29) until he had the fire in the barley to send him to Absalom in a hurry. Absalom was impatient for action, and Joab was too cautious in playing this waiting game. Reading between the lines one senses that at this point Joab recognized the fatal danger of going along with the vain and reckless Absalom. He calculated that he would be safer to stay with the ageing King a little longer. It was not yet opportune to show his hand. The reconciliation of David and Absalom was a mockery of plain hypocrisy. Absalom bowed his body but not his heart. David's kiss of peace ignored the truth 'There is no peace, saith my God, to the wicked'. The stage is now set for Absalom's daring revolt and David's deepest humiliation.

DOCTRINE:
In contrast to David's kiss, the cross takes sin seriously.

TWO PROVERBS

The New Hebrides islanders have a proverb, 'He's an old hawk and can no longer get off the ground.' That was what Absalom thought of David. He reckoned that his old father was heading for senility, had lost the confidence of the people, and would go to pieces in the face of a determined coup. But another Melanesian proverb says 'The old dog has grey hair, but beware of its bite!' And it was this reality which the coming drama would confirm. There *had* been steady deterioration in David. Civil cases were delayed and it was hard to get justice (4). His people saw too little of him for his own good. The harem had grown and effeminacy had partly conquered him (16). The image of Absalom as the youthful reformer had captured the imagination of the puzzled populace. The forty years of verse 7 should read four years – a copyist's slip accounts for the difference – and should be counted from Absalom's return from exile. Allowing for the two years of restraint (14: 28) Absalom had apparently had two years in which to sow the seeds of rebellion far and wide (12). When the trumpet sounded in Hebron and reverberated from Dan to Beersheba it looked as if Absalom could not lose. David recognized that, humanly speaking, his end had come (14). Flight was the only thought. But no sooner had king David resolved upon flight than the old dog with the grey hair began to show that he could still bite. With superb loyalty his foreign bodyguard (18) stood by him to a man. They passed over the brook Kidron (23), across which great David's greater Son was later to pass with his tiny escort of perplexed disciples on the way to the Garden of Gethsemane (John 18: 1). In both cases apparent defeat was to issue in victory.

[183]

VINEGAR TO DRINK

The bitterness in David's cup was compounded from the nettles of his son's treachery, the sorrel of his people's fickleness (12, 13), the docks of Ahitophel's disloyalty (31), and the convolvulus of Shimei's cursing (16: 5). David drained the cup to the dregs. His greater Son would taste and drink a yet more bitter cup compounded of the weeds and poisons of humanity's sin (Mark 14: 36).

It was at this darkest hour that David's heart began to sing. You will find his song in Psalm 3. As the first pangs of humiliation passed David turned instinctively to God:

'Thou, O Lord, art a Shield about me;
My glory, and the lifter up of my countenance'.

As he sang light broke. First gallant Ittai scorned all disloyalty and pledged his sword in life and death, to his master (19–22). Then David saw the mute concern of his weeping people lining the way of his escape (23). Next came the two high priests complete with ark and Levites. They knew where they belonged (24). By directing them back into the city David was intimating his confidence that God would fight for him and restore him to his throne. The ark was the visible pledge of his return (25). The high priests were safe from civil strife by virtue of their Divine office. They, with Hushai, must play their part boldly in the king's secret service, and the young runners could be trusted to carry the dispatches (36).

CONSIDER:
David's impulsive prayer about Ahithophel (31). Do you find yourself using this kind of urgent prayer in the midst of a difficult situation? How was it answered (see 17: 14, 23)?

ZIBA THE OPPORTUNIST (1–4)

Ziba the Opportunist (1–3). When a government looks like
falling the political vultures appear from nowhere. Ziba was one
of these. He was manager of Saul's estates which David had
restored to the crippled Mephibosheth. He now reckoned that
David was ousted for ever, and would not even have time to
verify the slander about the lame man's treason (3) and
ingratitude. King David gave his hasty decree in favour of Ziba
(4), but lived to revoke it in part (19: 29, 30).

Shimei, the turncoat (5–14). In this incident with its sequel
(19: 16–23), we see the true greatness of a man of God. Abishai
reflects our natural irritation and resentment under heckling
and provocation. A wife often resents reflections upon her
husband and has to be pacified by her husband! Here David
steadies his hot-headed champion with a tight rein and a sober
self-judgment. When we suffer some churlish insult or sneak-
ing innuendo we give God his highest advantage when we look
first into our own imperfect lives, as David does here (11, 12);
we can afford to say 'Let him alone and let him curse!'

Hushai the actor: Espionage is as ancient as war and with
espionage goes lying as a science. Hushai had been made the
nerve centre of David's Secret Service and the record shows
with what cool-headed counsel he carried out his delicate task.
God often has his chessmen in strange positions on the
chessboard.

IN REAL LIFE:
*It was a quiet-spoken travel agent who once helped me out of a tight
spot in the Middle East. I kept saying to myself, 'As for God, his
way is perfect'. But I did not dare to ask how the little travel agent
got me on that plane!*

[185]

ANSWERED PRAYER

To pray is one thing; to keep our meddling hands off the complex circumstances is another. David was now dependent upon God's sovereign control of events. The lesson of the reading is given in verse 14. This is no easy lesson for a Christian to learn. We tend to adopt Oliver Cromwell's motto, 'Trust God and keep your powder dry' as an excuse for helping God to help us.

Ahithophel's counsel was normally taken as final (16: 23). And his shrewd advice to pursue and kill David while his little force was disorganised was no doubt sound. It appealed to the men who had to make the big decision (17: 4), and should have been conclusive. But here God showed his hand. Hushai had not heard Ahithophel's advice until Absalom rehearsed it to him. He therefore needed divine wisdom in his extemporised advice. As we read Hushai's cautious use of 'do' and 'don't' we see how skilfully God used him to unnerve Absalom (8–10) and then to embolden him (11–13). His word-pictures of fateful defeat and then of total victory were vivid and telling. Here we see confirmed the Bible declaration that the heart of the king is in the hand of the Lord.

On 25/2/1750 George Whitefield wrote to the downcast James Hervey, one of the brilliant constellation of Oxford Methodists, and quoted these words:

'Leave to His sovereign sway,
To choose and to command;
So shalt thou, wond'ring, own His way,
How wise, how strong, His hand.
Far, far above thy thought
His counsel shall appear,
When fully He the work hath wrought,
That caused thy needless fear.'

[186]

ENCOURAGEMENT

Encouragement. The advice of Hushai was taken, but he was not present to hear the verdict of Absalom's privy councillors. That is why he sent the prompt despatch to David giving both Ahithophel's plan and his own, and urging the king to take the worst view of the situation and put the river Jordan between his own and Absalom's men. The adventures of the two runners indicate how precarious was their task and how Absalom's men were on the alert. David acted upon Hushai's advice, and got his entire force across the river by daylight.

Ahithophel's self-inflicted death is a commentary upon the words of Scripture, 'The sorrow of the world worketh death'. A disappointment, a loss of face, a deep humiliation is a terribly devastating experience to a man or woman who is living for this world and for what it can give. The growing prevalence of suicide and the pagan attitude to life and death are intimations that the most accomplished Ahithophels of our modern society are really very fragile, and crack under the stresses of a sick soul. Contrast the God-centred resolve of the humiliated king.

Hospitality (27–29). The gallant action of the three benefactors from such widely scattered areas must have heartened David and his men. Here were people who would risk their lives for David because they believed in his cause and in his ultimate triumph. David and his men were hungry for more than cheese and wheat. They needed the encouragement of these men of Israel's sturdy yeomanry; men who lived on the land and far enough from the intrigues of the court and the superficiality of the city to see things in their true proportions. Shobi, of Ammon is something of a mystery man (27) but not more so than Ittai of Gath and the loyal bodyguard of foreign troops who marched with the king to victory or disaster.

PRAYER:

'Preserve me, O God, from such eyeservice as would keep my soul in bondage to men and my will a slave to the opinions of men.' Amen.

[187]

WORTH TEN THOUSAND MEN

Worth ten thousand men. That was what these loyal veterans thought of their king. That is a pale reflection of what Christians think of their King. As the three little regiments passed out of the gates the 'eyes right' was no parade-ground formality. A glimpse of the king was life to their souls. Now they could fight as brave men in a righteous cause.

Cast into a great pit. This was the fate of the rebel son whose angel-like form and soft, seductive voice stole away the hearts of the people of God. Absalom's tomb still stands outside the eastern wall of Jerusalem, across the Kedron and close to Gethsemane. He planned his life grandly and built an ostentatious place for his bones (18). But a great pit received his mangled body and no burial honours were shown him. In all of this Absalom stands in the shadow of a more sinister figure who rebelled against his God and was cast out of heaven. In exile he planned the overthrow of the Father's kingdom, declaring, in Milton's powerful lines:

> 'All is not lost; th'unconquerable will,
> And study of revenge, immortal hate,
> And courage never to submit or yield,
> And what is else not to be overcome'

While temporary reverses are the lot of our King's men we have the Father's assurance that his kingdom is an everlasting kingdom. The fate of Lucifer and all his squadrons is determined. A great pit will receive him, and afterwards the lake of fire (Rev. 20). Then Christ shall stand forth in undisputed majesty and power. To him be glory and praise for ever. Amen.

PATHOS

In all the light and shadow of David's long and chequered life there is no moment of soul-anguish like this. He had often looked death in the face, stood side by side with greatness, read nobility in souls like Jonathan, and baseness in men like Shimei. He had come to the gates of hell, a moral leper on the brink of eternity, only to be rescued and restored. He had written out his penitential psalm (Psalm 51) in the indelible ink of a contrite sinner's tears. And now, in Absalom's death, he saw himself. He blamed himself. Absalom was too much like his father, too much like his pagan mother, too much conditioned by the luxury of the royal court, too much indulged and too little taught. In Absalom's wayward course David was tormented by the likeness to himself. Though long since forgiven by God, he watched the just sentence of God move inexorably through his household. First Tamar, then Amnon, now Absalom. When will this plague be stayed? 'Would that I had died for thee, O Absalom, my son, my son!'

Absalom had had the world at his feet. He had the charm and physique; he had wealth and position; his future was so full of promise. But he marred it all to serve that great tyrant – himself. Absalom's name means peace; but he died with a dagger in his belt and three darts in his heart.

THOUGHT:
There is an Absalom within every heart who only waits the right moment to renounce the King and usurp the throne.

BRINGING BACK THE KING

When I have wilfully sinned I have rebelled against my lawful King as much as Israel did when they followed Absalom. When the Holy Spirit has shown me the meaning of my sinful rebellion I am faced with a solemn choice. Either I may return at once, a red-handed rebel, to my King, depending upon his royal clemency and cleansing blood (1 John 2: 1, 2), or I may feel so ashamed and unworthy, so confused and upset, that I fear to seek his face. Thus I delay my confession and postpone my submission. This was Israel's feeling. The enemy Absalom was dead; the rebellion had ended in disaster. But 'all the people were at strife' (9). A modern version translates these key verses, 'And now all through the tribes of Israel, there was high debate. Here is a king, men said, who has rid us of our enemies, rescued us from the power of the Philistines, and he must be exiled from his kingdom to please Absalom! . . . Why is no voice raised for bringing the king back to us?' (9, 10b).

While Israel debated, the king acted (11). Thank God that our King knows how to do the same. He breaks in upon our guilty moods of diffidence, delay and fear with a direct word to our heart: 'You are my own kith and kin . . . Why do you hang back, instead of restoring me to the throne?' (12)

Perhaps this is a loving reprimand from King Jesus to our hearts this morning. He awaits our invitation.

FAIR WEATHER FRIENDS

For every clear-headed high-souled Christian who will stand up and be counted there are a dozen who will look this way and that to see what is expedient and safe. There is a little verse which Dr Martin Niemöller liked long before the crisis of National Socialism broke over his beloved country in the 1930's:

'One man will ask, "What comes of it?"
Another, "What is right?"
And this is what distinguishes
The vassal from the knight.'

The race of Shimei and Ziba is still with us; the race of yes-men with their facile grimace and nervous chatter. These are the men who can talk like Bunyan's Mr Talkative, and look like Bunyan's Mr Facing-both-ways. We marvelled at the old king's moderation with Shimei a little earlier in the hour of Shimei's insolence (16: 11–13). Now we marvel at his kingly grace in giving sentence upon the cringing suppliant: 'Thou shalt not die' (23).

Shrewd Ziba had to be silent in the presence of Mephibosheth, nor did he challenge the lame prince's testimony before the king (26, 27). 'The king has been criticized for not punishing Ziba's treachery, but it is quite possible that Ziba was acting partly in Mephibosheth's interest, under the impression that Absalom was likely to be victorious – the property which Ziba managed for his master would be safe from confiscation in either event' (Ronald Knox's footnote).

PRAYER:
Preserve me, O God, from the fear of man which brings a snare.
Amen.

MAN OF IRON

This is the meaning of Barzillai's name, and we cannot resist the conviction that it was a title of respect which his eighty years had earned for him. An army of Barzillais made up Oliver Cromwell's ironsides. For many more such men we cry, in Byron's words:

> 'Of the three hundred grant but three,
> To make a new Thermopylae!'

He liberally provisioned the king and his men in the darkest days of their misfortune (17: 27–29) and had scorned the perils of such an action. Now he arrives, a dignified figure with erect head and square shoulders, to show his fealty and offer manly encouragement. The noble sincerity of his words won the king's deepest respect (39). Where iron blends with human sympathy, and age ripens in unselfish dignity, there you see the aristocracy of the kingdom of heaven. 'Consider how great this man was!' (Hebrews 7: 4).

The royal escort swells as the king makes his triumphal return. The men of Judah came first (15). The men of Israel arrived at Gilgal, on the western side of Jordan to find that they had been forestalled and made to look tardy in their loyalty. The ensuing family quarrel revealed the unsettled condition of the nation and erupted in the abortive rebellion of Sheba. To bind such factions into a firm national unity once more was to prove no easy task.

DAVID'S SONG OF VICTORY

When David Livingstone died London *Punch* paid its tribute in two memorable lines:
> Marble may perish
> This is Livingstone.

The Psalmist-King, unlike his ambitious son Absalom, built no ostentatious monument to celebrate his greatness and his victories. He knew he was a God-made, not a self-made man, and that is why he turned his gratitude into imperishable song. The encore to this song will be found in the Psalter (Psalm 18), like The Old Hundredth which occurs in both the psalms and hymns of the Scottish Church Hymnary.

It belongs to an earlier period in David's reign when God had set him upon the throne of all Israel (cp. 2 Samuel 8: 1–14). The imagery of his fugitive years leaps to vivid life in the language of the rocky stronghold (2,3) and the raging wadi (5); the thundering heavens (14,15) and the massing nimbus clouds (12). But his meaning is never lost in a jungle of incoherent speech or hazy symbolism. God marches in triumph from the first verse to the last. He has a sharp ear for his servant's cry (4,7), a swift mount to come to his rescue (11), and a terrifying power when his arrows are sent winging towards his enemies.

Much of our Christian song is soft and plaintive and subjective. The honest heart needs the balancing language of majesty, the thunder of full-throated exultation, to do justice to so great a God as our God. That is why 'Ye gates, lift up your heads on high' to the tune St George's Edinburgh, and 'A safe stronghold our God is still' to Ein' feste Burg, are so magnificent and right.

QUESTION:
How do you account for the world-wide popularity of the hymn
'How great Thou art'?

[193]

WRITING HIS OWN TESTIMONIAL

When the writer of these notes applied for his first job, his father, who was also his minister, wrote out a reference. As the fifteen-year-old son read through his father's reference he was amazed how many good points his father could think of, and how many bad points he had forgotten! Here is David writing out his *own* testimonial and doing it for posterity to read and ponder. So long as he celebrates God's sovereign grace none will find fault (17–20). 'His great love befriended me' (20b).

But when he begins, in measured sentences, to recite his own virtues we are taken aback (21–25). 'Have I not kept true to the Lord's paths?' (22a). 'No task He laid upon me have I refused; ever stainless in His presence' (23b, 24a). This is the man who also wrote, 'Purge me with hyssop, and I shall be clean; wash me, and I shall be whiter than snow' (Psalm 51: 7).

These contradictory moods are really two sides of the believer's experience. He knows himself to be a sinner befriended by God's great love, and cleansed from the guilt and stain of sin. The fruit of this assurance is seen in strenuous endeavour to please God. By God's grace he is 'enabled more and more to die unto sin and live unto righteousness'. And it is this work of sanctification which David is celebrating here. The two sides are beautifully expressed in verse 27a, 'He that is Thy Own shall find Thee his very own.'

THOUGHT:
'As for God, his way is perfect' *(31). The Hebrew word translated 'perfect' occurs in verse 24 as* 'upright'. *It is a plural noun which is found again in the 'Urim and* Thummim', *lights and* perfections, *of Exodus 28: 30.*

BRONZE BOW AND BATTLE CRY

In Chapter 21: 15 we read the account of David's last battle. Only the swift intervention of Abishai saved the king's life. He was now too old for war and bowed to the will of his people. But the thrust and tumult of today's reading belong to an earlier time when the necessity of war kept David alert upon all the frontiers of his little kingdom. From strenuous campaigns and hand-to-hand fighting he emerged unhurt. Mighty armies hunted him down, only to be smashed upon the Rock of his Salvation. Famous heroes sought him out for single combat only to be stricken and crushed. David had a charmed life, and he never doubted why:

> 'Thy saving power, Lord, is my defence,
> Thy tender care fosters me' (36)

A little reflection will bring the same testimony to our own lips. Our battles have been spiritual; we have had to meet as varied enemies as king David. They have molested us upon all the frontiers of our daily life. Here and there a vicious foe has stood gloating over us as he did over Bunyan's pilgrim: 'I swear by my infernal den that thou shalt go no further; here will I spill thy soul.' With shame we confess to the spirit of rebellion which has sometimes seized upon our secret soul, though God alone saw this incipient treachery (44a). It is of the Lord's mercies that we are not consumed.

PRAISE:

> *'Blessed be the living Lord who is my God,*
> *Praised be the God who rescues me!' (47).*

CLEAR SHINING AFTER RAIN

'Dark, dark hath been the midnight
But dayspring is at hand'.

Yes, this last song, probably written from the brink of
eternity, is golden with the light from the Celestial City and
fragrant with the perfumes of Beulah Land. The threefold
tribute of verse 1 is from another hand. It is what we would call
the Foreword. The song opens with the fact of Divine
inspiration. While all ages celebrate the 'sweet psalmist of
Israel', he himself sees his exquisite poetry as the flowering of
the Holy Spirit's work within him (2; cp. 2 Peter 1: 21). It is
natural to praise the poet; supernatural to recognize the Spirit's
primary part in this and all of Holy Scripture. The song mirrors
the unflecked azure of God's perfection (3, 4). It is David's
closing testimony that in God is no darkness at all, no shadow
cast by turning. This truth only serves to deepen the wonder of
God's covenant grace. 'What worth has my kindred in God's
sight, that He should make an everlasting covenant with me,
sealed and ratified all of it?' (5). The Covenant continues. Jesus
is the Son of David on his human side (Romans 1: 3). And every
Christian inherits the benefits of the covenant, by faith in great
David's greater Son. David's kingdom has gone. The kingdom
of the Son of David has already been set up, and his kingdom
shall know no end.

FOOTNOTE:
*On verses 6, 7. The towering men of Belial who sought the king's
harm have shrunk to briar size; and they are as dry as tinder, ready
for the fire.*

[196]

DAVID'S MIGHTY MEN

Why were these mighty men so few? Each name is recorded on the king's honour roll with his exploit beside his name. Why have the élite been so few in the story of God's church? Is it that the record is incomplete? Is it that valour and cowardice are strangely intertwined in most of us? Is it that we love life, and the praises of men too well? Is it that God's servants are too earthy to survive gold-lettered mention upon the King's honour roll? Yes, all of these reasons operate decisively to restrict the inner circle to three; and the next circle to three, and the outer circle to thirty. Have we observed the motley nature of these men of valour? They were, for the most part, heroes of David's outlaw years, joint tenants of the cave of Adullam, men with a price on their heads. The gallant three who cut their way through to the Well of Bethlehem for water for their leader were performing a deed which declared ultimate and unquestioning allegiance. Mighty men they were, not only in valour, but also in devotion to their leader. Divided by race, upbringing, and a number of other circumstances, they were united by one single fact – and it was sufficient: they were *David's* mighty men. Loyalty to his person lay at the heart of their unwearied devotion, and at the root of their valour. It must be so with us under the Captain of our salvation.

> 'I have a Captain, and the soul
> Of every private man
> Has drunk in valour from his eyes
> Since first the war began.
> He is most merciful in fight,
> And of his wounds a single sight
> The embers of my failing might
> Into a flame can fan.'
>
> (T. T. Lynch)

[197]

THE CENSUS

The sin of Israel (1) F. W. Krummacher, the 19th-century German writer, suggests that this verse indicates that God was about to punish Israel as a nation for their successive acts of national treachery in following first Absalom and later Sheba. Certain it is that the judgment which David left to God's choice fell upon the nation as a whole rather than upon David's own family (14,15).

The sin of David. But it is also clear that David succumbed to the sin which Milton calls 'that last infirmity of noble mind' – the sin of pride. The taking of the census was clearly not an act of sin; Moses had already done this at God's direction (Exodus 30: 12, 13). Yet in this earlier census we have a hint of the sin which is implicit in all carnal counting of heads; the sin of vainglory, self-praise and subtle pride. Every man, on being counted, had to bring a money gift to make 'a ransom for his soul'. And the explanation is added, 'that there be no plague among them, when thou numberest them' (Exod. 30: 12). Joab must have had this warning in mind (3). And the king is represented as forcing his will upon the reluctant nation. It is an unhappy aspect of church work that statistics major on the number of baptisms, confirmations or new communicants in a congregation, as if these provide the only intelligible yardstick of success or failure. To the sensitive conscience this is all wrong. There is as much combustible pride in us as in David and we are just as prone to purr over publicity as he.

CONFESSION:
Unlike the earlier sin (chapter 12) David was brought to penitence and confession before the prophet arrived. This is clear from the Hebrew of verse 11.

'I GIVE IT ALL'

B.C. 1800. An ageing father walks slowly up the hill. Beside him is his son. 'Behold the fire and the wood: but where is the lamb for a burnt-offering?' The father's reply was spoken in faith and hope and love; 'My son, God will provide himself a lamb for a burnt offering.' (Genesis 22). The hill was mount Moriah. There Abraham gave his all.

B.C. 1000. Araunah the Jebusite was threshing corn on a flat rock outside the royal city. The prophet of God told King David that this was to be the place where God's plague would be stayed from the people. Araunah, though not a Hebrew, generously gave his oxen for the sacrifice, his land for the sacred altar and his yokes and implements for firewood. 'I give it all', he declared (1 Chron. 21: 23). The site of Araunah's threshing floor was the site of Abraham's Mount Moriah. Here on land purchased by David, Solomon reared the temple. Here Herod's temple was built. Here today the Mosque of Omar stands.

A.D. 26. 'Destroy this temple and in three days I will raise it up' (John 2: 19). The sign was fulfilled. Within sight of Abraham's Moriah, and Araunah's threshing floor, the Lamb of God gave his all. There the Father provided a lamb for a sin-offering. There the plague of sin was stayed from the people. There Christ in his resurrection body consecrated the spiritual temple whither we all are drawn in spiritual worship.

A.D. 1986. 'The hour cometh when ye shall neither in this mountain, nor yet at Jerusalem, worship the Father . . . God is a Spirit; and they that worship him must worship him in spirit and in truth.' (John 4: 21, 24).

[199]

THE GOOD LIFE

Today we pass from the life of David to a selection from the Psalms of David. Upon the threshold of the Psalter we are offered a priceless gift – the secret of happiness. The Psalms are the beatitudes of the Old Testament. Their first word is 'blessed' (R.V. marg. 'Happy'). Their entire theme is the blessed life. 'Blessed' (1) is a Hebrew exclamation. The Psalmist has been reflecting upon man's various recipes for happiness. He sees them reduced – fundamentally to two. The happy life is viewed from the standpoint of its relationships – human and Divine. If human relationships rule a man he will never be more than wind-blown chaff (4). If fellowship with God rules a man he will flourish like a deep-rooted tree. There is a calculated contrast between 'prosper' (3) and 'perish' (6). The contrast is so radical that the Psalmist breaks the silence of his own soul's wonder with the ejaculation 'Happy man! – you who walk not . . .' (1). The Hebrew verb for 'blessed' means straight or upright. Hence the etching out of the picture of the happy life is in terms of *character*. The blessed life is the good life, the happy man is the man of character. Underline the verbs which show that the happy life is the separated life (1), the satisfied life (2), the evergreen life (3). And if you are wondering how any one can speak of the happy life without speaking of forgiveness of sins look up Psalm 32.

CHRIST ON THE THRONE

This Psalm could have been written against the background of today's press headlines. The drama is timeless – plotting governments (2–3) seething peoples (1) a sovereign God (4–5) and a Saviour King (6–11). The 'Why?' of verse 1 is rhetorical. What folly to challenge God! While the 'heathen' (lit. the nations) mount their forces against King David, their real grievance is with almighty God. His yoke galls the unbroken spirit but is easy and light to the penitent. Down the vista of the years David sees the advent of the Messiah King. Since men and nations are by nature rebels Messiah's rule is resisted, and his cords of love are trampled underfoot (2–3 cp. Hosea 11: 4). Has he no champion? Yes, the Father who has decreed (6–9) that Jesus should have all power in heaven and in earth (Matt. 28: 18). The Father's absolute right and sovereignty are wrapped up in the emphatic 'I' of verse 6. 'My king' refers, in its obvious local sense, to King David; in its prophetic and universal sense to King David's greater Son. Thus there are three distinct kings in the Psalmist's mind: the kings of the earth (2), the eternal King of glory (4), and the Son, 'begotten of his Father before all worlds' (6–7) whom the Father calls 'my King'. Can we truthfully call him ours?

MEDITATION:
'Rejoice with trembling' (11) is a text which so gripped Augustine that he quotes it three times in his Confessions. *He would have linked it with such warnings as 1 Cor. 10: 12 and Rom. 11: 20.*

GOD'S MINORITIES

Ten thousand against one. These are heavy odds (3: 6). You must have noticed the contrast between the 'many' (3: 1–2; 4: 6) and David's 'I' and 'me'. These odds are the experience of the people of God still. You can think of situations when you felt as solitary as he, in a circle of gaping hostile critics (3: 6). But he has learned to set his troubles to music, and rousing music it is:

> 'Before the battle-lines are spread
> Jesus saves me now.
> Before the vaunting foe is dead
> Jesus saves me now.'

God's minorities are God's care. 'One man with God is a majority.' The whole Bible is full of the blessings of such secure solitariness. We learn to lean harder (3: 3), to pray better (3: 4) and to do without sedatives (3: 5; 4: 8). The local setting of these psalms is the treason of Absalom (2 Sam. 16–17) and the swelling roar of full-throated rebellion. It is amazing to recognize in these psalms David's evensong and matins on the first day of his ignominious flight from the royal palace and city.

Augustine tells, in his *Confessions*, how the Psalter 'discovered' him during his preparation for baptism. 'When I read the fourth psalm, how that psalm wrought upon me. I quaked with fear, and kindled with hope and with rejoicing in Thy mercy, O Father'.

MEDITATION:
'him that is godly' (4: 3) – one who lives under the influence of God's holy love.

'REMEMBER NOT THE SINS OF MY YOUTH' (7)

Those who live beside the open sea will know that it never wants for waves. Even when the wind is off the land small rollers fight their way ashore and you waken to their muffled music every morning. The Psalms are an ocean of spiritual experience, and always, whenever we listen, we hear the undertone of a sin-burdened heart at prayer (7, 11, 18). Hence this Psalm mingles testimony with confession; praise with awe; petition with humility. At verse 7 bitter memories overwhelm the psalmist. Has he no assurance of pardon that he thus turns back the pages of the past? Indeed he has! But he has learned that memory will not rest. It takes lively issue with the cleansing Cross. It disturbs and unsettles our peace in the Lord. There is therefore only one way to know daily assurance and that is to keep our eyes upon Christ amidst all unsettling memories. 'I possess assurance only so long as I see these two things simultaneously: all of my sinfulness and all of God's grace' (Prof. O. Hallesby).

A page from the past. Margaret Wilson, in 1685, at the age of 18, died a martyr during the Scottish covenanting struggles. She was tied to a stake and drowned in the tide in Solway Firth. Her last words were from the metrical version of Psalm 25:

> 'My sins and faults of youth
> Do Thou, O Lord forget;
> After Thy mercy think on me,
> And for Thy goodness great'.

'I HAVE NOT SAT WITH VAIN PERSONS' (4a)

These words describe a deliberate attitude to bad company. I once saw them written on the work-book of a New Hebrides lad who had proved a gifted helper in Bible translation. He was converted at the age of fifteen and grew rapidly in spiritual perception. He knew from experience that 'bad company is the devil's bird-lime' (Thomas Fuller) and had made Psalm 26: 4 his motto because it so aptly described his own resolve. He trusted in the Lord (1b) and loved the habitation of his house (8a). His life was full of promise. Then World War II brought a great Naval Base to a nearby island. With other islanders he visited this base for a few weeks to earn some money and see what he could pick up. They were welcomed by the Forces and entertained night after night at the cinema. This shattering introduction to western sophistication debauched his soul. He returned to his village with the light of his joy and testimony snuffed out. In spite of his motto he failed to keep his foot on level ground (12a). His experience has been that of thousands of promising young Christians. This explains the defensive palisade which the Psalmist builds about his soul in the resolve of this Psalm.

Consider Milton's lines put into the mouth of Samson's father:

> 'O miserable change! is this the man,
> That invincible Samson, far renowned,
> The dread of Israel's foes? . . .
> Select and sacred? glorious for a while,
> The miracle of men; then in an hour
> Ensnared, assaulted, overcome, led bound . . .
> Into a dungeon thrust, to work with slaves.'

[204]

THE BEAUTY OF THE LORD (4)

'It is an awful problem – a beautiful face with no true moral beauty below; a splendid physical grace – with no deeper grace beneath'. So wrote Forbes Robinson in one of his choice 'Letters to his Friends' published after his early death. And in another letter he says, 'Beautiful eyes where there is no beauty of soul beneath, are the eyes of others, long since dead, looking at us still.' Beauty had its fascination for the Psalmist as it has for all of us. He wanted time alone with God to see in God that perfection which is God (4). A great variety of Hebrew words is used in the Old Testament to give flexibility and depth to the idea of beauty. Here the word used means that radiance of beauty which flows from the perfection of God's being and God's ways. We speak of a 'radiant' bride because she looks so happy, so wholesome and so free. This is the kind of beauty the Psalmist found in God, as he spent time in the house of God. To behold the beauty of the Lord is to be made beautiful. Moses the man of God used the same Hebrew word in Psalm 90: 17 when he prayed: 'Let the beauty of the Lord our God be upon us'. The same Hebrew word is revealed in real life in Naomi – 'my lovely one' (Ruth 1: 20).

MEDITATION:
'In the true holy affections of the saints there is beautiful symmetry and proportion . . . There is every grace in them that is in Christ'. (*Jonathan Edwards in* The Religious Affections, *1746*).

MIRROR OF THE SOUL

'I have been accustomed to call this book "An Anatomy of all
the Parts of the Soul" for there is not an emotion of which
anyone can be conscious that is not here represented as in a
mirror' (John Calvin, in his preface to the Psalms). This prayer
begins with anxious petitions and closes with ardent praise (7).
If we stop to look closely at our own prayer-life we shall discover
that this order in prayer tends to be our own. It is not the ideal
order nor that which Jesus taught his disciples. Praise should
come first. But too often our present cares throng us so closely
that they furnish all the words for our poor unworthy prayers.
Take courage! In this we see ourselves in the life of the Psalmist.
He is a man of like passions with us. He is driven to prayer by
trouble rather than drawn thither by thanksgiving. But soon
from his bowed heart there rise not crying and complaining (1–
5) but confidence and rejoicing (6–9). His fears and anxieties
grow fewer and less troublesome as the 'saving strength of His
anointed' comes into fuller view in the soul. Prayer banishes
fear because it brings us into the presence of our Strength and
our Shield (7). We shall leave the crafty workers of iniquity to
him, in the spirit of the negro who sang:

> 'You can talk about me as much as you please;
> I'll talk about you down on my knees.'

[206]

THE VOICE OF THE LORD

God spoke to his fugitive servant Elijah in the wind and the earthquake and the fire, but all to no avail. It was only at the voice of gentle stillness that the prophet wrapped his face in his mantle and spoke with God (1 Kings 19: 11–14). With his own people the Lord does not need to employ the tempest and the crashing cedars (5). But with the heedless and the arrogant the unleashed fury of the hurricane and the unheralded convulsion of the earthquake are the authentic voice of the Lord. A nuclear scientist feels as helpless as a child during the sickening tremors of an earthquake. And how puny a pleasure yacht looks under the lash of the typhoon! The 'sons of the mighty' (1, R.V.) to whom the Psalmist addresses his challenge are, in our day, the secular moulders of men's minds. 'It is a diabolical science' affirms Calvin, 'which fixes our thoughts upon the works of nature and turns them away from God'. And he adds this comment, that to probe reality without taking account of God is like trying to recognize a man by looking at his fingernails. The voice of the Lord in the sevenfold manner of verses 3–9 may not save the sinner or humble the proud, but it does demonstrate to all that 'the Lord sitteth King for ever' (10b).

PRAYER:

> *'Let sense be dumb, let flesh retire;*
> *Speak through the earthquake, wind, and fire;*
> *O still small voice of calm!'*

THE UNBIDDEN GUEST

'Weeping may come in to lodge for the night . . .' (5 R.V. margin). Weeping is here vividly personified. She is the unexpected visitor who arrives late at night in dripping clothes and brings dismal tidings. All night long she holds our eyes waking, pouring out distressing thoughts, predicting dark calamities and holding out no hope of respite. As day breaks she is still in the house. Then, with the first rays of the sun, a knock comes upon the door. Here is Joy, fragrant as the dawn and with the shafts of the eastern sky about her. She is the herald of new hope. She banishes doubt and distress of soul. The uninvited guest slips silently from the house without so much as a nod; a new atmosphere fills the place. Our hearts are glad. Our tears are wiped away. A new spirit takes hold of us. Who has not played host to this unbidden guest? David does not detail for us the occasion of his distress (1). He leaves us liberty to recollect our own. From his night of weeping he writes for us this verdict:

> His anger is but for a moment,
> His favour is for a lifetime (5, R.V. marg.)

MEDITATION:
'The covenant of grace is as firm as the covenant of the day.'
(Matthew Henry)

'I AM IN TROUBLE' (9)

The law of libel and slander gives little protection to a Christian. He can be defamed in such subtle ways that he has no human redress. And he needs no such protection. In some such way as this David was suffering from mischievous slanders (13) which eroded the confidence of former loyal friends and left him no redress, except in God (11). This is all he needs (1), and all he asks (2). This is all that we should ask. To commit our spirit into God's hand (5), as David does so deliberately, is no narrow action of the soul. It is a comprehensive alliance of our cause with God's, of our impotence with his power. To say the words of verse 5 is to commit our reputation to God, our vindication in the thick of lying calumnies and repeated personal humiliations. It is to renounce all retaliation as unworthy of the Christian's witness, and to leave God to take his time with us and with our detractors. This confidence of ultimate vindication arises from the fact that God knows our trouble better than we do (9), and has pledged himself to be our house of defence.

FROM A MINISTER'S DIARY:
'Some very wicked letters sent me ten days ago now help me strangely. My enemies have been compelled to forward my soul's interest.' (Diary of Dr Andrew Bonar)

A PROSPEROUS LIFE

'By nature all men greatly desire to be in a prosperous or happy state; but while the greater number are fascinated by the allurements of the world, and prefer its lies and impostures, scarcely one in a hundred sets his heart on God.' This is Calvin's comment upon verse 23. 'O love the Lord, all ye his saints'. It is a fitting thought for this day. What solid sense of gratitude is mine today as I look back over the way by which God has led me? Have I joined with the Psalmist in saying, amidst all disconcerting events, 'I have trusted in thee, O Lord' (14)? Could I honestly say that under severe testing, 'I have called upon thee' (17)? Amidst many mercies did I gladly declare 'How great is they goodness!' (19)?

Has each new deliverance from trouble and temptation evoked this testimony, 'He hath shewed me his marvellous kindness' (21)? Only such liberty of spirit will keep us positive and prayerful from day to day. Only a deepening experience of the love of God will keep us from vulgar dependence upon men and events. Only the quiet entrusting of our life, our loved ones and our cause to God will invest our testimony with that 'good courage' (24) which marks out the man of God.

A PRAYER:
(*based upon verse 15a*)

> '*Our times are in Thy hand;*
> *Why should we doubt or fear?*
> *A Father's hand will never cause*
> *His child a needless tear.*'

GUIDANCE

At the heart of today's reading is the Lord's promise of personal guidance for the humble believer. 'I will instruct thee and teach thee in the way which thou shalt go: I will guide thee with mine eye' (8). The R.V. expands this last sentence: 'I will counsel thee with mine eye upon thee'. We stand, this day, in felt need of this promised guidance. There are certain conditions for those who would experience God's guiding hand. (i) We must first know the meaning of forgiveness (1), and of our acceptance by God through the imputation of our sin and guilt to Christ and of his righteousness to us (2). (ii) This presupposes an honest confession of all known sin to the God who alone can forgive sin and reconcile the sinner to himself (5). (iii) From such a fellowship confidence is born within the believer's soul which sustains him amidst every threatening calamity (6–7). (iv) We must renounce all mulish stubbornness of spirit (9). (v) A devout and teachable spirit 'finds nothing but mercy all around him' (10b).

MEDITATION:
Ponder Vinet's words:

> *'To have sought God's will is to have found it.'*

A NEW SONG (3)

A skilled scientist in his laboratory and a cook in her kitchen both have a modest sense of mastery. But if they should change places this sense of mastery would quickly disappear. David lived in a little kingdom, but it was part of a big world. His God was a great God, the God of the universe (6) as well as the kitchen. He was also the God of the trusting heart (21). David's new song is just another endeavour to put into poetry this paradox about God. The psalm celebrates a God who is

> 'Centre and soul of every sphere,
> Yet to each loving heart how near.'

To him the vast oceans are like imprisoned waters in an underground cistern (7). The restless movement of un-numbered peoples is stilled at a syllable from his lips (8–10). Effortlessly he takes note of all the sons of men (13). He has 'fashioned each man's nature and weighs the actions of each' (15). Does this bring terror to the heart? Certainly not to the trusting heart. Verses 18–22 are the Psalmist's tribute to this great God whose greatness is no less seen in his intimate and personal concern for each one of his people. The reader who can make these words his own has learned a new song for this a new day.

MEDITATION:
'All that is good, all that is true, all that is beautiful, be it great or small, perfect or fragmentary, natural as well as supernatural, moral as well as material, comes from God.' (John Henry Newman)

[212]

ALPHABET OF THE SOUL

You will notice that this Psalm has twenty-two verses, answering to the twenty-two letters of the Hebrew alphabet. Like Psalm 25 it is an acrostic on these letters, with this detail, that one letter has been omitted and another substituted in the closing verse. One translator calls Psalm 25 An Alphabet of Trust and Psalm 34 An Alphabet of Right-doing. In each Psalm he skilfully works his way down the English alphabet achieving a translation which conveys both the form and the sense of the original. Our recollection of schoolboy acrostic rhymes should not disturb our estimate of the quality of these two Psalms. There is grandeur and simplicity in both. We have often heard verses 1–3 as a call to worship. Verses 4–17 may give colour to the headnote of the Psalm regarding David's escape from the king of Gath who is here called by his hereditary title, Abimelech. In I Samuel 21: 10–13 he is referred to by his personal name Achish. This is one of the Psalms used in the Jewish morning service for sabbaths and for festivals.

MEDITATION:
'If you wish to see the holy Christian church depicted in living colours, and given a living form, in a painting in miniature, then place the Book of Psalms in front of you.' (Luther's Preface to the Psalms)

[213]

'THE RIVER OF THY PLEASURES' (8)

The big service car, with its variety of passengers, travelled north from Amman (Jordan) towards the Syrian border along a modern highway. The countryside was burnt and shimmering in the midsummer heat. Then we began the long winding descent to the 'brook Jabbok'. Oleanders were blooming along its narrow course. As we sped across the low bridge I craned my neck to see how much water this 'brook' carried at the height of summer. The driver remarked, 'plenty fish in that river!' It was clear and clean and swift – not at all like the slow-moving Jordan as it twists and turns on its way to the Dead Sea. This refreshing picture was surely in the Psalmist's mind as he wrote, 'Thou shalt make them drink of the river of thy pleasures'. This metaphor is a favourite with both Psalmist and Prophet. The word 'pleasures' is from the same Hebrew root as 'Eden' and is meant to convey to the Christian, who has learned the secret of abiding in Christ, that deep and satisfying joy which is found only in God.

MEDITATION:
'Where can one find nobler words to express joy than in the Psalms of praise or gratitude? In them you can see into the hearts of all the saints as if you were looking at a lovely pleasure garden, or were gazing into heaven.' (Luther's Preface to the Psalms)

WORKERS OF INIQUITY

Who are these 'workers of iniquity' who lurk in the shadows of
the Psalter and harass the man of God? We may guess, but we
are never told. This fact makes the Psalms more securely our
own. To humiliate the Christian, to taunt him, then more
boldly to menace him, and if possible to destroy him – nothing
less is in the heart of the 'workers of iniquity'. We are here told
what not to do: Not to 'fret' (1a), a rare Hebrew word meaning to
become heated, or 'het up', not to envy the successes of his
apparently charmed life (1b); not to chew the cud of our just
grievances (8b). We are also told *what we must do*. Trust in the
Lord (3), 'David begins with the doctrine of faith' (Calvin). Go
on doing good, and stay right where we are (3). 'Dwell in the
land' is a command, for we are to seek safety not in flight but in
trust; we are to revel in the perfect will of God, for when we
delight in him (4) he will delight in us (23). We are to roll our
heavy burden upon the broad shoulders of Omnipotence (5), to
learn to be silent and still, with eyes upon his sceptre (7). We are
then told *what God promises to do*: To supply our modest needs
(3b, and see 16 and 25), to grant our heart's prayer (4b), to
vindicate the justice of our cause (6), and to show us how swiftly
the wicked pass away (10).

THE GREEN BAY TREE

The Green Bay Tree (35) bears a striking resemblance to the tropical banyan. Beginning as a tiny parasite lodged in the fork of a forest tree, it slowly overpowers the supporting tree, dropping aerial roots and thrusting out great horizontal branches. These in turn are propped up by vertical limbs and so the king of the tropical forest dominates all growth in its vicinity. Yet the banyan is shallow-rooted. I have seen them prostrate after a hurricane, the great expanse of roots clutching in death the torn-up surface of the ground now vertical like the wall of a church. The little trees will live again sending life from their shorn-off stems; but the banyan will wither until the villagers set it burning with their firesticks and plant bananas and sweet potatoes in its ashes. Our own turbulent quarter century has grown its own crop of green bay trees and we do not need to be very old to affirm with the Psalmist:

'Until yesterday I saw the evil-doer throned high as the branching cedars; then, when I passed by, he was there no longer, and I looked in vain to find him' (35).

MEDITATION:
'If open punishment were now inflicted for every sin it would be supposed that nothing would be reserved till the last judgment. Again, if God now did not openly punish any sin it would be presumed that there was no divine providence.' (Augustine)

[216]

Psalm 39: 1–13

'HOW FRAIL I AM'

The Psalmist prays to know his frailties. Most of us pray that our frailties will not be known. He is thinking first of his ungovernable tongue which so often got him into trouble and dishonourable defeat (1–2). He is thinking also of his turbulent feelings leading him to brooding resentments and hasty speech (3). And he is thinking of corrected perspectives, to see the brevity of life (5a) the insignificance of man (5b) and the transience of wealth (6). At verse 7 he reaches a point of resolve which ends his inward-looking mood and brings his thoughts to repose in God. To be able to say 'My hope is in thee' (7b) is at one and the same time the complete answer to our sins (8a), our fears (8b), our chastenings (9–11), and our forebodings of approaching death (12–13). The Christian is not a self-made man, proud of his power to rise above his frailties, but an honest pilgrim perplexed by his frailties, who has learned to look at these very frailties in the light of Calvary and Pentecost.

Contrast with verse 13b Milton's noble lines:

> . . . *'so death becomes*
> *His final remedy, and after life*
> *Tried in sharp tribulation, and refined*
> *By faith and faithful works, to second life,*
> *Waked in the renovation of the just*
> *Resigns him up with heaven and earth renewed'*
> *(Paradise Lost)*

THE FOOL HATH SAID . . .

This Psalm touches a profound fact when it gives us the fool's verdict (1). Since the Fall man is not only *without* holiness, he is in revolt against holiness. And since God is the symbol and author of all holiness, the sinner is in revolt against God. This revolt lies deeper than mere words. Its language is the language of deliberate deeds (1b). Moral atheism may strangely co-exist with lip-service to God. It is what a man is in his heart that determines what he is before the all-seeing eye of God (2). The terrible totalitarianism of evil, emphasized in verse 3, finds frightening re-affirmation all the way through the Bible. See Genesis 6: 1–6, Romans 3: 10–12 and Revelation 6: 15–17. Four Hebrew words are commonly used in the Old Testament for 'fool'; that used here has the thought of emptiness, worthlessness. Such people give themselves away. They are hollow, metallic, without weight of judgment or worth of character. Their saying is the projection of their being and their doing. God is not mocked. He sees (2); He scatters (5); He rejects (5).

MEDITATION:
'*Atheists deserve not curses, but tears. He who can deny God on a starry night, or beside the graves of his dearest ones, or in the presence of martyrdom, is greatly unhappy or greatly wicked.*' (*G. Mazzini*)

QUESTION:
Compare the Bible's verdict on the other fools of Scripture. (Prov. 14: 9; Matt. 7: 26; Lk. 12: 20; Rom. 1: 22; 1 Cor. 15: 36).

BETRAYED

The title to this Psalm points us back to an incident in David's life as an outlaw when fellow tribesmen of Judah betrayed his presence to Saul (1 Sam. 23: 19; 26: 1). Saul set out to destroy David, accompanied by 3000 veteran troops. In his predicament David cast himself upon God's intervention. He had long since learned that a believer is never out-numbered if he has God as his 'ally' (4, A.V. helper). 'How should one chase a thousand and two put ten thousand to flight except their Rock (i.e. Jehovah) had sold them, and the Lord had shut them up?' (Deut. 32: 30). David's Psalm was a cry of faith and trust (4–5) as well as a plea for protection (1–3). And he seems to have written the closing verse (7) in anticipation of God's intervention, as if the crisis were already past. God's intervention is described in 1 Samuel 23: 27–29. David had not to strike a blow. Have we learned this lesson? It is so easy for us to resort to the meddling methods of those who may wish to humiliate us or cripple the Lord's work. But the attitude of true faith is to rest our confidence in the 'Name' (1), symbol of the character of God. We should do what the hymn suggests:

> 'Have we trials and temptations?
> Is there trouble anywhere?
> We should never be discouraged –
> Take it to the Lord in prayer.'

FALSE FRIEND

'If only I could get away from it all! (6–8). They are all on to me!
I'm not appreciated as I should be. I think I'll resign. I'll leave
home; then mum will be sorry!' This was not quite David's
mood, but it is a common mood among us. We have less reason
than he. David was betrayed by an intimate friend (12–14, 20–
21), upon whose loyalty and worth he had long leant for
encouragement. Now this friend has 'broken his covenant'
(20), become double-tongued (21) and spread sharp slanders
and cruel criticism to David's hurt. What should one do when
this treatment is ours? The answer is at hand in verse 22, 'Cast
thy burden upon the Lord, and he shall sustain thee.' With this
is linked submissiveness in prayer (16–17).

QUESTION:
*Who was this false friend in David's life? Was it Absalom? Was it
Ahithophel? Christ knew this experience too (John 13: 18).*

MEDITATION:
*'When our window is opened towards heaven, the window of heaven
is open to us.' (C. H. Spurgeon)*

OLD AND GREYHEADED

To grow old gracefully calls for more grace than nature can provide. Old age is a new world of strange conflicts and secret fears; the fear of being left alone, the fear of being a burden to loved ones, the fear of becoming a helpless invalid, the fear of losing one's grip, the fear of being imposed upon. These fears are not new. The psalmist is here thinking aloud for the encouragement of all who are in the autumn of life. 'I am old and greyheaded, O God forsake me not' (18). 'Cast me not off in the time of old age' (9). Two great realities sustain God's people through their eventide years. The first is *gratitude for past mercies*. He looks back over a long pilgrimage to the home where he was welcomed as a babe (6). He remembers the timely disciplines of his youth (17). The memories of later years are blurred, but those of childhood and youth are as vivid as if they belonged to yesterday. The second mark of gracious old age is *confidence in the faithfulness of God*. 'My tongue shall talk of thy righteousness all the day long' (24). Gratitude for the past and quiet trust for the future (8) are the psalmist's recipe for contented old age. There will still be secret fears and conflicts and the peculiar temptations of old age (10, 11) but these will never be allowed to rob us of our song (22–24).

FOR CONSIDERATION:
The golden years. *Eventide is the flowering time for the believer's life of prayer. He is free to devote more time to prayer. He wakens early and his waking thoughts are all turned into prayers. And this is a true vocation from the Lord.*

CHRIST'S UNIVERSAL KINGDOM

Napoleon's words are well-known: 'Everything in Jesus astonishes me. Alexander, Charlemagne and myself founded empires. But upon what did we rest the creations of our genius? Upon force! Jesus Christ alone founded his empire upon love; and at this hour, millions of men would die for him'. This psalm for Solomon looks to a greater than Solomon, and engraves the features of his world-wide kingdom upon granite rock.

The power of God is behind it (1). 'God hath spoken once; twice have I heard this: that power belongeth unto God'. (Psa. 62: 11) 'There is no power but of God' (Rom. 13: 1).

The justice of God is within it (2–4). And how does God use his power? In very practical ways. Look at the threefold character of his absolute justice in verse 4: to judge, to save, to break.

The glory of God is around it (6–11). There is spiritual prosperity (6), national righteousness (7), world-wide influence (8, 9) and universal sovereignty (10, 11)

The love of God is throughout it (12–14). These verses are simply an outline of Christ's earthly ministry. They are to be continued in the ministry of his people, for love is active mercy and untiring compassion.

The blessing of God is upon it (15–17). 'Long shall he [God's King] live!' Men shall 'make themselves happy' in him. This is the happiness of redeemed hearts.

THOUGHT:
The idea that we can find happiness without holiness is the great delusion of our day.

THE PROSPERITY OF THE WICKED

This prosperity (3) has always been a cause of perplexity to the Christian, and a matter for comment by the observant man of the world. The latter assumes that the silence of God suggests that he must have gone out of business. The Christian, on the defensive at such a suggestion, admits to himself privately that he sometimes wonders about it all too. Zophar reminded Job that the triumphing of the wicked is short (Job 20: 5) but Job was wrestling with deeper problems than the facile Zophar had faced. With prosperity there comes brazen arrogance, and when this arrogance is harnessed to the will to power, its typical expression is violence (6). Prosperity to most people means 'increase in riches' (12). Men who put their trust in riches tend to despise any other God than gold (11). This attitude gives a man a false sense of security. He takes risks, confident that he can carry them off (7b A.V. margin). He does not quite dismiss God as a possibility to be reckoned with, but he organizes God out of his life (11). This long-drawn-out drama of the apparently charmed life of the ungodly (12a) worries the upright person. He finds himself looking back over his shoulder, and furtively thinking that all would have been well if he had not become a Christian (2, 3). Repentance and an upright life scarcely seem to pay off (15). Indeed the Christian seems to have a raw deal most of the time (14).

FOR SELF-EXAMINATION:
When one finds oneself in this wistful mood concerning the past, what can one do? Paul's recipe is given in Philippians chapter 3.

'UNTIL . . .'

Something always happens when we go into the sanctuary (17). There are the perceptible consequences of corporate worship in the house of God, the elevation of our thoughts, the purifying of our affections, and the directing of our obedience. But there are deeper and less perceptible consequences; and this is one reason for the apostolic warning to forsake not 'the assembling of ourselves together, as the manner of some is' (Heb. 10: 25). One of these unconscious consequences of coming into the presence of the living God in his sanctuary is the gaining of proper perspectives. Things imperceptibly alter. The *fear* which we could not shake off withers as we say, 'I have put my trust in the Lord God' (28). The *ferment* in our thoughts ceases to work when we confess that God is our portion for ever (26). The *wavering loyalties* are established as we cry 'Whom have I in heaven but thee?' (25) Heaven! Why the very reality of heaven fades when we habitually desert the sanctuary. There is always a price to pay for absenting ourselves from the corporate worship of God's people. And there are profound adjustments of soul and mind and body, of our relationship with God and our neighbour, and of our reactions to sudden and shattering events, when we do as Jesus did and go into the house of God on the weekly day of worship. The whole nagging problem of the apparent prosperity of the wicked was answered for the troubled psalmist when he submitted his thoughts to the deep therapy of the Lord within the sanctuary.

WARNING:
Beware of those forms of Christian activity which rob you of regular worship in the house of God.

O GOD, WHY?

This psalm is a wail of anguish from the bleeding heart of the people of the captivity, and springs from their sense of dereliction. Its New Testament echo, if we may reverently make this comparison, is the Saviour's 'Why hast thou forsaken me?' from Golgotha's cross. The suffering servant in the first case is the remnant people, in the second case the redeeming representative God-man. The same cry goes up today from the uneasy soul of younger churches under terrible stress and travail. But we must remember that the triumph of Babylon was in God's plan. Nothing is too costly when the purging and purifying of God's people is the end in view. The smoking ruins of the temple (7), the decay of true religion (8), the disappearance of the preacher (9) – all these deepen the dismay in the hearts of the devout few who cry, 'O God, Why?' But the heavens are silent.

'*O God, how long?*' (10). We read church history, covering two thousand years in a few hundred pages of compressed events. But every generation in that crimsoned pilgrim story has echoed the same cry, 'O God, how long?' (Rev. 6: 10). And the most moving plea has ever been 'Have respect unto thy covenant' (20). '*Arise, O God*' (22). The psalmist and his suffering people have learned to trample down self, even in the midst of their afflictions. Their final cry is for the Lord's vindication of himself before a haughty and a heedless world.

PRAYER:
Help me, O God, to leave all questions of the 'why' to be answered by thee in thine own way and in thine own time. Amen.

Psalm 75: 1–10

IT IS GOD WHO RULES ALL

To live with our eyes on the headlines in the morning paper, our ears alert for the 7 o'clock news, is a sure way to lose a sense of proportion and perspective in human affairs. 'It is God who rules all'. That is why the Psalmist has something to sing about; that is why God is the theme of his praise (1). The worshipping soul alone can hear the mystic harmonies of heaven. Verses 2–5 are a recording of the voice of God. Translate verse 2, 'When the time is ripe I [emphatic] will judge uprightly'. And when is the time ripe – when 'earth rocks to its fall, and all that dwell on it' (3a)? Surely history unfolds example after example since the time of the Flood (Gen. 6–9). The law of the rise and fall of nations is that power brings arrogance (4), and arrogance luxury, and luxury decay, and decay is buried beneath the silent sands of history. Witness the spent might of Assyria, Babylon, Macedonia and Rome. Witness the vaults of the dying nations of our own day, ready to receive the bones of their lost sovereignties. 'It is God who rules all' and he reserves the right to administer the foaming cup of judgment to the lips of the braggart nation (8). 'It is God who rules all'; he putteth down one, and lifteth up another (7).

THE CUP:
As a symbol of God's wrath – Psalm 60: 3; Isaiah 51: 17; Revelation 14: 10. As a symbol of God's mercy – Psalms 16: 5; 23: 5; 116: 13.

[226]

THE WRATH OF MAN

Verse 10 refers to the military arrogance of Assyria as Sennacherib stood poised for the final wipe-out of Jerusalem (see 2 Kings 18; 2 Chronicles 32). King Hezekiah had sought to reassure the people with the words, 'There be more with us than with him: with him is an arm of flesh; but with us is the Lord our God to help us and to fight our battles' (2 Chr. 32: 7, 8). Now, in retrospect, the psalmist celebrates this great deliverance (1–3) in the only proper way: he attributes it wholly to God. In verses 4–6 he describes God's sudden onslaught under the figure of a lion leaping on the enemy from the mountains of prey. Then in verses 7–9 the psalmist draws his lesson from the irresistible might of God. 'Who can resist thee, so terrible, so sudden in thy anger?' (7). Finally, in verses 10–12 we are reminded that the believing heart will show its gratitude in the adoration of such a God. It is deeply reassuring to turn from abstract discussions on a remote God, or from clinical data on a dead or dying God, to the pulsating realism of this song which celebrates a living, acting, saving and keeping God; a God who laughs at the clouded minds of men and takes the latest 'finding' about God as the starting point for his intervention in a new visitation of his power. We need to remember that the real answer to the Deism of the late 17th and early 18th century was God's gift of the Evangelical Revival.

Worried about the world? We look for God's intervention again, in our own day.

I WILL REMEMBER (10, 11)

God never forgets; but often he appears to have forgotten. There are people like this. We inwardly think they have forgotten our kindnesses and help. Then our miserable thoughts are one day dispelled by a golden shaft of bright remembrance – a letter, a 'phone call, a hurried visit when passing in their car. We then feel so much better and reproach ourselves for our hard thoughts about them. 'Hath God forgotten to be gracious?' (9). The psalmist's faltering voice may echo your own thoughts this morning. He had been faithful in remembering God (cp. Ps. 63: 6). He was regular in his devotions. Yet here he is overwhelmed with a sense of Divine neglect (3)! He can look back upon times of rich and intimate communion (6). From these came his best thoughts in prayer and praise. Now the tide is out and his little craft lies on its side upon the sand (7, 8). Samuel Rutherford knew this experience: 'I have not now, of a long time, found such high spring tides as formerly . . . I wait on upon the shore-side till the Lord send a full sea.' Perhaps the psalmist had yet to face the fact that the heart which can praise and commune with a silent God has reached a maturity unknown to the buoyant years of our spiritual adolescence. There is something deceptive about the desire to feel the presence of God in the day of trouble (2). It is better to count our blessings in a quiet session of grateful remembering. This is what the psalmist did, and how quickly his spirit was animated! Praise banishes complaining in the latter part of the psalm, and all the questionings sink to rest upon the bosom of God.

DARK SAYINGS OF OLD (2)

These are those riddles of God's providence which look wintry and bleak but are turned by the hand of God into the bracing disciplines of a well-ordered spiritual, moral and communal life. The history books which a hundred years ago were on the shelves of Scottish homes were all animated by such a motive. Israel's homes were her universities, and all her sons and daughters were expected to qualify in history. For the Hebrew, history is no accident. It is the platform upon which God works out his irresistible purpose of redemption in the face of man's stubbornness and hell's hate. Hence the frequent historical psalms with their ballad-like narrative, vivid language, and blunt honesty. 'Dark sayings of old' (2) are therefore those unveilings of the ways and works of God which show him triumphant as Redeemer and Saviour in spite of the waywardness, folly, rebellion and short memories of his covenant people. And the lilt and picturesqueness of the language are calculated to teach history in an easily assimilated form to the youngest children in the household. If they later failed to 'set their hope in God' (7) and became 'a stubborn and rebellious generation' (8) they were sinning against light. It is the terrible misfortune of multitudes today to be living in a moral sandstorm where darkness is called light and light darkness.

CONSIDER:
Verse 7 as an Anchorage for Life in the confused conditions of our day.

MERCY AND WRATH

The moral axis of God's government of his creatures has two
opposite poles – his mercy (v.1–29) and his wrath (30–64).
These twin realities are present in all the Bible's unfolding of
the nature of God, the thoughts of God, the ways of God. They
are before us in vivid technicolour in the life of God's Son.
Their ultimate, clear-cut vindication will take place at the Last
Day. When we try to disentangle the crimson threads from the
gold we tear the fabric woven on the looms of God. To create a
God without anger and wrath (38) is to invent a caricature, to
make a graven image. His wrath is not like man's wrath; it is
free from cruelty, caprice and lawless passion. His mercy is not
like man's mercy, it is persevering, disinterested, and from the
heart. As Israel cheaply traded on God's mercy, so do we. God's
people of the old covenant confused election with licence to
choose their own way. God's people today stand in need of the
reminder that judgment must begin at the house of God, and
that our God is a consuming fire. The great mystery which the
psalmist celebrates here is the willingness of God to deal in
mercy with his people who oft provoked him and grieved him
(40); turned back and tempted him (41); remembered not his
hand, nor the day when he redeemed them from the enemy
(42).

THOUGHT:
'All his wonderful deeds left them faithless still' (*32*).

A DECEITFUL BOW

This is a bow which 'plays the archer false' (57). Beautifully fashioned and finished, powerful to the grip of the experienced bowman, without any visible flaw, it nevertheless shoots off target and does so persistently. Such a bow is useless, mocks the skill of the archer and betrays him in the hour of battle. No matter how long he experiments with it his calculations are always out. It is the despair of its owner. This metaphor of the deceitful bow occurs again in Hosea 7: 16. In both instances the bow is Israel and the Archer is God. He patiently fashioned his people. In his confident hands he planned to use this bow to wing the arrows of his purposes home to the hearts of men and nations. There is no lack of skill in the Archer. But the bow is perverse and quirky. Taut in his mighty grip it looks invincible. But the arrow leaps from the bowstring like a child's plaything, darting and swerving to no purpose. That such a Warrior should have such a bow is a mystery which inhabits all of Israel's history. That the Great Archer should continue to feather his arrows, and tightly tie the string of such a bow is the supreme miracle of the Old Testament. That the new and larger Israel to which through grace we belong should prove a bow 'which plays the Archer false' is all so plain as we look out upon a lost world, a confused church, and perplexed Christians. When will the Warrior awake as one out of sleep (65)?

PRAYER:

> 'O Lord, I have heard thy speech, and was afraid:
> O Lord, revive thy work in the midst of the years,
> in wrath remember mercy'. (Hab. 3: 2).

A CRY OF ANGUISH

The bombs on Rotterdam and Belgrade are forgotten. Few recollect the rape of Nanking. But Israel's anguish has given us a timeless cry. It is the cry of the violated for vindication. The siege of Jerusalem has ended in the sack of the city and frightful realism meets us in the stark recital of those dark events (1–3). 'How long, Lord?' is a universal cry. The hungry refugees in the camps of Africa and Southern Asia; the homeless civilians, the helpless multitudes of half the world echo their inarticulate question. Israel was a world in miniature and on the screen of its recorded story we see a preview of humanity's turbulence and sorrows. There is no easy answer. Humanity's sorrows, like Israel's before us, are the reaping from our corporate sins and common crimes (8, 9). Every famine victim in Ethiopia, every frightened widow who checks the doors and window locks at night, is sharing in the consequences of our long endeavour to run our lives, our homes, our cities and our nations without God. There had to be a day of reckoning, though it took 400 years to come. Jerusalem, smouldering under the torch of Nebuchadnezzar's executioners, is not mere history; it is bedrock truth, granite reality, inescapable cause and effect.

'VISIT THIS VINE'

This prayer (14c) is beautifully rendered in another version: 'Look to this vine, that needs thy care. Revive the stock which thy own hand has planted, branches that by thee throve, and throve for thee'. The vine out of Egypt (8) is the Hebrew people, God's elect nation of the old covenant. The planting of this vine in a pleasant land, and its luxuriant growth, were God's work (9–11). The psalmist is thinking back to the spacious and prosperous reigns of David and Solomon (Psa. 72). The devastation which has accompanied the later history of the monarchy is acknowledged to be God's work, and a just judgment (16). The boar and the wild beast symbolize the predatory nations which have ravaged the vine and reduced it to a leafless stump. 'The man of thy right hand' is best taken as a further reference to Israel typified no longer as a vine, but personified as the chosen individual. The threefold refrain (3, 7, 19) calls upon God as the victorious Ruler to exert his sovereign strength. The shining face is a beautiful figure of speech for the smile of God's life-giving favour; conversely the frown of God (16b) is the intimation of death.

A SUGGESTION:
The pictures of the Shepherd (1) and the Vine (8) reappear frequently in Scripture (e.g. John 10 and 15). Link up a few such references as the basis of a Bible Study.

THE PERIL OF GETTING
OUR OWN WAY (12)

No success is more empty than to demand our rights and to get them. Moral strength, maturity of mind and personality, are the fruit of duty cheerfully acknowledged and honourably discharged. But in a soft age duty is unwelcome, and everyone clamours for his rights. Mazzini, the Italian patriot, in his sensitive essay on 'The Duties of Man', warned the Italian working-classes to beware of the man who keeps talking about rights. This had become Israel's ground of agitation (11, 12). At Sinai, with their eyes wide open, they entered into covenant with God. They soon began to weaken, grizzling about their desert rations, and throwing off the yoke of their obligations. Stubbornness became a habit, fed by the fuel of resentment, murmuring and ingratitude. The more God did for them the more they demanded of him and the less they cared about him. 'I spoke, but my people would not listen; Israel went on unheeding, till I was fain to give their hard hearts free play, let them follow their own devices' (12, 13). The bitter fruits of this cheap liberty are mentioned in the closing verses of the psalm: Israel's enemies now menace them; her oppressors, whom God would have smitten, now triumph; the sands in Israel's hourglass are fast running out. The finest of the wheat and the honey dripping from the rock (17) are reserved by God for those who have yielded up the government of their lives to him, for those who have learned to say 'Not my will, but thine be done.'

QUESTION:
Israel learned these lessons the hard way. How can we, as Christians, help our friends to learn them without getting hurt in the process?

'YE ARE GODS' (6)

In a menacing situation in our Lord's encounter with the Jewish
leaders he deflected their charge of blasphemy by quoting these
extraordinary words from Psalm 82. See John 10: 31–36: 'gods'
translates the Hebrew *elohim* which is here clearly used of
ordinary people. But there was something extraordinary about
the people here addressed as 'gods'. They had stood in a
privileged relationship to God as his covenant people, 'children
of the most High' (6). While *elohim* most frequently occurs as
the Divine Name, occasionally we find it used of the rulers and
judges of the people (e.g. Exod. 21: 6, 22: 28). This is well
illustrated in the first verse of the Psalm which reads: 'See
where he stands, the Ruler (El) of all, among the rulers (*elohim*)
assembled, comes forward to pronounce judgment upon the
rulers (*elohim*) themselves'. In verse 6 the emphatic pronouns
require some such translation as this: 'gods you are; I myself
have declared it'. Yet the shattering thrust of these exalted
words, as applied to Israel, is one of unmitigated judgment:
'The doom of mortals awaits you, you shall fall with the fall of
human princes' (7). These favoured 'elohim' had abused their
privileged office (2); had ignored the poor and fatherless and
had therefore forfeited their office with its high privileges (7, 8).

QUESTION:
*In the light of the context in this Psalm and of our Lord's use of 'Ye
are gods' in John 10: 34, may we not recognize a solemn hint that
Jesus' accusers were about to forfeit their national privileges?*

DOOR DUTIES

A doorkeeper (10) in the house of the Lord has the lowliest of offices; but how enriching! He sees the worshipper as he mounts the steps and reads the mood of his soul. To that mood he adapts his salutation. When he meets a rebuff he is not dismayed. That is why only mature Christians need ask to be doorkeepers. In Solomon's temple they were the sons of Korah. Jesus was a doorkeeper in the temple of Herod. He observed how the rich came in with their gifts, and noticed the downcast eyes of the widow. Jesus stands beside the doorkeeper still, cautioning him against ever taking his duties lightly or coming to them prayerlessly, or arriving for them unpunctually, or defaulting from them for any cause save such as the Lord of the door (John 10: 7) would approve. Such a sense of holy privilege ruled this poet's soul. It is no over-statement when he says that one such day is better than a thousand days of empty chatter and of sterile busy-ness. I cannot understand the young fellow who does not pray for the day when his minister or deacons will say to him, 'Friend, come up higher!' Then he will stand at the door as one who has a Divine charge, and he will appear to every worshipper as the very personification of the anonymous doorkeeper of Psalm 84. His handshake, his manly greeting, his keen eye will all declare 'I had rather be a doorkeeper in the house of my God than to dwell in the tents of wickedness' (10).

THOUGHT:
Women can be doorkeepers too – see Acts 12: 13.

REVIVAL

Revival is God's work, hence the emphatic *thou* of verse 6. Revival is rare and there are many Christians who have no personal experience of its mighty ministry. The Psalmist was grateful for the intervention of God which had brought the remnant of Jacob back from Babylon (1). He saw in this migration a ministry of grace to their souls (2, 3). But he longed for more. 'Mercy drops round us are falling, but for the *showers* we plead.' And all over the world countless prayers are mingling with yours this morning to cry, 'Wilt thou not revive us again: that thy people may rejoice in thee?' The freedom to talk about the living Saviour, which is a sure accompaniment of revival, springs from that flood-tide of God-given joy which flows in such times of blessing. Revival brings a clear message on the central realities of God's great salvation (8–11). Mercy and truth are the twin realities upon which our salvation depends, for these two words tell us that what God's justice demands his love provides. These qualities find their harmony in the heart of God. That is why Revival transcends all argument and all questioning, and sets forth Christ our righteousness as its whole theme. Revival always brings moral fruits in its train (11–13). Truth springs out of the earth and God's people learn to walk once more in the way of his steps (13). But God is sovereign in revival, and that is why this Psalm is one long cry for revival.

HOW TO PREPARE FOR REVIVAL:
Robert Murray M'Cheyne of St Peter's, Dundee, used to read to his mid-week meeting extracts and news concerning revival and blessing in other countries. This helped his people to pray for like blessing, and at last it came.

[237]

'I AM HOLY' (2a)

The word 'holy' here is from the Hebrew word for God's loving-kindness, His leal-love which occurs as 'mercy' again in verses 5, 13 and 16. The Psalmist is declaring that he knows himself to be the object of God's gracious dealings. Poor and needy as he is, he is not on that account passed by. The great Jehovah has set his heart upon him saying, 'I have loved thee with an everlasting love' (Jeremiah 31: 3). Does this not make him holy? Indeed it does! He knows himself to be the Lord's concern, the Lord's property, the Lord's precious jewel. And since he is now 'not his own', but the Lord's, he relaxes his tenacious grip upon the straw and tinsel of a dying world. He trusts himself in life and death to his great Redeemer. This intimate relationship gives meaning to his prayers (1–4), depth to his confession of shortcoming (5), confidence to his cry for help (6, 7).

Why has 'holy' become a mis-used word? 'Holy Joe' is a tag fastened round the neck of the Christian by a frivolous and spiteful world. A 'holier than thou' attitude is talked about as if it were inseparable from the modest testimony of the most genuine Christian. Let us be clear about this: holiness is God's very nature. Without holiness no man shall see the Lord. As a redeemed people we are to be 'holy and without reproach' in the midst of a talkative world. Our holiness is a gift from God. It cost God the Cross. Let us not join the parrot-cry against it, nor think there is virtue in smearing our testimony with sufficient camouflage to make our holy life look like that of the secular society in which we live and work.

THOUGHT:
Holiness and salvation are inseparable (Vinet).

THE CITY OF GOD (3)

'A terrible rumour reaches us out of the West' wrote Jerome in Bethlehem; 'the Eternal City has fallen!' The rumour proved to be true. The Goths had captured Rome (410 A.D.). The ageing Augustine, bishop of Hippo in North Africa, had been working on his greatest book, *Civitas Dei*, the *City of God*. He had seen the disaster in prospect. Above the rise and fall of empires he saw the greatness and glory of the kingdom of God. He opens his Book with the words, 'The glorious city of God is my theme in this work . . . I have undertaken its defence against those who prefer their false gods to the Founder of this city, – a city surpassing glorious.' This vision of faith is nourished by the 87th Psalm, by the 72nd Psalm, by the 46th Psalm, and by the imagery of the Apocalypse. Bernard of Cluny saw the same prospect beyond the travail of his own times, and bequeathed the hymn 'Jerusalem the golden' to the universal Church. Martin Luther was nerved and comforted with the same bracing conviction when he gave us his bold paraphrase of Psalm 46. And John Newton, joint writer with William Cowper of the *Olney Hymns*, has given the hymnals of Christendom his version of this Psalm in the lines:

> 'Glorious things of thee are spoken,
> Zion, city of our God;
> He whose Word can not be broken
> Formed thee for his own abode.'

They all concur in two respects. The City of God is the true home of the people of God; the City of God in its perfection still awaits us. 'There we shall rest and see, see and love, love and praise. This is what shall be in the end without end' (closing words of Augustine's *City of God*).

[239]

THE COVENANT PSALM

This Psalm is like the golden clasps which bind firmly together the themes of the Third Book of the Psalter (Psalms 42–89). It is fitting that the clasps should snap firmly shut on the doctrine of the Covenant – God's binding contract with David and his house. The close of the Psalm shows that it is written in days of national disaster, long after the glory of David's kingdom has departed (38–48). The Covenant is placed before the Great Covenanter to remind him of his obligations. Hence verses 1–4 are a cluster of bright jewels which reflect the *character of the God of the Covenant*. Pick out these jewels: those which reflect the *heart* of the God of the Covenant (1a, 2a) and those which reveal his unwavering *purpose* (1b, 2b). When the heart of God and the will of God are at work on behalf of the people of the Covenant they may rest assured of its fulfilment, despite all appearances to the contrary (4–14). The short film-strip of grand events in the Covenant history (9–12) is meant to feed the faith and hope of discouraged believers. David's greater Son is on the throne of his Kingdom. He has already made captivity captive and taken his seat at the right hand of God. In spite of all appearances he already has all authority in heaven and on earth. This is why we can affirm with greater reason than the anxious Psalmist: 'Blessed is the people that know the joyful sound: they shall walk, O Lord, in the light of thy countenance.'

EXPLANATION:
The Covenant with David (3, 4; 35–37) is referred to in Acts 15: 15–17. The presence of believing Jews in the early church is here insisted upon as proof of the fulfilment of the Covenant with David.

RESPONSIBILITY

The stray dog which wanders around the village knows no
discipline. But the faithful collie whose co-operation means
everything to the farmer will be disciplined at the least sign of
slacking. The God of the Covenant requires of the people of the
Covenant a fine sensitivity to his voice and will. He has invested
so much in them. His own reputation is at stake. He cannot
afford to leave them to play fast and loose with his commandments. Therefore, side by side with the generous expressions of
his settled Covenant with David (19–29), we read the reference
to the rod and the stripes by which God chastens those sons of
the Covenant who swerve from his commandments (30–32).
Privilege goes hand in hand with responsibility. The responsibility is not easily discharged. As the privilege is a high and holy
one, 'higher than the kings of the earth' (27), so the duties of
love and loyalty are high and holy ones. Our conscientious
Covenant-keeping God watches with jealous concern. But, you
say, This is all about David and his descendants; what has that
Covenant to do with me? The answer is that the Lord's
Covenant with king David is the preface and picture of a deeper
reality – God's Covenant with great David's greater Son. Since
Jesus is the Mediator of the new Covenant, and since his people
inherit the promises made to David, we are to read this Psalm as
directly applicable to the privilege and responsibility of our
being sons of the living God (cp. Hebrews 8: 6–13).

QUESTION:
*On the New Testament uses of the rod, look up Hebrews 12: 5–11.
What Old Testament quotations are here used? What evidence of
'chastening' can you find in your own life?*

CAST OFF AND ABHORRED

The Psalmist who has just celebrated the constancy of God's Covenant (1–18) now complains bitterly at his repudiation of his Covenant. On all sides he sees the broken walls and desolated landscape of Judah. Everywhere their enemies are victorious and arrogant. Only God is silent. Every sentence in this last section of the Psalm (38–45) reads like the repudiation of those grand assertions with which the Psalm began (1–18). Does the Psalmist contradict himself? How can he put together such contradictory themes in one poem? The answer lies in the way we look at things. Amidst the desolating events of human tragedy it so easily appears to sorrowing hearts that God has denied his Covenant and finally deserted us. But while weeping may endure for a night, joy cometh in the morning. The sun rises and scatters the darkness. And in our soul the remembrance of the faithfulness of God brings back the equilibrium of our feelings. The same soul who cries, 'Lord, where are thy former loving kindnesses?' (49) will soon sing again, 'Blessed be the Lord for evermore' (52). And over the broken hopes, and brief joys of life he will come to cry, with the obscure poet Ethan the Ezrahite, 'Amen, and Amen'. The seeming contradictions of the opening and closing moods of this Psalm therefore point to a profound reality in human life – the inconstancy of feelings and human hopes; and to a profound reality of the life of God – the unswerving constancy of his covenanted love and mercy.

MEDITATION:

> *'I change, He changes not,*
> *The Christ can never die.*
> *His love, not mine the resting place,*
> *His truth, not mine, the tie.'*

[242]

A WELL-TESTED RECIPE FOR RETIREMENT

'Moses the man of God' knew no retirement and, for the last forty years of his life, no holidays. For men and women who have to face retirement, loneliness and the thought of being unwanted, he has written this Psalm. Though we often hear it read, rather gloomily, at funerals, the Psalm belongs to life, not death. Now is the time to learn its elemental truths and begin to live by them. *The Psalmist begins with God* (v.1–2). This is where he lives. He is at home with God. God and he have reached a deep and secure relationship from which life has gained immensely in meaning. *He now sees the brevity of life* (3–6). Moses lived 120 years and packed into them the best achievements of a dozen other outstanding lives. Yet both years and achievements shrink into nothingness against the eternity of the life of God. *He sees the moral bond* which unites us to God, both in life and in death (7–10). We are answerable to God, accountable, responsible. This imparts a solemn *view of the stewardship of time* (12). The pagan numbers his years; the child of God numbers his *days*. Like his Master he remembers that there are twelve hours in the day, and the night cometh when no man can work. His prayer, 'O satisfy us *early* with thy mercy' (14) is a prayer for the flowering of spiritual affections at the dawning of life's day, and not belatedly as evening shadows fall and the mourners go about the streets. *He wants to see God at work in his family* (16) and knows that the deepest solace of the eventide years is the evidence of Christ honoured in the lives of children and of children's children. This crowning blessing will put the burnished gold upon the autumn of our lives, and will prepare us for the climax of the believer's pilgrimage, when he will see the King in his beauty and behold the land that is very far off.

[243]

THREEFOLD CORD

The careful and helpful marginal notes in the Newberry Bible suggest that we have in this Psalm the threefold testimony of the Spirit (1), the Messiah (2–13), and the Father (14–16).

(1) *The Spirit* testifies first of all (1) to the safety of the pilgrim who passes the night (A.V. abides) under the protecting care of Shaddai, his almighty Guardian.

(2) *The Messiah* corroborates the Spirit's testimony (2–13) about God; He is our 'safe stronghold' (2), offering to us present and perfect protection from a thousand perils (3–7). God did this in the life of his Son. The reference of the tempter to verses 11, 12 shows that Satan recognized that the primary reference in these verses is to the Father's guardianship over the life of the Son of his love (Matthew 4: 6; Luke 4: 10, 11). How much more confidently may we make these promises our own who have made the Lord our refuge, and the most High our habitation!

(3) The testimony of the Spirit and of the Messiah is confirmed by *God* the Father (14–16). Here are 'exceeding great and precious promises' whose words God's people daily verify. This threefold cord is securely fastened by the triune God to the life of the most shy and faltering believer, however much one may feel like Bunyan's Mr. Despondency or like his daughter Miss Much Afraid.

DISCUSSION:
'The blessing of the Old Testament is prosperity, of the New Testament adversity'. Which of these blessings have you known more of? Which is more likely to help the Christian to keep close to his Lord?

Psalm 92: 1–15

LIKE THE PALM TREE

Although the fruit of the palm tree is not mentioned in the Bible, the date-palm seems to be meant in this Psalm and frequently elsewhere in Scripture. The visitor to modern Jericho will find some magnificent specimens thriving in the hot conditions of the Jordan Valley, laden with golden berries in summer. They give a good idea of what the Psalmist means in this Psalm. The palm is a picture of the righteous man. The spring waters nourish it and the warm winter of the Jordan Valley protects it from set-backs. Under these conditions the date-palm becomes a more impressive tree than the specimens which often meet us in photographs of Egypt and Mesopotamia (2). These conditions illustrate the spiritual benefits to a believer of being 'planted' in the house of the Lord. It is always a temptation to the Christian to feel that his church is not just what he would like it to be. He can easily become critical, instead of entering more devotedly into its life and witness. There were great evils associated with the temple worship in Israel. But this 'Psalm for the Sabbath day' does not pause to reveal them. It points out the positive growth in grace which marks the life of the Christian who gets his roots well down in regular church life and can be depended upon to be in his place, with his Bible and hymn book, regardless of the weather, the preacher, last-minute visitors or his own moods and feelings.

QUESTION:
Which verse suggests that the Psalmist was a 'twicer' at worship on the Sabbath day?

TO GOD ALONE BE GLORY!

At the close of World War II a New Hebridean chief encouraged his people to replace their old thatch church with a bigger and better structure. The five-hundred village folk worked with a will. One day the dignified old chief called on the missionary doctor to ask his advice about suitable wording for a tablet to commemorate the opening of the new church. The doctor wisely asked the chief what he himself thought. His prompt reply was:

THIS CHURCH WAS BUILT BY CHIEF NGANGA

The doctor quietly asked if he had done the work single-handed. 'Oh no! My people worked too. Everyone helped.' He saw the point and decided it would be good to add the words AND HIS PEOPLE. Gently the doctor sowed his final thought. 'Why have you done all this work, and given all this money? Why have you built the big new church?' The chief went away to think it over. Whose church was it? For what reason had they all worked so eagerly? When he finally came back the inscription read:

TO THE GLORY OF GOD

THIS CHURCH WAS BUILT

BY CHIEF NGANGA AND HIS PEOPLE.

The chief had taken God for granted; and so do we. This Psalm is written as a reminder of God's regal majesty, of his present sovereignty, of his creative power and providence, of his eternity of Being, of his control of the stormy events of history, of his mastery in the storms of our own life.

THOUGHT:
God cannot be 'defined'; but the answer of the Westminster Shorter Catechism is worth memorising: 'God is a Spirit, infinite, eternal, and unchangeable, in his being, wisdom, power, holiness, justice, goodness, and truth.'

[246]

'O LORD GOD . . . SHOW THYSELF' (1)

Four decades have passed since the world trembled under the shock of the atom-bomb. Fear has stalked the councils of the nations ever since that blast ushered humanity into a new era of potential self-destruction. Yet we are still here. We have somehow survived the first forty years of the nuclear age.

Readers of these pages in all parts of the world are alive to pressures and perils which are peculiarly local and unknown to the rest of the world. There are other perils which the press shares with the world and, so far as we in other lands are able, we rejoice with those who rejoice and we weep with those who weep.

But who that has lived through the past forty years can doubt the presence in national and international affairs of the One spoken of in this Psalm? Are you waiting for the Lord to come and reign in some future Messianic age? He is reigning now! He has all authority in heaven and upon earth and he has it now, and he will never cease to have it. This authority is his by virtue of his redemptive work upon the Cross (Phil. 2: 9). We do not *need* the evidence of historic events in our own time to exhibit the truth of his present sovereignty; but we believe that discerning observers of recent events should be encouraged by the kinds of proofs which the Psalmist, in today's reading, so earnestly desired to see, and which we see.

A GUIDE TO PUBLIC WORSHIP

It is possible to enter the house of God still worrying over whether we have turned off the electric stove. A thousand irritating and adhesive cares stay with us as we take our place in the pew. The Hebrew temple worship had a remedy for this. The choral services of praise engaged the attention of the worshipper and compelled participation. Psalms 95–100 form a cluster of 'pieces' with their own individuality, which together make up an anthem of adoration and praise of God. Just as it is impossible to sit unmoved and unresponsive through a rendering of Handel's Messiah, so this ancient Jewish anthem was meant to engage the thought, heart, will and affections of every Hebrew in the house of God. Once the worshipper was thoroughly attuned to the theme, God then dealt with him upon two important facets of all God-honouring worship:

(1) *The object of our worship is God* (1–7). These verses picture a reverent, happy band of worshippers approaching the temple, their hearts overflowing with gratitude. There is here no suggestion of trifling or cheap praise, and this is a warning for any of us who, alas!, become accustomed to irreverence and lightness in the worship of God.

(2) *The attitude of our worship is sincere* (7d–11). Verse 7 closes with a sudden intrusion. 'Today if ye will hear his voice . . .' It is the voice of the priest or prophet warning all worshippers against the fatal peril of hypocrisy, of hearing with hard hearts, of being rejected from the rest that remains to the people of God.

QUESTION:
How much does the duty and joy of worship draw you to the house of God? Are you among those who think of worship as occupying the whole of the service, or of those who brush worship aside as merely the 'preliminaries' of the service?

[248]

A NEW SONG (I)

A new Song should accompany *salvation*. The Psalmist sings
this new song in Psalm 40: 3 and there he gives the steps in the
Lord's deliverance of his sin-sick soul from death. A new song
should accompany every new *victory of faith*. The Psalmist sings
such a song in Psalm 98: 1 and he attributes all the honour and
the credit to God. And a new song should be upon our lips at the
dawning of *each new day* 'because his compassions fail not; they
are new every morning' (Lam. 3: 23). For the pilgrim on the
King's highway his song is an authentic evidence of his
salvation both to himself and to his fellow-pilgrims. To lose our
song is to lose our testimony. Yet it may easily be lost. A
doubting Christian has no song; a disobedient Christian has no
song; a double-minded Christian has no song; a diffident,
timorous Christian has no song. Whatever songs we learn to
sing in our pilgrimage here, will assist us in the singing of the
grandest new song of all (Revelation 5: 9, 10):

'Thou art worthy to take the book,
And to open the seals thereof:
For thou wast slain,
And has redeemed us to God by thy blood
Out of every kindred, and tongue, and people, and nation'.

Dante, in *The Paradiso*, imagined that he heard this heavenly
song of this universal choir: 'no voice exempt, no voice but well
could join melodious part, such concord is in heaven'.

THE LORD REIGNETH

One hundred years ago, when noblemen thought and wrote about God, the Duke of Argyll wrote a thoughtful book which won wide acceptance. He called it *The Reign of Law*. He argued the evidence for a Creator and Sustainer from the uniformity of nature and the consistency of natural laws. In a thousand unobtrusive ways the observant Christian sees that God rules. He sees this in the unwritten book of his personal life-story. Who ever could have subdued our touchy pride and vanity but God? Who ever could have brought good out of the wanderings and twistings and turnings of our restless hearts but God? Certainly 'light is sown for the righteous and gladness for the upright in heart' (11). But there are some who point to the confused world about us in sheer despair, saying 'Look at the plight of the hungry and the homeless, and the movement of political refugees'. The Psalmist had lived long enough to see that, although 'clouds and darkness' veil God's majesty from men's eyes, yet 'righteousness and judgment' never cease to be the habitation of his throne (2). Not only does he preserve the souls of his saints (10); he also burns up his enemies round about (3). As surely as this twofold exercise of his kingly rule will mark the day of final Judgment, so surely does it mark the history of his present sovereignty in the lives of saints and sinners alike, and in the destinies of nations.

PRAISE:
> *'Thine be the glory, risen, conquering Son,*
> *Endless is the victory thou o'er death hast won.'*
> *(trans. from the French of Edmund Louis Budry.)*

[250]

'A JOYFUL NOISE'

One Sunday evening I found myself at an undenominational church hall with a floor of Oregon pine, on the outskirts of a city. Ten minutes of praise introduced the service. The electronic organ and the piano were yoked in exuberant song. The church steadily filled. Still more chairs were brought in. The praise swelled. Even the babes in their push-chairs seemed to be singing. We were all obeying the Divine command 'Make a joyful noise unto the Lord'. The theme warrants a joyful noise; the Lord rejoiced in a loud, reverent noise. Even the people of God falter when the praise of God fails, or sinks to a half-hearted muttering or a self-conscious undertone. The psalmist has learned his lessons from nature. He has heard the billowing storm pull out all the stops and thunder the praise of God in the rhythmic roar of the breakers (7) and the steady reverberation of the cataracts in the gorge (8). The hills catch the theme and shout for joy. The orchestral accompaniment mounts and swells with harp and trumpet and cornet fully engaged. This hilarious and uninhibited praise is what our God deserves. It is what our God commands. When royalty drives by in a Rolls-Royce we want no desultory clapping, no subdued applause. And here is Royalty. Let us not dishonour Him with sealed lips or muted praise.

A new song

> 'New every morning is the love
> Our wakening and uprising prove;
> Through sleep and darkness safely brought
> Restored to life, and power, and thought.
> (John Keble)

'GOD THAT . . . FORGAVEST THEM' (8b)

He was a quiet helpful fellow, active in his church and entertaining thoughts of Christian work. Now he had come to his minister in great anguish of soul to tell him he had to get married. They knelt in prayer, and at the minister's request he uttered a few faltering words of confession. The minister prayed, quoting the words of 1 John 1: 9, Isaiah 1: 18, and 44: 22. Then they rose and the minister talked with him and wrote out the Scripture passages which he would need to go over with his girl friend. She too was a church girl and a professing Christian. Before he left, the young man had found assurance of cleansing, absolution and acceptance in the words of Jesus the sinner's Friend. The Psalmist knew this experience. Out of just such a situation as this he testified, 'Thou forgavest them'.

'Thou tookest vengeance' (8c). But the Minister had to point out to the young man that the hardest years of his life lay before him. Though God had forgiven him, he would never be able to forgive himself. Though Christ had accepted him, others would now talk about him. Though he had had thoughts of full-time service, these must now be laid aside, at least for the time being. In their home, following marriage, they would need grace to avoid recrimination and to bear with misunderstanding and the rejection of some. They would have to learn that sin exacts its vengeance, though the guilt of sin is fully expiated in the atoning blood of the Lamb of God.

'HE . . . NOT WE'

The universal appeal of this Psalm lies in its grand God-centred chorus of praise. The Lord is its centre and soul and, as a result, his people have found a worthy theme for their songs. You must have noticed that early in the Christian life one delights in the hymns of experience, the themes which spell out the language of our own longings after holiness, or express our gratitude for a clean heart and a new song. Later you find yourself unconsciously moving to hymns which celebrate God's majesty in nature and in grace. This is the keynote of 'The Old Hundredth'. This explains its timeless appeal. Here we have God, not self, at the centre of our thoughts. He, not we, is the subject. This explains the unguarded language which lifts the Psalm to so lofty a height of pure praise.

> 'All people that on earth do dwell
> *Sing* to the Lord with *cheerful voice*;
> Him serve with *mirth*, his *praise* forth tell,
> Come ye before him, and *rejoice*.'

Public worship which begins with man-centred petitions and supplications is thin and unsatisfying. Our hearts need to be elevated in proper adoration. This will produce a fitting order for our private devotions, and will preserve us from the spiritual decay which results from prayerlessness.

CASE HISTORY:
A Sydney (Australia) lawyer, converted in the 1959 Billy Graham Crusade, used the Nicene Creed in his early morning devotions. He found that its God-centred affirmations lifted prayer into praise and supplication into adoration.

SOMETHING TO SING ABOUT

God's mercy gives us something to sing about. Elsewhere the Psalmist is even more explicit in his song than here (1–4). His entire life was a proof of this fact. 'It is of the Lord's mercies that we are not consumed.' Our waywardness and stubbornness, our short memories for God's mercies and long memories for our misfortunes, our abuse of holy privileges and neglect of God's commandments – all of these should remind us today that we are not worthy of the least of his mercies. God's mercy is too high for our poor shallow hearts to know. That is why the Word still conquers all translators and forces them into paraphrases. It was George Adam Smith who popularised the phrase 'leal-love'.

God's judgment also gives us something to sing about, though many find in this an occasion for murmuring and contention (5–8). His judgment upon our wild schemes of self-pleasing – it is time to sing about that! His judgment upon our lukewarm church life – it is time to sing about that! His judgment upon our national idolatries – it is time to sing about that! Unless God loved us enough to chasten us we would be without a song of any sort. To celebrate his judgment is to praise his faithfulness, his fatherly disciplines of sanctity and love. That is why we have learned to sing of both mercy and judgment.

THOUGHT:
A heart which celebrates both God's mercy and his judgment is a heart which is learning to 'behave itself wisely in a perfect way' (2).

THE PELICAN, THE OWL
AND THE SPARROW (1–11)

These ill-assorted birds have a role to fill in this 'prayer of the afflicted, when he is overwhelmed, and poureth out his complaint before the Lord.' Dereliction, loneliness, and a sense of awful nothingness are often part of God's way of preparing us for grace. Sometimes this experience comes to believers who are older in the Christian life, sometimes to young Christians upon the threshold of great spiritual discoveries. The Psalmist was a keen bird-watcher. The grotesque pelican, ridiculous at any time, is what the Christian feels he looks like; one huge misfit, isolated from his fellows. In this melancholy mood the night-flying owl, shunning society, is the true expression of our fugitive soul. The nameless sparrow, commonest of common-places, is what the Christian often feels like in the big bustling world about him. But the Psalm does not end here.

The everlasting God (12–28). God carries this lonely soul out of the silent sand-dunes of his anguish up to the mountains of eternity and he puts a song of grandeur and strength upon his bloodless lips and makes him say:

> 'Maker of worlds of old, the starry sky;
> Thou shalt their glories fold, and lay them by.
> Yet thy years never fail; endless thy fame;
> Thy mighty power we hail; thou art the same.
> (from the French of E. L. Bevir, 1847–1922)

SINNERS AND ANGELS SING IN UNISON

Here is a Psalm to be learned by heart. Its verses can be our song in the house of our pilgrimage. The writer of these notes was taught it as a child in his parents' manse. Now he cannot forget it. The words spring to one's lips in prayer; water one's soul in drought; furnish one's table with daily bread. All God's 'benefits' (2) begin with forgiveness. Even the body is profoundly affected by grace and a Christian is quick to make God his true physician (3). The Kinsman-Redeemer of verse 4 comes to us in the verb 'redeemeth' to show us his hands and his side. He adds in the same instant the assurance 'they shall never perish' (4). He who yesterday was a solitary sparrow upon the house-top is now an eagle, vital with youthful energy. Conversion induces resilience into our whole personality and brings a new springtime to old age (5). A God who can do all these miracles is great in every way. He is magnificent in his mercy (9–11). He is exquisite in his gentleness (13, 14). He is everlasting in his covenant-keeping; sweetly consistent, and so good to children's children (17). Is it any wonder that his children long to keep his commandments and to prove worthy of his covenant love (18)? Though few mortals pause to praise their God, all nature sings, all angels, all the armies of heaven, all ministering spirits, all works in all places of his dominion. It is time for us to do the same (22b).

'ALL GOD'S WORKS'

The mechanistic interpretation of nature has robbed us of more than we know. Our children are taught to worship science and how early they tire of their text books. The nature poem which we have just read is alive with the Presence of God. Not the God of the Deist who, having created the universe, retires from it. Nor the God of the Pantheist, who is prisoner within his own creation. No, we have here the God of the Genesis creation, delighting in the work of his own hands, clothed in light (2), moving majestically upon the wings of the wind (3) with angel escort (4), scanning the seven oceans at a glance and taming them with a word (6–9). He who made the beasts of the earth after their kind (Gen. 1) now provides for the wild asses and the lion's cubs (11, 21). He who caused the oleanders and the cypresses to grow solves the housing problems of the stork and the starling (17). Our garden lettuces are his gift (14). Earth is satisfied (13) but man continues to worry and to grumble. God puts the light on our face, the joy in our heart and the marrow in our bones (15). How good of God to make the darkness! The evening rings the curfew on man's work (23) and draws the curtain of night about his loved ones. For the hidden furry world night cannot come too soon. It is the signal for half of God's great creation to venture forth in search of food (20, 21).

'THOU SENDEST FORTH THY SPIRIT' (30)

Yesterday we spoke of this Psalm as a superb nature poem celebrating God's intimate concern for his whole creation. Today, in this key verse (30) we are told that God uses his Holy Spirit as the personal Agent in the complex mystery of sustaining the entire creation in life and harmony. There is no free-lance process in God's universe, no ungoverned corner of his entire creation, no rebel area in nature. His Spirit proceeds from himself, not as mere breath (though that is the root idea in the Hebrew word) but as life-giving Person. At the dawn of all God's works he used his Spirit to brood over the primeval chaos and bring order and life to birth (Gen. 1: 2). Now, with unwearying and intimate concern he breathes his Holy Spirit through the entire nerve-system of the created world – animate and inanimate; man and beast, visible and invisible, intricate and simple. This important but overlooked truth lifts nature from the domain of the secular and links it with its maker and sustainer. The world becomes a sanctuary. All nature is at worship. God is the object of that worship; the Holy Spirit is he who makes all nature supernatural. But higher than the ministry of the Holy Spirit in nature is his work in the hearts of redeemed men and women. By that gracious ministry we are able to say with the Psalmist. 'My meditation of him shall be sweet; I will be glad in the Lord' (34).

'REMEMBER HIS MARVELLOUS WORKS' (5)

But how can we 'remember' when we so infrequently read of them? Israel was systematically taught its history, and this is one of the great poems which helped the younger generations to 'remember'. It was Augustine who said, 'History is a Divine poem'. No one believed and honoured this reality more than the Jews. The late Chief Rabbi, J. H. Hertz of London, said 'History is the thought of God'. Here in our reading today we are everywhere confronted with the Lord of history. His name vibrates through every part of the Psalm. The pronouns 'he' and 'his' (of God) occur more than 40 times in verses 5–45 (R.V.). History is written in Divine deeds (1); in wondrous works (2); in God's judgments (7) and in God's everlasting covenant (10). From small beginnings he has watched over his covenant people, providing (11), protecting (14), preserving (17), promoting (21). Always the history lesson concludes with the same compelling urge, 'Glory ye in his holy name' (3).

QUESTION:
Compare the use Stephen (Acts 7), Peter (Acts 2) and Paul (Acts 13 etc.) made of the history of Israel in their greatest utterances in the book of Acts. Do we root our testimony deeply in the history of our redemption? And do we illustrate sufficiently from the history of the church?

MEDITATION:
'Conservatism is the disposition to be historical, to attach oneself to those opinions which have stood the test of time and experience.' (W. G. T. Shedd)

THE LORD IS KING

The beat of the drum throbs through this victorious narrative whose purpose is to show that the Lord is King. He alone is sovereign in history. It has been said that any understanding of history must reckon with these three factors: God's sovereignty; man's will; and the permitted operation of a power of evil (the devil). It is important to see that this poem allows no loss of sovereignty to God in the interests of men or devils. On the contrary the epic of his Divine government finds its true glory in the fact that God holds in derision all his opponents (Psa. 2: 4). The detailed record, in melodious poetry, of the plagues of Egypt (27–36) and of the miracles which accompanied Israel's deliverance (37–44) must have had the same powerful effect upon Jewish homes as an illustrated copy of Foxe's *Book of Martyrs* or Smellie's *Men of the Covenant* had on many a God-fearing household in England and Scotland. Indeed this very form of concrete instruction through vivid events in Old Testament history has proved itself on many a missionfield to be the ideal introduction to the gospel.

QUESTION:
Divine history is taught for a purpose expressed in verse 45; and it evokes a response (also in verse 45). Find a similar purpose expressed in the New Testament, and a similar response (see, for example, John 13: 17; Eph. 2: 10; Rom. 11: 33–36; Rev. 4: 10–11; 5: 11–14).

'THEY SOON FORGOT . . .' (13)

While Psalm 105 impresses us with the power of God this Psalm impresses us no less with the mercy and long-suffering of God in view of the repeated treachery of his chosen people. National songs are accustomed to celebrate victories and fine traits, but here is a nation which weaves into memorable poetry their recurring acts of disloyalty and shame. What possible motive could they have? Clearly to magnify the grace of God in his compassion for his covenant people. He saved them in spite of themselves. And he is the same in his saving of us. 'While we were yet sinners Christ died for us.' The Psalmist therefore begins with his Te Deum of praise (1–5) and celebrates the mercy which unceasingly flows from the heart of God (1). This is followed by confession (6–39), and, as we trace the dark stream of Israel's ingratitude, swollen by every tributary of wilful rebellion, we sense something of the awe with which the poet records, 'many times he caused them to be delivered'. 'He regarded their distress.'

EXERCISE:
Note down in one column the verbs which speak of Israel's sin, and opposite these in another column the verbs which speak of God's mercy. You may like to distinguish, also, between Israel's sins of omission (e.g. 7a, 13, 21) and sins of commission.

MEDITATION:
'The worst of all heresies is indifference' (Vinet).

'MANY TIMES . . .' (43)

While we marvel at God's patience with his covenant people Israel under all the provocations of their wicked works, we can see here the mirror of our own ill-deserts; even since we came to Christ. We too have been to Baal-peor if not in act, then in secret thought (28) (cp. Num. 25: 1–3), and have had to look again to the mediation of our great High Priest – a greater than Phinehas (30) (cp. Heb. 10: 19–22). We too have murmured at Meribah (32) (cp. Num. 20: 1–13), and have embittered others thereby. We too have mingled with the peoples of the land (35) and have learned to be conformed to this world (cp. Rom. 12: 2). In our destitution we have hastened back to prayer and to new pledges of obedience and 'many times he has delivered' us (43). When we were brought low we cried out and 'He heard'; 'He remembered'; 'He relented' (44–45).

Thus we join with grateful Israel in this prayer of confession, and with Israel we raise our song of adoration and praise to God our Saviour (47–48). These two verses also appear in 1 Chronicles 16: 35–36 at the close of the special hymn of praise which was composed to be sung on the occasion of the bringing up of the ark of God to Jerusalem. And we are told that on that occasion all the people, having heard the song, said 'Amen' and praised the Lord.

MEDITATION:
Here is Samuel Rutherford's testimony: 'New washings, renewed application of purchased redemption, by that sacred blood which sealeth the free covenant, is a thing of daily and hourly use to a poor sinner.'

DECLARE HIS WORKS
WITH REJOICING

The printing and publishing firms have found a profitable and popular line in marketing 'Thank You' stationery. These little notes, with their Japanese cherry blossom or glimpses of the Canadian Rockies, are popular for one simple reason – the ever-recurring need to say 'Thank you'. How clumsy our thoughts are when we try to write our own thank-you letters! How poor and inadequate our best sentences look in the light of what we *should* say, and would say if we could!

The fifth book of the Psalter opens with praise and the thoughts of the psalmist come thick and fast from his inspired heart. He seems to be so free with his pen, so fresh and honest with his praise. Vivid pictures are painted which tell their own grateful story (4, 5). Tears and laughter are both here. Every word makes sense. The reason for this note of integrity is the depth of the humiliation and the grandeur of God's deliverance which followed upon it.

The structure of the Psalm is noteworthy. The nation's history is sung over in four stanzas: 4–9; 10–16; 17–21; 22–32. Each stanza opens with a recollection of perils now past, and flows into praise for God's deliverance. We see in quick succession the perils of the desert, the bondage of the prison, the solemn approach of death, and the terror of the stormy sea. Threaded through this tapestry of thanksgiving are the twin choruses which are sung four times (6, 13, 19, 28 and 8, 15, 21, 31).

THOUGHT:

> *First the cry of felt need (6, 13, 19, 28)*
> *Then the cry of heartfelt gratitude (8, 15, 21, 31).*

[263]

'DOWN TO THE SEA IN SHIPS'

In all our great ports there are Missions to Seamen with the atmosphere of a home away from home. And these never fail to attract the mariners of many lands and languages. They know that they can have a shower, drink a cup of tea and find a welcome. The men who go down to the sea in ships are often superstitious; but often they are religious, like Jonah's crewmates, and sometimes they are men of deep and simple faith. The writer's mother was reared under such a father. Many times he brought his full-rigged ship from Scotland to New Zealand round the Cape of Good Hope, and took his ship home again by Cape Horn, and never lost a man. These full-rigged ships of two thousand tons, crowded with migrants from the Old World to the Southern seas, were at the mercy of icebergs and fickle winds, of smouldering cargo fires and of fierce gales in the 'roaring forties'. Men of the sea, like men of the land, had time to think of God. They depended upon the stars for navigation, upon the winds for a swift passage, upon a higher Hand for safety amid a thousand perils. This made many of them men of deep religious faith and simple and inflexible character. The Psalmist who wrote this passage knew the anguish of suspense as cross seas tossed his wooden ship, and violent winds screamed through her rigging. He writes an eyewitness account, as vivid in its way as the account which Luke gives us of the storm and the shipwreck in Acts 27. The sense of gratitude and intense relief in verses 29 and 30 is meant to prompt the chorus of verse 31.

VAIN IS THE HELP OF MAN

In the first five verses of this Psalm David is engaged in praise. At verse 6 this passes imperceptibly into a cry for help. Then God speaks, and what follows is a declaration of the sovereign rights of God over the nations (7–9). We can follow readily the train of thought through verses 7 and 8 because here God speaks of his very own. But how do Moab, Edom and Philistia come up for notice? The references all imply ownership. To cast out the shoe over Edom was to take legal ownership over it (cp. Ruth 4: 7). This is exactly what David, by God's help, achieved. Moab and Edom were reduced to tributary vassals. Philistia, the traditional foe, was crushed. Thus David puts into the mouth of God the language of verses 7–9 to signify the fact that he recognised he owed these conquests to God, and received the dominion from God. The strong city of Edom had daunted all its enemies, so David asks dramatically, Who will lead me in there? (10). He answers his own question on a note of triumph which may mean that the victory was already won, or that he sees God's support as deciding the issue in his favour. One thing is certain. Master strategist and able soldier and brave leader of men as he is, David disowns all self-confidence; and no less firmly does he renounce any trust in the arm of flesh, for 'vain is the help of man'.

My motto must be 'I can . . . through Christ' (Phil. 4: 13).

[265]

DAVID SINGING THE PRAISE
OF CHRIST

Here is a little song from a millennium before Bethlehem's holy Child was born, yet written in adoration of God's 'everlasting, true and only Son'. If any reader of these pages has found his confidence in the prophecies and prefigurings of Christ shaken by the reading of some popular introduction to the Bible he can usefully spend the next few minutes doing this simple exercise:

Christ as King (1). Read verse one and jot down from the marginal references the places where this verse is appealed to in the New Testament. You should have these references:

Matthew 22: 41–46. Here Christ quotes Psalm 110: 1 to jolt the Pharisees out of their low views of his Person, and to shock them into recognition of his Eternal Sonship, and his pre-existent glory at the right hand of God. The Pharisees were out of their depth. But there is no good reason why we should be.

Acts 2: 34. Here Peter, speaking to Bible-loving Jews on the Day of Pentecost, has already quoted Psalm 16 as Messianic (25–28), and now endorses his point from Psalm 110: 1 to prove that Jesus is 'both Lord and Christ'.

Heb. 1: 13. Here the Epistle opens with a dazzling array of quotations from the Psalms, all setting forth the glory of Christ. The climax is reached in the quotation of Psalm 110: 1.

Christ as eternal High Priest is pre-figured in Psalm 110: 4. Your marginal references should take you to Hebrews 5: 6, 6: 20, 7: 17, 21.

For a setting forth of his two offices as Priest and King see Zech. 6: 11–13 where Joshua the priest-king is a type of Christ.

THE A TO Z OF GRACE

In ten verses the Psalmist celebrates God's grace, and works his way through the twenty-two letters of the Hebrew alphabet – from Aleph to Tau. One or two recent translations skilfully use the letters of the English alphabet to preserve the Hebrew structure. Here is a fitting way of showing that language, when fully stretched, still fails to do justice to the goodness of God.

The song opens with a mighty Hallelujah – the literal Hebrew for 'Praise ye the Lord'. Not only does the theme require the whole alphabet, it engages the 'whole heart' (1). The Psalmist then fastens our attention upon the works of God which are an unending delight to the inquiring heart of the Christian (2). The probing microscope and telescope only serve to confirm the Psalmist's experience that the more we know of life's mysteries the more we enter new fields of wonder and of mystery. 'Honourable' and 'glorious' are therefore fitting tributes, for they see and celebrate the sovereign Hand which rules all and does all things well (3). How does God use his power? In redeeming us (4), in feeding us (5), in preserving us (6), in assuring us of his character (7, 8). Because he took the first decisive steps for our salvation, while we were in the far country of our own ignorance and folly (9), his people can trust him to complete the plan of their redemption and bring them safely to the city which has foundations, whose Builder and Maker is God (6). Only godly fear can give a man these satisfying perspectives. That is why the psalmist says that the fear of the Lord is the ABC of all true learning. Every well-taught Christian holds a divinity degree (10).

AN ACROSTIC ON THE HAPPY LIFE

The twenty-two letters of the Hebrew alphabet are again pressed into service to describe the happy life. The key word 'blessed' is itself plural and from the many facets of this jewel there shine forth rays of God-given happiness. There is no other root for blessedness than a cleansing and ennobling 'fear' of the Lord which goes hand in hand with a love for his commandments (1). The order of what follows is instructive. Beginning with the witness and strength of the family (2) God adds the further blessing of prosperity (3) linked with uprightness (3). The blessed life has its dark valleys but the Sun of righteousness arises even there with healing in its wings (4). Shakespeare may counsel us to be neither borrower nor lender but the blessed life has learned to open its hand (5). Length of days and a fragrant legacy of memories belong to the godly man (6), and peace of mind amid all sudden calamities (7). He leaves his critics in the hands of God (8). He is remembered for his liberal care of the needy (9). God will 'lift up his head in triumph' (9c) to the chagrin of his detractors whose envy and threats can do him no real harm. The life of the blessed is the concern of the Lord.

NEW TESTAMENT ENDORSEMENT:
Look up 2 Corinthians 9: 9 for a revealing amplification of verse 9.

HAVE YOU LEARNED TO SING?

Some worshippers do not sing, and a few cannot sing, but many more should sing than do sing. The worship of the Hebrews assumed that all the congregation knew the Psalter and would enter cheerfully into the act of corporate praise. Psalms 113–118 form a little hymnal of their own, linked with the religious festivals of the church year. Just as we find special hymns for Christmas and Easter and Whitsuntide, so they found these Psalms appropriate to the feasts of Passover, Pentecost and Tabernacles. In the Gospels we learn that the Lord's Supper closed with the singing of a hymn (Mark 14: 26) and this is thought to have been selected from the Psalms 113–118. What makes today's Psalm so suited to this sacred use? First, its emphasis upon the praise of God as the universal duty and privilege of all people. In verse 2 we see the timelessness of his kingdom; in verse 3 its world-wide dominion. The second portion (5–9) lays its emphasis upon the intimate concern and amazing grace of the High and Holy One who inhabits eternity (5, 6). Our Puritan fathers were quick to see in the vivid metaphors of the poor picked out of the dust, the beggar plucked from the dunghill, and the barren woman happy with her children, true pictures of what God has done for us who have believed in Jesus.

John Ellerton's hymn may well have sprung from verse 3 of this Psalm.

> 'As o'er each continent and island
> The dawn leads on another day,
> The voice of prayer is never silent,
> Nor dies the strain of praise away.'

A NATION'S TESTIMONY
TO ITS SAVIOUR

When a nation bears testimony to its Saviour it is right that it should say what God has done for it corporately. Many of the Psalms are of the nature of personal testimony. This Psalm is a nation's testimony compressed into eight dramatic verses in which the seas flee, the mountains skip and the flinty rock runs with water. We see in these verses the effortlessness of God's power on behalf of his people, and the proprietary interest which he has in them. The word 'sanctuary' points to his dwelling among them as their God, the word 'dominion' to his ruling over them as their King. Both terms describe the church's relationship to its Lord. The use of two unusual Divine names in verse 7 is instructive. 'The Lord' is Hebrew *Adon*, a word which occurs only 30 times in the Old Testament and which carries the emphasis on God's proprietary rights as Ruler and Owner of the entire earth. The 'God of Jacob' is *Eloah*, a word which occurs some 56 times and is derived from a Hebrew verb meaning 'to worship'. The Psalmist wants to present God as the supreme object of our adoration. This emphasis is based upon his proprietary rights over us and his saving acts on our behalf.

THOUGHT:
'Each separate title of God may be regarded as one letter, complete indeed in itself, yet, when arranged and combined together, spelling out in full the grand and wondrous Name of the God of the Bible' (Newberry).

THREE CLASSES . . . THREE
DIVERSE REACTIONS

The Psalm opens with the glad confession that all that we are and have is from God's mercy and for the honour of his Name. We are prone to lose sight of this regulative truth and to filch a little of the credit for ourselves. We speak expansively of 'our' promising youth work, 'our' new church, 'our' recent converts. This is a degradation of the truth. It is robbing God of his due. Not unto us, but unto his Name we give glory!

The heathen, i.e. the surrounding nations, watching Israel's calamities, taunt her for her absentee God (2). Israel answers, that because God is invisible he is not therefore absent. On the contrary his heavenly throne guarantees his omnipotence (3). Their little gods invite the satire of verses 4–8 and the profound diagnosis of verse 9.

The dead of verse 17 are the nameless generations of the past who have lain down with sealed lips and silent tongues. *Sheol* here carries the thought of eternal silence. This verse is not a theology of the intermediate state but an emphasis upon the important truth that if God is to get his due praise he must get it from the living, not the dead.

Israel (9–16), and the house of Aaron, and the blessed of the Lord are of another spirit. And it is exhilarating to imagine with what fervour the pilgrims burst into song as they sang the mighty refrain '*He* is their help and their shield' (9, 10, 11).

'I AM THY SERVANT; THOU HAST LOOSED MY BONDS'

With the words of verse 16 Augustine opens Book Nine of his immortal *Confessions* immediately following his account of his conversion in the garden at Milan. His *Confessions* are in no way to be compared with magazines of our day which carry the same title. Augustine's purpose was to bear ardent testimony to the grace and love of God in Christ, and he does this most frequently in the language of the Psalms. This Psalm is deeply personal. Its inclusion in the liturgy for the festivals of the Hebrew church points to the inescapably personal nature of all public worship. We each have our own private and intimate reasons for saying 'I love the Lord' (1); 'I was brought low' (6), 'I was greatly afflicted' (10). And one of the unfathomed mysteries of grace is that God had an ear for *my* voice (1), helped *me* (6), dealt bountifully with *me* (7) and loosed *my* bonds (16). He acts towards *me* as if he had no other name laid upon his heart. And yet his family is so vast that only God knows them all. He knows them all as intimately as he knows me. He deals with them all as bountifully as he has dealt with me (7). Let us not neglect to pay our vows in the courts of the Lord's house, in the presence of all his people (18).

HALLELUJAH (PSALM 117)

Handel has shown that the key word of this Psalm is part of the language of redeemed men everywhere. The Hallelujah Chorus of *The Messiah* has its anticipation in this smallest of Psalms and rolls on like a deep accompaniment through Scripture to find its climax in Revelation Chapter 19. It is surprising that Psalm 117 has not found the same wide use as Psalm 100 which it resembles.

'*His mercy endureth for ever*' (Psalm 118: 1–14). This chorus points to the nature of the Psalm as one associated with Israel's great festivals, when crowds made their way to Jerusalem, singing as they went. The word 'mercy' sparkles like a jewel against the background of torn velvet which made up Israel's later history. There is the mercy which points to our High Priest (3) and the mercy which springs from our prayers (5). There is the mercy which garrisons us amid all fears (6), and the mercy which never forsakes the weakest of God's unworthy children (7). We need the reminder of verses 8, 9. Amid a world where everyone desires a friend at court (9) the Christian steadfastly refuses to panic or to trust the arm of flesh. He *has* a Friend who presides over the Court of Heaven and rules among the nations of the earth (10).

> 'My times are in Thy hand,
> Jesus, the Crucified;
> Those hands my cruel sins had pierced
> Are now my guard and guide.'

MESSIAH'S HYMN BOOK

We recognize in today's portion familiar quotations which take our thoughts to the closing events of our Lord's earthly ministry. 'Blessed is he that cometh in the name of the Lord' (26) is to be Jerusalem's cry amidst the excitement of his triumphal entry (Matt. 21: 9) and it is to be his people's cry as they welcome Christ at the last Advent (Matt. 23: 39).

'The stone which the builders refused' (22) is to find frequent reference in the New Testament. Jesus quoted verses 22 and 23 to the chief priests and elders of the Jews in the tense moments which followed the parable of the vineyard let out to husband-men (Matt. 21: 33–46). And his words were an announcement to apostate Jewry that God had made him both Lord and Christ. The apostle Peter quoted the same words in his defence before the Sanhedrin (Acts 4: 11) and he directly applied them to Jesus and his rejection by the Jewish 'builders'. Many years later the apostle Peter quoted the same words in his first Epistle (2: 4–7) and expanded the application by cross reference to two related quotations from Isaiah 28: 16 and 8: 14. 'The Stone' became, in the early fathers, a Name for Christ. As such he is still precious to those who believe; still a Stone to trip over to those who reject his Person and his saving cross.

GOD'S WORD (1)

The Centrality of God's Word. At the heart of our Bible is Psalm 119 whose 176 verses are in praise of God's gift of his Word. The theme unfolds systematically and with grace. Each of the 22 sections of eight verses is headed with a letter of the Hebrew alphabet. The eight verses of each section all commence with a word beginning with that letter. It would seem an impossible task to achieve a translation which reproduces this Hebrew acrostic, but Ronald Knox has done it with skill and not a hint of clumsiness of language. In our notes on this Psalm we are going to look at facets of the Word revealed by each successive section.

The royal Word (1–8). The keynote is *authority*. We are to keep it, not question it (2); to walk in it, not ignore it (3); to observe it, not obscure it (4); to respect it, not resent it (6); to see it as a book of judgments, not of opinions (7); of statutes, not suggestions (8); of precepts, not puzzles (4); of commandments, not discussions (6).

The cleansing Word (9–16). Here is the way to a clean life (9), a clean heart (10, 11), clean lips (13), a clean mind (15), and clean pleasures (14–16). The devout Borden, of Yale, whose biography stirred a generation of young men, made verses 9 and 11 his motto while at University. Verse 9 he had illuminated on the wall of his room, and verse 11 inscribed in the front of his Bible.

GOD'S WORD (2)

The gracious Word (17–24). The grace which bestows *life* is unveiled in verse 17. Grace was exhibited in God's dealings with the Psalmist. Grace lies behind every aspiration after God, every impulse to pray, every endeavour to lead others to himself.

The grace which bestows *light* is unveiled in verse 18. Every time we bow in prayer we are confessing our dependence upon God for light to see the hidden riches of his grace.

The grace which bestows *love* is unveiled in verse 20. Love for God is love for God's law, God's will, God's commandments. This love is not in us by nature. It becomes ours through God's gift of grace.

The reviving Word (25–32). '*Quicken* thou me' is the cry of a desolate heart, forsaken by others and crushed under a sense of failure and hopelessness. The reviving word is our remedy at such times. How often has the writer of these notes given strength at a sick-bed or in the house of sorrow by simply taking a blank envelope from his satchel and writing on it the verse of Scripture which seemed most apt and personal. He has often needed the ministry of the reviving word for his own heart and he has learned to find it in the daily reading of Holy Scripture. Let us seek to the Divine Physician amidst all feelings of failure (25), unworthiness (28) and leanness of soul (32).

GOD'S WORD (3)

The guiding Word (33–40). Guidance springs from the Holy Spirit employing the Word (33). This guidance presupposes the enlightened mind (34). This guidance assumes prompt and glad obedience on our part (35). There is always the danger of our misreading or misconstruing this guidance through some disease of the heart and conscience. *Covetousness* is such a disease; it affects the whole man (36). And there is the inevitable blurring of the guidance of God's Word when the reader is under the spell of *Vanity Fair* (37). The more we submit ourselves to the Word the more we shall prove the reality of its guiding ministry (38–40).

The liberating Word (41–48). What is it to 'walk at liberty' (45)? It is to find that God's Word liberates us from public opinion (42), from panic about our uncertain future (43), from fear to testify to the saving work of God in Christ (46). This liberty, like Luther's, is bound to the Word. This liberty does not come to most of us in a moment but gradually as we pray daily the prayer of verses 47 and 48. There is no true freedom in having our own way. Christ's service is perfect freedom. We are never more free than when bondslaves of Jesus Christ. Only then do we 'walk at liberty'.

GOD'S WORD (4)

The peremptory Word (57–64). When God's Word convicts us of some shortcoming, some sin of omission or commission, our response must be prompt and unquestioning. The Psalmist was a man of surrendered heart (57) and prayerful obedience (58). As he walked with the Lord in the light of his Word, rays of revealing truth uncovered unsuspected sin in his life (59). What did he do? He thought on his ways, like the prodigal (Lk. 15: 17). He turned from sin to the Word and will of God. He made haste, allowing no second thoughts to compromise his obedience. He delayed not to put into immediate practice what God had so clearly shown him (60). If this means getting up at midnight in order to seal our response in a new surrender we shall do this gladly (62).

The chastening Word (65–72). 'Before I was afflicted I went astray, but now I observe Thy word' (67 R.V.). We cannot do without our Father's hand whether in comfort (50) or in chastening (71). Our sensitive flesh shrinks under the rod of affliction. But without its corrections where would we be? Chastening keeps us on the path of obedience (67). Chastening teaches us more about God (68). We learn the deeper meaning of that word 'good' both in relation to who God is and what God does (68). We discover that chastening is one of the higher diplomas in the University of Christian Experience (71). Our heart's verdict becomes more firm and settled the longer we travel with God, and we learn to say, 'Thou hast dealt well with thy servant' (65).

GOD'S WORD (5)

The silent Word (81–88). One of the striking things about these verses is the accurate way in which they plot the rising and falling of our feelings in the face of trials and temptations. The Psalm opens with a man fainting under his burden, but hoping in spite of all despair (81). We see a man prostrate beneath a brazen sky yet looking to God for comfort still (82). Job 30: 30 may shed some light on the metaphor of the bottle in the smoke. He senses the break-up of his powers, his loss of grip on life (83, 84, 87). He entreats God to come forth from his silent heavens and rescue him (84, 86).

The enduring Word (89–96). 'For ever' is a long time, but so long will God's Word have God's seal upon it. So long will God's truth remain unchanged and unchanging. All human perfection has an end (96) but 'thy law has a boundless range'. The enduring earth is a shadow cast by the enduring Word, a kind of reflection of the eternal validity of God's laws and God's faithfulness (90, 91). Our eternity is wrapped up in our relationship to this enduring Word (92). Through its convicting work God quickened and saved us (93). Through its sanctifying work God keeps us close to himself (92).

An interesting thought arises out of verse 89: will the language of heaven be essentially the language of Scripture learned and loved here and understood in its breadth and depth hereafter?

GOD'S WORD (6)

The intellectual Word (97–104). Who is this man who makes this threefold claim? He claims to be *wiser than his enemies* (98). Hosea 4: 1, 6, 11 gives a hint of the answer. Harlotry and wine take away the brains. All sin blurs the moral judgment, closes the lenses of perception, and seals off the soul from the loftier flights of understanding.

Wiser than his teachers (99). His teachers had the knowledge of facts, techniques, method. But God's man has understanding. He sees all knowledge from the aspect of that posture of godly fear which is the beginning of wisdom.

Wiser than his seniors (100). In primitive societies the village elders are the custodians of the oral tradition. They carry the conscience of the tribe. But there is more real understanding in the soul of the submissive Christian than can be gained by the mere accumulation of years. The Bible is a University Course. Enrolment comes at our conversion. The Course will last our lifetime.

The enlightening Word (105–112). The Bible sheds light on our solemn vows (16), light on our afflictions (107), light on life's uncertainties (109), light on the pitfalls in our pathway (110). 'In vain is the net spread in the sight of any bird.' The daily access of light for the faithful reader of Scripture shows up the glory of his Lord, the grandeur of his inheritance and the nobility of his calling. To turn from that light is to love death.

GOD'S WORD (7)

The exacting Word (113–120). The Word of God stands over
against all human shuffling and evasion. The more we read it
the less we are capable of saying one thing and meaning
another. James has said that a double-minded man is unstable
in all his ways (Jas. 1: 8). He was reflecting the Psalmist's
declaration in verse 113. The Word of the Lord sifts our inner
motives, shows up the duplicity which others cannot see, and
makes us hate double-mindedness in ourselves and in others.
Some seek security in deceit (118). We shall seek it in him who
is our shield and hiding-place (114). It is a wholesome fear
which produces this kind of integrity in the faithful reader of
God's Word (120).

The jealous Word (121–128). The Psalmist sums up this
section by declaring 'I hate every false way.' He is jealous for
God's way and God's honour. This is a right kind of jealousy
imparted by God's Word to obedient readers. Love for God's
Word kills that self-love which has slain its thousands. But it
does more. It takes the glitter off the false ways of a fallen world
which would otherwise hold us spellbound. The more God's
Word works its way into our thinking and our behaviour the
more we shall be grieved at all who treat it unworthily and at
those who make void God's law (126).

GOD'S WORD (8)

The confirming Word (129–136). If you want to know what an author thinks of other writers in the same field of learning look at his footnotes. They are often bristling with brass tacks. The Bible writers are free from any sniping at earlier writers and books. They all build upon their predecessors, and do so without seeking to score points off them. This is beautifully illustrated in today's portion. The Psalmist is so honest and so sincere in confirming the deep and satisfying truth of all the Scripture which was before him. The clue to his attitude to Scripture is found in his attitude to the Lord of Scripture. To love the Name is to love God (132).

The righteous Word (137–144). Jehovah-tsidkenu is the name of God which embodies the opening word of this section, 'righteous'. Jehovah-tsidkenu means 'the Lord our righteousness' (Jer. 23: 6). God's Word, like himself, is righteous (137). All that he has spoken is true to what he is in his own incorruptible integrity and truth (138). Because God is not subject to change and decay his Word is clothed with the same timeless quality (142). It is just as precious to us as it was to David (140). It is just as necessary for 'man come of age' as for Israel in ancient times. The neglect and rejection of God's Word is a commentary on man's hostile heart, not upon God's timeless Word (139).

GOD'S WORD (9)

The prayerful Word (145–152). There is much to be said for reading the Bible upon one's knees. In this posture prayer blends imperceptibly with the word of Scripture. Each aids the other and creates the ideal attitude of obedience and responsive love. It is the function of this portion to bring out the intimate and mutual bond between prayer and Scripture-reading. In verse 145 we see earnest prayer, 'I cried'. In verse 146 obedient prayer, 'I shall observe'. In verse 147a diligent prayer, 'I prevented the dawning of the morning'. In verse 147b expectant prayer, 'I hoped'. Then notice the imperceptible transition as the Psalmist glides from prayer to meditation in verse 148.

The considerate Word (153–160). Does the Lord take notice of my particular and personal circumstances? Today's portion very clearly insists that he does. He considers my affliction (153). He pleads my cause (154), not as a mere acquaintance but as my Kinsman-Redeemer, my 'goel'. He puts new life into me when I am taunted and ready to give up (157) or surrounded by treachery (158). This quickening is so personal that every believer can depend upon him to do so, regardless of all depressing conditions. This quickening does not come from some mystical experience but from God's dealing with me in and through his Word (154, 156), the vehicle of his loving-kindness (159).

GOD'S WORD (10)

The satisfying Word (161–168). In these eight verses we hear sweet music played upon an instrument of seven strings. Let us call these seven strings by the singer's own names. There is *awe* of God's Word (161), *joy* in God's Word (162), *love* for God's Word (163), *praise* to God for his Word (164), *peace* from God's Word (165), *hope* in God's Word (166), *obedience* to God's Word (167). These seven strings spell out the perfection of the Word in its satisfying ministry within the heart of the believer. Worship may be thin and unsatisfying or it may be rich and rewarding. All depends upon the bond which our soul has established between God and his Word.

The sovereign Word (169–176). The Psalm opened with God as sovereign in giving us his holy law (1–8). It closes fittingly with God as sovereign in showing us his saving grace (169–176). For years we were like a frightened child separated from his parents, lost in the swiftly moving crowd, terrified and exhausted. At last we stopped in our tracks and ceased to run and breathed the prayer, 'I have gone astray like a lost sheep; seek thy servant' (176). Now, from the vantage ground of salvation we can look back and read the record clearly. It was God who imparted the first longings after him (174). It was God who imparted life to my dead soul (175). 'I had not sought thee hadst thou not first sought me' (Augustine).

KEPT

An only son was leaving home as a teen-ager. He was going to the city for his first job. His parents had a final word as the train pulled in at the country railway station. He never forgot his mother's parting encouragement. It was just the one word, '*kept*'. She was pointing her son to Psalm 121 and the security of those who put their hand in God's hand. Both parents have finished their journey and the teen-ager is now an elder in his church. But the unchanging God who neither slumbers nor sleeps has proved that he is as good as his Word.

The hills of verse 1 ('mountains' in R.V.) should be linked with Mount Zion in Psalm 125. From the steadfast hills the Psalmist's thought travels easily to the steadfast God. It is one of his favourite metaphors for the security of the believer. Our God is also the God of the silent hours (3, 4). We may lay ourselves down and sleep, for he makes us to dwell in safety. And he is the God of the secret places (5). Because he is at our right hand we shall not be moved (Psa. 16: 8). Even the sun and the moon are told to do the believer no harm (6). And he is the God of the lonely road to whose keeping we commit all the untrodden way. We are poor keepers of ourselves, both in body and in soul, and need very much the security of his guardian arm and his vigilant eye. The French Reformers gave us the motto, 'Et teneo, et teneor' – '*I keep*', yes, but, better still, '*I am kept*'.

[285]

THE PILGRIM PSALMS

Psalms 120–134 belong to a class of their own and are headed songs of degrees, or songs of ascents. Probably the title refers to the going up of Israel to Jerusalem at the annual religious festivals. Possibly some belong to the time of the return from the exile. There are frequent allusions to the exile (Psa. 120) and to the terrible experience of the nation's chastenings (Psa. 124). However in today's Psalm a happier note is struck as we see the hosts of pilgrims thronging the highways to Zion and singing as they go up to Jerusalem. We may call this Psalm 'A Hymn for God's House' and its language can easily fit our own mood and duty as we make our preparations for church attendance. In verse 1 we see the invitation and watch the willing guest as he responds with eagerness. In verses 2, 3 he visualizes himself already standing within the gates of the holy city. In verse 4 we see the deeper meaning of our relationships within the church. Our going to God's house is a testimony to all the people of God. A Christian who stays away from church for whatever reason is silencing one of God's chosen witnesses in the world. Our King presides as Judge over his house and rules it by his Word and Spirit (5). We must safeguard the threefold cord of prayer, prosperity and peace (6, 7). And we must be more than passengers and spectators. The church of God places its holy obligations upon all the people of God (8, 9).

OUR STEADFAST HELPER

Psalm 123. A descant on devotion. The true attitude in our devotion is the upturned face (1). The true object of our devotion is the exalted Lord (1). The true hallmark of our devotion is our sensitivity to his least behest (2). The true test of our devotion is our patience to await the moment of his mercy (2). The best fuel for the fires of our devotion is the scorning and contempt of those who reproach us (3, 4). This scours the rust off our armour and puts purpose into our soul. The imagery of the Psalm is eastern. The servant receives her orders by signs, often scarcely perceptible. The servant's eyes must rest constantly upon the hands of her mistress.

Psalm 124. God in the contingencies of life. First we read what might have been (1–5). Our enemies set themselves in opposition (2), sought our utter annihilation (3), planned to drown us in oblivion (4, 5). Next we read what God did (1–8). He took our side (1, 2). He kept us safe (6). He proved our strong and steadfast Helper (8). What came of this terrible contingency? Why, we are still here! We have escaped the well-laid nets of our enemies (7)! This Psalm was often sung in persecuting times in Scotland. The most notable occasion was perhaps on the release of John Durie, a faithful minister who had been imprisoned. When he was set free in 1582 and entered Edinburgh, the people came out to meet him. As they moved up the High Street they sang the metrical version of this Psalm, 'Now Israel may say, and that truly'.

[287]

IN PRAISE OF REAL PEACE

To be 'somebody' does not bring contentment. To have things does not give peace. Then let us look again at the Psalmist's recipe.

Peace comes from our having our feet firmly planted upon Mount Zion. Geography undergirds theology in verses 1 and 2, and tells us that the immovable man is God's man.

Peace comes from our having a sovereign Protector, vigilant, ever-present, absolutely unconquerable (2).

Peace comes from our seeing God at work extricating us from the calculated take-over of powerful enemies (3). The God of the righteous will not suffer the power (i.e. the rod or sceptre) of the wicked to lie heavily upon them.

Peace comes from confidence in God's observant eye and swift mercy. His eyes are upon the whole earth, beholding the evil and the good. This fact comforts the Christian (4) as it disturbs the most cynical of sinners (5). The heart has good reason to breathe the prayer, 'Peace be upon Israel' (5b). This peace is assured by Israel's Prince of Peace. But such are the fears of our false hearts and the ferocity of our unseen foes that we do well to say it over and over to ourselves until we possess the certainty of its message, 'Peace be upon Israel!' Yes, let us say it again as the Psalmist does in Psalm 128: 6, 'Peace be upon Israel!'

HIS MERCY ENDURETH FOREVER

This Psalm sings its own way into our heart even though we have to hear it, muted, in English. We can sense the lilt of joy and the deeper note of a people's thanksgiving. The song moves from the theme of the wonder and greatness of God's Person (1–3) to the wonder and greatness of all God's works of creation (4–9), redemption (10–15), and providence (16–25). The refrain 'for his mercy endureth forever' is meant to be a congregational response from all the worshippers after the choir has chanted the respective verses. Compare Psalm 118: 1–4, 29.

The simplest way to relate this Psalm to our own experience of God's mercy is to look quietly and steadily back over the scroll of his mighty acts on our behalf. There are his acts of creation. Think of how he has opened our eyes to see the wonder of the world around:

> 'Something lives in every hue
> Christless eyes have never seen'.

Thank the Lord by saying 'For his mercy endureth for ever.' Then think of his works of redemption on our behalf. Name again the particular victories when God showed his 'strong hand' and his 'stretched out arm' (12) on your behalf. Who was your Pharaoh? Who your Og, king of Bashan (15, 20)? What is your heritage from the Lord (21–22)? Certainly we need to repeat our refrain often: 'For his mercy endureth for ever'. We have met and vanquished as many giants as Bunyan's Pilgrims. It is time to set our story to music.

John Milton's well-known metrical version of this Psalm was composed when he was a student at Cambridge:

> 'Let us with a gladsome mind
> Praise the Lord, for he is kind;
> For his mercies aye endure,
> Ever faithful, ever sure.'

[289]

IN A STRANGE LAND

In the communes of the People's Republic of China there is, we gather, no time to sit down by the rivers and weep; and there are no harps. Then what is this Psalm about?

It is not a complaint against the harshness of Israel's captivity in Babylon. In some ways the picture is sadly idyllic, with its slow-moving waters fringed with poplars (A.V. willows). The severity of Israel's earlier bondage in Egypt is absent here.

Nor is it the weeping of conviction of sin or the tears of guilty and contrite hearts (Ezra 10: 1).

No! Here we have grief of a different kind – the weeping of God's people robbed of the ordinances of worship. 'There is a distinction between us and God's ancient people, for at that time the worship of God was confined to one place [the temple on Mount Zion], but now he has his temple wherever "two or three" are met together in Christ's Name' (Calvin). The acuteness of their agony lay in the Babylonians' insistence that these captive Jews should entertain them with that form of praise which was consecrated to the worship of God and tied to the sacred ritual of the temple. 'The captors ask for the songs of Zion as the Philistines asked for sport from Samson, to amuse them.'

We too are strangers in a strange land (4) but we have our 'Jerusalem which is above' (Gal. 4: 26). Of this we sing, with the medieval Bernard of Cluny:

> 'Jerusalem the golden,
> With milk and honey blest,
> Beneath thy contemplation
> Sink heart and voice oppressed.'

ELOHIM

'Before the gods' (1) does not mean that David acknowledged the living reality of other gods, the 'gods many and lords many' of which the Apostle Paul speaks in 1 Corinthians 8: 5. The Hebrew word *elohim*, here used for 'gods', occurs 2500 times in the Old Testament and is usually translated 'God'. Gen. 1: 1 is the first reference. But occasionally *elohim* is used in a more general sense, as in this Psalm. Young's *Analytical Concordance* shows the following alternative renderings in the Authorized Version. *Elohim* is translated 'angels' once; 'goddess' twice; 'judges' four times; 'gods' 240 times. The first part of *Elohim* – *El* – is used as a proper name for God 212 times in the Old Testament and derives from a root which signifies 'strength', 'might'. The Hebrew plural ending – im – hints at some such plurality of Persons as we see in the doctrine of the Trinity. See for example Genesis 1: 26 where *Elohim* is followed by the plural pronouns 'us' 'our' 'our'. It is difficult to find an English concept which embraces these facets of the Hebrew *elohim*. In one of the Melanesian languages of the New Hebrides *elohim* answers to the idiom for the corporate authority and powers of the chiefs. The chief was called 'supwe ni navanua', god of the land. But he received this authority together with his title to the tribal lands from 'Supwe ni elangi', the high God. The word 'Supwe' was thus used both for God and for the chief, as was *elohim* in the Old Testament. It would be fair to translate verse 1, 'Before the *rulers* will I sing praise unto thee'.

MEDITATION ON VERSE 6:
'Lowliness and humility are the court dress of God: he who wears them will please God well.'

[291]

TOO WONDERFUL

Here is David's hymn to his omnipotent, omniscient and omnipresent God. But he would not have dreamed of using such cold and flinty terms as these. He has learned that God is all-knowing through the quiet voice of conscience testifying that from him no secrets are hid (1–2). He has learned by experience, in a thousand different circumstances, that what men call 'coincidences' are the particular providences of God (3–5). When first the full solemnity of the truth of God's ever-present Spirit broke upon his conscience David wanted to hide his faults from such pure, all-seeing eyes (7–12). But where could he hide from such a God as this? Where (7)? Where (8)? Where (9–10)? Where (11–12)? Though he were to fly as fast as the light of dawn shoots from the east he could not outdistance God.

Then his mind turns to the mystery and miracle of the origin of life, his life, every single human life, your life and my life (13–16). Every birth is a Divine creation; 'thou' in verse 13 is the emphatic Hebrew pronoun. The words 'curiously wrought' (15) seem to refer to the art of embroidery (Exod. 28: 8). They beautifully portray the perfect symmetry, delicate artistry and chaste loveliness of the human body; which beauty we should not despise however much it is today exploited. God does not speak of the unborn babe in terms of so many months but in 'days' – as another translation runs – 'the days that were formed for me'.

Such sensitivity to God means sensitivity to sin (19–24). 'A good man desires to know the worst about himself.' (Matthew Henry).

TRUE PRAYER

'David complains of the implacable cruelty of his enemies, and of their treachery and calumnies. In the close, having besought God's help, and expressing his persuasion of obtaining favour he comforts himself with the hope of deliverance, and just vengeance being executed upon his enemies' (Calvin's headnote to his comment on this Psalm).

Anxiety (1–5). Note the words used to describe this anonymous pressure-group who were set on destroying David's reputation (3) and his very life (4–5). 'Evil', 'violent', 'arrogant' are three aspects of sinful human nature. The technical words for snares in verse 5 are interesting. The Authorized Version uses 'snare' for *seven* different Hebrew words, an indication of the vivid homeliness of David's metaphor in a land where children learned how to snare sparrows, and kings amused themselves by snaring savage beasts.

Trust (6–8). 'Thou hast covered . . .' (8) 'David comes forth, not as a raw and undisciplined recruit, but as a soldier well tried in previous engagements.'

Retribution (9–11). Verse 10 seems to have in mind the fate of Sodom and Gomorrah (Gen. 19: 23–28). Verse 11 uses the hunting metaphor, so closely linked with the activities of David's enemies in verse 5.

Confidence (12–13). 'I know' is the language of Christian assurance. Look up its use by the Apostle Paul (e.g. 2 Tim. 1: 12) and compare John's 'we know' in 1 John. Four descriptions of the believer occur in verses 12–13. How many of them fit our personal case?

MEDITATION:
'Till we have a persuasion of being saved through the grace of God there can be no sincere prayer . . . Doubtful prayer is no prayer at all.' (Calvin)

[293]

THEIR DAINTIES

We may well take to heart the prayer of verse 3 of this Psalm. The writer of these notes remembers how often his father used this petition when the family knelt in prayer after breakfast. This had the effect of making me ask myself, as a boy, What does it mean to 'set a watch . . . before my mouth'? Gradually the picture formed itself of the Lord standing beside me and listening to every word. This solemnizing thought has its New Testament parallel in Matthew 12: 36–37. 'Every idle (thought-less) word that men shall speak they shall give account thereof in the day of judgment. For by thy words thou shalt be justified and by thy words thou shalt be condemned.'

While verses 1–2 are concerned with prayer, verse 3 applies to all that we say, and to all that we are tempted to say. But since it is 'out of the abundance of the *heart* the mouth speaketh' (Matt. 12: 34 cp. 15: 18), David now traces temptation to its inner spring (4). A Christian may seem well-disciplined in speech and yet be afflicted by many evil and ungoverned thoughts. Hence our need of God's timely grace and guardian-ship at the very centre of our life.

'Their dainties' (4) are the 'kick' which the happy pagan gets out of his particular way of life. Even a committed Christian can secretly cast a wistful glance over his shoulder and say in a moment of weakness, 'Lucky fellow!' In fact the Hebrew word for 'dainties' – manammim – is plainly onomatopoeic. Say it to yourself slowly two or three times. What do you hear? The lip movements of secret gratification. Look up Psalm 73: 2–3.

THOU KNOWEST MY WAY

I write this on a warm summer's morning in the sub-tropical north of New Zealand. I have enjoyed a good night's rest. The study window of my manse looks out upon an arm of the Manukau Harbour. It is all so quiet and peaceful.

How then can I 'think in' to David's predicament? He writes as an outlaw with a price on his head. His hideout is a cave (1 Sam. 24: 3). Humanly speaking he has no prospect of life. Comforts have fled from him. Any day his enemy Saul expects to overwhelm him with sudden destruction.

The verbs in the Authorized Version are in the past tense; certain other translations give them in present tenses. This gives added vividness to David's experience. It also enables us to live through it with him. The Bible's message is supremely for us. The history is ours. The primary author, the Holy Spirit, had you and me in view in this Psalm, as elsewhere in Scripture (1 Peter 1: 12).

The Psalm reveals a beautiful symmetry. Four expressions of anxious prayer are followed by a cry of assurance – '*Thou* (emphatic Hebrew pronoun) knowest my way'. Then four desolating experiences are mentioned, to be followed by another cry of assurance 'Thou (again the emphatic Heb. pron.) art my refuge' etc. (5a). Then three further pleas for God's help are uttered with a reason annexed in each case (6–7a), again to be followed by a cry of assurance (7b).

MEDITATION ON VERSE 4A:
'I looked on my right hand . . .'. The allusion seems to be to the Jewish courts where both accuser and advocate stood on the right hand of the accused (Psa. 109: 6). David felt he had no man to plead his cause (cp. Is. 53: 7–8, and 2 Tim. 4: 16–17).

[295]

THY GOOD SPIRIT

The reference to the Spirit in verse 10 is to God's Holy Spirit, though the A.V. writes spirit without the capital 'S'. 'Let thy good Spirit lead me' (10) is an acknowledgment that the believer's whole life calls for and is granted the guidance of the Holy Spirit (Rom. 8: 14). The Spirit taught David to pray this prayer (cp. Rom. 8: 26–27). The Spirit taught David the gospel truth of justification by faith (v.2 cp. Rom. 4: 6–8). The Spirit supported David in his deluge of trouble and despair (3–4) by pointing his spirit to God's mighty acts (5) and by causing him to seek God's help alone (6–9). The Spirit taught David the appropriate attitudes and desires of the contrite heart (10–11). Write down the four expressions which sum up his consecration hymn in these two verses. Notice that each has a reason annexed, which is rooted in the character of God: 'thou', 'thy', 'thy', 'thy'.

'The term Spirit is opposed to that corruption which is natural to us; for all men's thoughts are polluted and perverted until reduced to right rule by the grace of the Spirit . . . David assigns the praise of whatever is good, upright or true to the Spirit of God' (Calvin's comment on this Psalm).

MEDITATION ON VERSE 12:
'I am thy servant'. 'This is equivalent to David making himself God's client, and committing his life to God's protection' (Calvin) (cp. Ps. 116: 16).

GRANDFATHER OF THE REFORMATION

Habakkuk begat Paul and Paul begat Luther. When Paul asserted that the just shall live by faith (Rom. 1:17; Gal. 3: 11) he was quoting Habakkuk 2: 4, and when Luther found peace in these words he found them in the Epistle to the Romans. Said Luther: 'Habakkuk has a right name for his office, for Habakkuk means a heartener, as one who takes another to his heart and arms'. Verse 1 tells us two things about him: he was a man who could *feel* and a man who could *see*. The world he looked out on was a tottering world, red with carnage and rotten with corruption. In 612 B.C. the Chaldeans had crushed Assyria, and in 605 the Egyptians were cut to pieces at Carchemish. Judah was ripe for judgment at this time. Habakkuk cried out to God to deal with his own people (1: 1–4). God answered in an unexpected way by sending the savage Chaldeans as his scourge (1: 5–11). Habakkuk is numb with anguish but celebrates God's holiness and justice in this terrible event (1: 12–2: 1). God then disclosed phase II of his purposes – five woes upon the Chaldeans (2: 2–20). Habakkuk's reply is a song of praise and prayer to God (Ch. 3). He begins with a wail of despair (1: 2) and ends with a shout of triumph (Ch. 3). This chapter unveils *the prophet's fear*; first in what he *saw* (1–4), sin rampant in Judah, justice and judgment fled; *second* in what he *said* (2). This is the age-old problem of the silence of God (cp. Rev. 6: 9, 10). *Third*, in what he *heard* (5–11), for God's use of the Chaldeans seemed incredible and too terrible to contemplate. *Fourth*, in what he felt (12–17), for how can a holy God use such base instruments?

20TH CENT. CHALDEANS:
'Communism is but an instrument which God is using to deal with His own people' (Dr. D. M. Lloyd-Jones).

THE PROPHET'S FAITH

In verses 1–5 we have the heart of the prophecy and its key word is faith.

The place of faith (1) is the watchtower which looks over the turbulent scene of human conflict and disorder to the throne of God. As Habakkuk does this a strange composure settles on his spirit. The storm of agitation (1: 2, 12) has sunk to rest at the sight of God's face.

The patience of faith (1b). God's judgments have not been revoked. Judah's vices and vauntings have not been rebuked. Yet the prophet has learned to see that God has His Own perfect time, and no delays are accidents. He gives up questioning, wailing, protesting and rests content in God.

The vision of faith (2–19). Faith rests on revealed facts of which the tablets are the evidence (2). Faith rests on fixed events of which the Word of God is the guarantee and the counsel of God is the secret source (3). The five 'woes' of this section are intimations of God's social and moral concern. Note down the areas of this concern.

The clue to this life of faith is 'the just shall live by faith' (4). This is the way the life of the believer begins and continues. There is no moment and no situation along the journey to the Celestial City when we shall not have to live by faith. The alternatives are that we should live by our wits, or by our works, or by our moods and emotions. To live by faith is to live normally, as God means us to live. For confirmation glance again at Heb. 11.

HABAKKUK'S SONG

'Habakkuk excels in this passage everything of its kind in Hebrew poetry' (Orelli). Here we come from the wail of sorrow to the shout of triumph. God's coming in judgment, which the prophet now sees in clear and vivid outline, throws all nature into trembling agitation (4–15) and should be compared with the revelation of the Law at Sinai (Ex. 19: 16–24), and the convulsion of nature at the Lord's second advent (Mt. 24: 27–31). Figures of speech leap from the chapter to testify to God's sovereignty over all human events and over nature in all her stubborn consistency. The cry for the reviving of God's work (2), which has been on the lips of God's people in every generation, is answered in the declaration of verse 13, 'Thou wentest forth for the salvation of thy people, for the salvation of thine anointed' (13 R.V.). Now we notice two moods in the song which appear contradictory. Habakkuk confesses that he trembles while he waits for God's judgments to break upon Judah and upon the Chaldeans (16 'waiting for the day of trouble' R. V. Margin). But faith can sing while it trembles (17–19). Faith lives above the clouds. Faith has a song amidst all alarms and uncertainties. 'Joy' and 'rejoice' are its keynotes (18), and this is not bravado but the imparted gift of God (19) to the believer who has learned to say with Habakkuk 'the just shall live by his faith'.

CHRIST'S BIRTH CERTIFICATE

In the time-honoured words of the Authorized Version we commence today the reading of 'The New Testament of our Lord and Saviour Jesus Christ'. We are slowed down by this long genealogy featuring forty-two men and four women. These men and women are recorded in the pages of history that they may share in the honour of belonging to the ancestry of the Saviour.

While Luke's genealogy (Luke 3: 23–38) shows Mary's descent from Abraham and David, Matthew's serves a different yet complementary purpose. He writes for the Jewish people and gives the legal descent of Jesus through His foster parent Joseph who ranked as legal father. Joseph would register Jesus as his legal son. Thus Jesus was entitled to be regarded as the successor to the rights and privileges which flowed down from King David through his descendant Joseph. The genealogy had to prove that Christ was the successor to the throne of David. But the presence of the four women (underline them as you read) proves that this genealogy is more than a list of hard names. It is a perfect introduction to the saving work of Christ. Tamar (v.3), Rahab (v.5), Ruth (v.5) and Bathsheba (v.6) all declare that 'by grace ye are saved, through faith, and that not of yourselves' (Eph. 2: 8). Before God used four men to write Four Gospels in the New Testament, he used four women to write the gospel in the Old Testament. The forty-two men were necessary to Matthew's genealogy; the four women to Matthew's Gospel.

BETHLEHEM

Four times today we have read the place-name Bethlehem. We may well ask – Why was Christ born in Bethlehem? (i) *There was the prophetic reason* clearly stated by the chief priests and scribes who quoted Micah 5: 2 as their proof text. Seven centuries have passed since the Holy Spirit spoke through Micah words which must have made the prophet search his own utterance (1 Peter 1: 10–12). Christ was born in Bethlehem because God foretold the event, and the Scripture cannot be broken. (2) There was the *political reason.* Under the census decree of Caesar Augustus (to facilitate taxation) Herod the Great, as King of Judea was permitted to determine how best he might give effect to this decree. He directed that each family head should proceed to his tribal city. This obliged Joseph to journey 80 miles south from Nazareth. Augustus and Herod thus unwittingly secured Joseph's presence in Bethlehem at the very hour of Jesus' birth. (3) *There was the personal reason.* Mary's babe was now due (Lk. 2: 5). Joseph could have registered her in her absence. But Mary was a spiritual woman. She knew Micah's prophecy. She had for months been singing over to herself the prophecies of Isaiah chapters 7 and 9. She insisted upon accompanying Joseph. She was the handmaid of the Lord along every weary mile of that harsh winter's journey. (4) Perhaps profounder than these is the fact that Beth-lehem means 'house of bread' and the Lord Jesus is the Bread of Life (John 6: 30–35).

QUESTION:
Can you find a hint of another profound reason in 2 Sam. 23: 14–17 (cp. John 4: 13–14)?

SORROW AS WELL AS JOY FLOWED FROM THE BIRTH OF JESUS

The joyous message of the angel to the shepherds in Bethlehem's fields mingles with the voice in Ramah of Rachel weeping for her children (2: 18). Heaven and hell are already in conflict over Messiah's cradle. The miracle of the incarnation of the Son of God blends with the miracle of the preservation of the Son of God. The warning given to the wise men (12), the supernatural guidance given to Joseph (13), the later direction to return to Israel (20), and then to proceed north to Galilee (22), were all evidences of a sovereign hand upon the life of the holy Child. The God who gave him to us, was the God who kept him for us until that hour when Jesus said 'I have finished the work which thou gavest me to do' (John 17: 4). Why has his obscure birth excited such contrary feelings as joy and weeping, such different reactions as angelic songs and Herod's fury (16)? The answer lies in the very reason for the Saviour's birth. 'Herod trembled', says Calvin, 'because he saw that he was reigning in opposition to Christ'. This enmity followed Jesus from the manger to the Cross and finally slew him. But the Hand that shielded the infant Babe finally moved away the stone from the sepulchre and made the Cross the symbol of Christ's triumph and the deepest explanation of his birth.

THE PREACHING OF JOHN AND
THE BAPTISM OF JESUS

So this was the place of John's baptism! I stood in the shade of a pepper tree. Twelve feet below me the Jordan flowed noiselessly between its soft and steeply-shelving banks towards the Dead Sea. A couple of rowing boats were tied to the nearer side. The river was narrow and discoloured – perhaps fifty feet wide. A large fish broke the surface, leaving ripples on the sluggish current. Nearby, beneath an awning, was a stall for chilled pepsi-cola. We were only a few miles from Jericho. The August sun beat down from a cloudless sky. I tried to be still. In imagination I saw the jostling crowds (5), and listened to the preaching of the Baptist (2–3). Cries of prophetic fire mingled (7) with the sobs of the penitent (6). The Pharisees and Sadducees, smug men of a dead religion, are drawn to the spectacle. They criticize it harshly. 'They were like snakes . . . fleeing from a field when the scythes were mowing down the crops, or escaping from a desert fire' (R. V. G. Tasker). John points to a greater than he and to a deeper and transforming baptism (11).

After the threshing-sledge has done its bruising and its crushing work the Lord's winnowing-fork (A.V. 'fan' 12) tosses the littered contents of the threshing-floor to separate the wheat of his people from the chaff of the impenitent whose dependence upon race (9) and ritual (7) has blinded them to the need for a clean heart (11) and a good life (10).

MEDITATION:
'Like a dove' (16). Why not like an eagle (Ex. 19: 4) or a peacock (2 Chr. 9: 21) or even a hen (Matt. 23: 37)?

CHRIST TEMPTED

'Though he was a Son, yet learned he obedience by the things which he suffered' (Heb. 5: 8). Here we see the humanity of our Lord under the same sustained attacks of Satan as we experience in our humanity. Under these temptations Jesus 'learned obedience', not as God, for God cannot obey – God rules – but as man, for he has just declared at his baptism that he must 'fulfil all righteousness' (3: 15), that is, comply with all that God requires of him. This includes sinlessness, and implies victory over all temptation, and the personal defeat of the tempter. Christ here confronts Satan as heaven's champion 'led up by the Spirit'. Campbell Morgan, in his *Crises of the Christ*, goes so far as to say that if Satan could have escaped from the necessity of this conflict he would have done so. Satan thought Jesus' fasting had enfeebled him and hence selected cunningly his first fiery dart (3). But he soon learned his mistake. Jesus' fasting had fortified him for the conflict, and furnished him with armour-piercing weapons (4, 7, 10). What key words did the devil omit in his glib quotation of Psalm 91: 11–12 (verse 6)? Every Christian, and certainly every preacher, is tempted to 'sell' himself to popularity, cutting the corners to the goal of cheap success (5–7). The rapier-thrust which broke all Satan's defences was the keen-edged expression 'the Lord thy God' (7, 10). He spread his black wings and, dripping blood from many wounds, left Jesus in possession of the field. This is the theme of Milton's *Paradise Regained*.

MEMORISING:
Jesus had probably memorized the entire Old Testament. Try to memorize a verse a day, taking Hebrews 4: 15 today.

THE GOOD NEWS OF THE KINGDOM

We have just read the title-page of Jesus' ministry in Galilee. First we see him pressing his advantage over Satan by miracles and exorcisms (23–24). Next we note his emphasis on repentance (17), a radical transformation of life rooted in a personal faith in Christ. Thirdly we note the terms 'kingdom of heaven' (17), 'the gospel of the kingdom' (23). 'By "kingdom" is meant "kingly rule" rather than the sphere in which that rule is exercised' (Tasker). Hence Jesus is beckoning men of all classes and of every felt need to enter his spiritual fellowship, the society of his followers who live under his holy laws, and help forward the spread of his good news. The four disciples (18–22) here step into the record by Divine intention to remind us that the kingdom includes lowly folk (18), involves the surrender of self (22) and offers a satisfying and life-long vocation (19). Matthew is careful to head this title-page with the testimony of the Old Testament (14–16). Isaiah 9: 1–2 is quoted as if the prophet is standing in far-off Assyria and looking out upon the ravaged lands of Galilee. From that vantage point 'the sea' is the Mediterranean; 'beyond Jordan' means west of Jordan (15).

KEY TO INTERPRETATION:
This Gospel provided the early church with an indispensable tool in its threefold task of defending its beliefs against Jewish opponents, of instructing converts in the ethical life of a Christian, and of helping its own members to live a disciplined life.

THE BEATITUDES

The lonely tableland where Jesus gathered his disciples and gave them the laws of his kingdom, was undoubtedly in Galilee. The Sermon on the Mount is a practical way of life only to those who are already members of that kingdom. Hence it leads straight to the foot of the cross and to the necessity of a heart at rest in the will of God. As we spend the next few days reading the Sermon we shall remember that one Man once lived like this. He knows how hard it is, and how rewarding. Every verse needs to be read with the prayer upon our lips, 'Lord, is it I?' Here we can learn our duties, and our calling as disciples of Christ.

There are nine beatitudes and we suggest three groups of three: verses 3–5 unrecognized blessings; verses 6 unclaimed riches; verses 9–12 uncommon privileges. They all belong together, like diamonds set in a cluster. Yet the verses are progressive, the thought in each leading on to the next. Entering the kingdom by the low gateway of a broken heart (3) we see ourselves as we really are; we mourn, and are comforted (4). The King stoops to give us the ornament of a meek and quiet spirit (15). How strangely our values have now changed! We hunger and thirst after God's will, not ours (6); are given a selfless compassion for every broken, bitter life (7). We yearn for purity of inward thought and motive (8). We work for peace among men (9). And we can 'take it' when, because of our zeal, we are despised (10–12).

MEDITATION:
'The name of the judge was Lord Hate Good' (the trial of Faithful in Vanity Fair).

CHRIST AND HIS BIBLE

The influence of Christians (13–16). Among the jungle tribes of Santo Island, New Hebrides, there is no ready source of mineral salt. So great is the craving for salt that they burn certain vines and palms for potash. When the evening meal is ready water is gently poured over the dirty handful of ash, allowing the salty solution to trickle onto the cooked food. After two or three applications of water the gritty potash has lost its savour. The jungle-dweller throws it out the narrow door of his thatched hut where it is quickly trodden into the damp clay. Salt works by secret penetration from within. Light works by clear illumination from without. Together these complete the two aspects of a Christian's influence. The 'bushel' (15) was a tub for measuring meal.

Christ endorses the entire Old Testament (17–20). On this important section try to read Tasker (*Tyndale Commentary on Matthew* pp. 64–67). The rest of chapter 5 is made up of a series of controversial questions in which Jesus takes to task the Jewish rabbis for their wresting of the Old Testament Scriptures. Lest it should seem that Jesus is himself about to question the Old Testament Scriptures, he carefully safeguards the ensuing discussions with the plain declarations of verses 17–19 and hints at the source of the church's disorders in the false teaching (19) and unworthy lives (20) of its professional leaders. By 'the law, or the prophets' (17) Jesus means the entire Old Testament Scriptures.

COMMENT ON VERSE 18:
'There is nothing in the Old Testament which is unimportant, nothing that was put there by random; and so it is impossible that a single letter should perish' (Calvin).

MURDER AND ADULTERY

'To hate is to kill' (Vinet): verses 21–26. Murder is an ugly word. But every vulture came out of an egg. And murder is hatched from the secret smouldering sins of anger, hate and contempt. Jesus as very God, here takes the sixth commandment, passes it through the prism of his knowledge of the heart of man, and shows its sweep and inwardness. The error which he confronts is the 'decent' man's tendency to say 'I'm O.K., don't worry about me', a self-approving judgment which we tend to share in common with the liberal rabbis of Christ's day. There are several eggs in the vulture's nest: anger (22), abuse (22), alienation (23–24), tardiness (25–26). 'Thou fool . . . equivalent to Raca, an Aramaic word, like "nitwit" ' (Tasker).

Soul-surgery (27–32). Adultery is another ugly word. But modern life works hard to make it decent. The liberal rabbis did the same. They restricted the seventh commandment to the sin of a man who seduces a *married* woman. Jesus here shows that the design of the commandment is to condemn all unchaste thoughts, words and deeds. Symptoms of this are over-familiarity with the other sex; fickle emotions and unstable friendships; allowing the heart to dwell in a dream-world of illicit love. The complicating factors are our own capacity for self-deception, our failure to distinguish spiritual and sensual emotions, and our unconscious acceptance of the low morality of a lust-ridden society. Thank God for the truth of William Cowper's words: 'The Cross, once seen, is death to every vice.'

Ponder Thomas Fuller's words:
'Anger is either heavenly, earthly or hellish'.

VOWS & OATHS (33–37)

'Forswear' (33 A.V.) means 'perjure thyself'. This is not a veto
against Christians taking oaths in civil actions, for Jesus himself
was put on oath at his trial before the high priest (Matt. 26: 63–
64). The liberal rabbis of Jesus' day laced their conversation
and undertakings with the absurd oaths instanced in verses
34–36 which studiously avoided the use of God's name. They
thus reasoned that no harm was done if they broke such
undertakings, since God's name had not been invoked. Such
casuistry Christ sweeps aside with a word which is pertinent to
our evil usages (By Jove! etc) verse 37. *'An eye for an eye'* (38–
42). Read Leviticus 24: 17–22 where *lex talionis* is made a
principle of jurisprudence in the Old Testament. The liberal
rabbis took this principle, given by God to restrain the lust for
vengeance, and widened it to justify personal retaliation and
private vendettas of every sort. Calvin is probably right in
regarding the injunctions of verse 39–42 as illustrations of verse
39a, *'Love thy neighbour'* (43–48). These words are from
Leviticus 19: 18. The words 'and hate thine enemies' were dug
up by the evil inventiveness and casuistry of the rabbis. They
had attached them as a corollary to Leviticus 19: 18. Jesus
shows that their inference was utterly mistaken (44) and their
corollary merely another indication of their hardness of heart.

GOOD WORKS

'Alms' is rendered 'righteousness' in the margin of the Authorised Version and in the Revised Version. Tasker views this as the key word in this sentence in which Jesus is about to distinguish true righteousness from the prevailing marks of Jewish piety – almsgiving, prayer and fasting, in that order of importance. Jesus does not question the rightness of the actions, but only of the motive – to gain praise and respect from men (2). The word 'have' in verses 2, 5 and 16, is used in secular Greek for an account which is receipted as 'paid'. For those who are influenced in what they do by a desire to build up credit among men, Jesus says the reward has been paid in full here and now. The Father will reward such self-centred motives (4). 'Closet' (Authorized Version) should now be rendered 'inner chamber'. The Greek word means a store-room for riches. We are never richer than when we are upon our knees possessing our possessions in Christ, and calling down the riches of his grace upon others. 'Vain repetitions' (7) translates an obscure word. Tyndale has 'babble not much' and the old Syriac version 'do not say idle things'. 'Daily' bread (11) may mean 'our bread for the coming day' (R.V. marg.). Verse 13 loses its difficulty if we understand 'temptation' in its broader sense of testing or outward trial. 'Evil' is literally 'the evil one' (R.V.).

MEDITATION:
'Although the disciples are to be seen doing good works, they must not do good works in order to be seen.' (Levertoff, as quoted in Tasker)

THE LIGHT OF THE EYE

Chapter 6 falls into two halves at verse 19. The first half warns
us of the perils which confront the Christian in living his
spiritual life (1–18). The second half warns us of the perils which
confront us from the side of our *secular* life (19–34). Today's
portion closes the first half with a warning about spiritual
ostentation and window-dressing (16–18). Fasting is symbolic
of the place of self-discipline in the believer's daily life. By it we
say 'No' to ever-present appetites which seek to rule and
regulate our time and interests and responses. To discover how
far you are ruled in this way, try giving up a meal to spend the
time in Bible study and prayer. Two facts will emerge: the
struggle needed to break the routine of the meal-hour; and the
unexpected satisfaction through closer communion with God
(18). To arise early for our quiet time involves self-denial and is
a kind of fasting. But to let all our friends know how early we
rise is to fall into the sin of the Pharisees. A word on verses 22–
23. We speak of the eyes as the windows of the soul because of
their power to express personality and emotions. For 'light' (22
A.V.) the Revised Version has 'lamp'. By a kind of spiritual
refraction the healthy eye not only shines outwards, but also
inwards, chasing away brooding and morbid thoughts and
imparting an antiseptic quality to the whole inner life. The
converse is also true (23).

MEDITATION:
*'An "evil eye" was a Jewish metaphor for a grudging or jealous
spirit' (Tasker).*

WORRY

The ghost of John Bunyan's Man with the Muckrake hovers over verse 24. Golden crown and broken stubble point up the ultimate contrast found in the words 'hate' and 'love' (24). 'Serve' (24) is the Greek word for the kind of service slaves give, dominated by the will of the master, belonging body and soul to him. 'Can' and 'cannot' (24) are also strong terms. The totalitarian demands of the master bring the slave to utter yieldedness, whether for good or for evil. 'Whoever gives himself up as the slave of riches must abandon the service of God . . . Covetousness makes us the slaves of the devil' (Calvin). The only way to deal with covetousness at its tap-root is to yield our whole life to God, allowing the greed in our soul to be crucified with Christ; and watching the birth of selfless love for others. Yet even as surrendered Christians we shall have to face progressive and subtle tests along these very lines of money, ambition and success.

But it is possible to worship mammon out of our very poverty and want (25–34). All excessive anxiety, all worry which arises from lack of trust in our heavenly Father (25–31), all worldly fear of the future (34) are here expressly forbidden. They too are cloaked forms of mammon-worship. 'Worry is an indication that we think that God cannot look after us' (Oswald Chambers).

MEDITATION:
'*Christ does not forbid every kind of care, but only what arises from distrust . . . from unbelief*' (*Calvin*).

THE CRITIC CRITICIZED

What is condemned here by the lips of Jesus is religious censoriousness. You can expect this in the noisy business of 'religion', but not in the fellowship where Christ is known, loved and exalted. Criticism is a disease which begins so quietly that we do not notice ourselves suffering from it, but it grows so steadily that we gain the unenviable reputation of being keeper of everyone's conscience. Calvin points out that these words are not meant to be an absolute prohibition of judging. The power of seeing into character is to be coveted and cultivated, and the absence of this discernment makes us simpletons, not saints. Fault-finding is presumptuous (1) and quickly invites retaliation (2); it speedily loses all sense of proportion (3), and leads inevitably to self-righteousness (4); it violates the family relationship of Christians, for 'brother' (3–4) is a sacred word. It calls for stern and prompt measures – 'first cast out . . .' (5), points to a moral revulsion which prompts us to confess the sin of fault-finding and once and for all (Greek tense) renounce its evil power. *Pearls before swine* (6). Dogs and pigs were unclean animals to the Jew and suggest people who are out of sympathy with Christ's message. Christ never taught without first taking account of his audience. Luther tells the fable of the lion which made a banquet and invited all the beasts, including the pig. Looking over the rich dishes and costly food the sow demanded, 'Have you no bran?' 'Even so,' adds Luther, 'we set before men and women the richest gifts of God – and they grub for guilders.'

MEDITATION ON VERSE 7:
'Christ knoweth the knock of his friends.' (Samuel Rutherford)

[313]

THE TREE IS KNOWN BY ITS FRUIT

In Jonathan Edwards' *Treatise on the Religious Affections* we find these words: 'Hypocrites may much more easily be brought to talk like saints than to act like saints . . . Words are cheap; Christian practice is a costly laborious thing.' 'False prophets' (15) is one Greek word whose root meaning is 'liar'. Not that the prophet-cum-liar preached his lies, though that is terrible to think of; he *lived* his lies, and got away with it. Sheep's clothing was the typical garb of the Old Testament prophet, a symbol of innocence and honesty of heart. But wrapped around a false prophet integrity is only skin-deep. We are to recognize the false prophet, not by his preaching (22) but by his behaviour (16–19). Recognition will take time; a tree has to grow to bear fruit. The fruit is according to the real nature of the tree. '*I never knew you*' (21–29). Jesus' warnings here are not directed to gangsters and the promoters of syndicated crime, but to professing Christians. The 'many' of verse 22 should be underlined, and compared with the 'many' of verse 13. These closing verses of the Sermon on the Mount remind us of the terrible possibility of self-deception, of building a lifetime of religious activity upon a foundation of sand. There is only one rock-foundation – Christ.

CHRIST'S POWER AND MAN'S FAITH

Chapters 5–7 show us the authority of the King in his teaching (7: 29). Chapters 8–9 show us the authority of the King over sickness, over demons, over the forces of nature, over death and over the hearts of man. Nine miracles are here selected by Matthew, and grouped in threes; the theme is always the same: our King Jesus has all power and authority in heaven and in earth (28: 18). We worship him today as we see the power of his touch (3, 15) and of his bare word (8, 13). Over today's portion is engraved the lovely quotation from Isaiah 53: 4 'Himself took our infirmities and bear our sicknesses' (17) to show that 'all this activity of Jesus was evidence that he was filling the role of the ideal Servant of God' (Tasker). Tasker takes the verbs in verse 17 in the sense of 'removing' or 'carrying away', adding, 'Though Jesus bore the burden of men's *sins*, there is no evidence that he endured physical maladies on their behalf'. *Healer of leprosy* (1–4). The first miracle deals with deep defilement, and significantly shows that Jesus is both able and willing (2, 3) to save to the uttermost those who 'come' (2). *The faith of the centurion* (5–13): Bengel comments: 'From this first mention of faith in the New Testament we may gather that faith (as well as unbelief) is in both the understanding and the will . . . Of all the virtues evinced by those who came to the Lord, he is wont to praise faith alone . . . In proportion to the greatness of humility is the greatness of faith.' The faith of this centurion (10) and the unbelief of the people of his own country (Mark 6: 6) alike made Jesus marvel.

QUESTION:
Four centurions find mention in the New Testament: Matt. 8, Matt. 27, Acts 10, Acts 27. What had they in common?

[315]

THE COST OF DISCIPLESHIP (18–22)

For many professing Christians today it is much easier to be a churchman than to retain membership in a lodge. How different this situation is from that which Jesus envisaged when he urged upon these eager young men, serious second thoughts! The request of the would-be disciple in verse 21 could be paraphrased in the idiom of the South Sea Islands: 'My father is very old; it is my filial duty to stand by him and see him out. Then, after the proper period of mourning has elapsed, I shall be ready to follow thee.' The reply of Jesus sharply contrasts conventional decencies with loyalty to himself.

A great calm (23–27). The boat has come to be widely used as a symbol of the universal church, and is sometimes depicted with Peter at the helm. Here we see plainly enough that there is no ultimate security on *the boat*, however sturdy (21). Nor is there any security in *the men* who man the boat, however experienced and devoted (25). The only security is in Christ, the Lord of the church, the Ruler of all the turbulence of human events (27). He alone can bring a great calm to an anxious heart and to a stricken conscience.

Possessed with devils (28–32). The true believer enjoys the society of Christ and of his people. But demonic powers hound society in the opposite direction, making men and women and young people misanthropic, sadistic, fierce, predatory and violent.

QUESTION:
Connect Christ's victory over Satan (4: 11) with his authority over demons (8: 16, 32) and John's declared reason for his coming (1 John 3: 8).

[316]

THE MAN SICK OF THE PALSY

Not all religious audiences are responsive to Christ's teaching (3) or to a convert's testimony (11). Luke 5: 17 gives us a glimpse of the unsympathetic Jewish leaders who packed a house in Capernaum. Jesus knows all hearts. He recognized the faith which moved the four friends (2). He discerned the despair which gripped the paralytic. He reckoned on the scribes' reaction before ever he spoke the words, 'Thy sins be forgiven thee.' He spoke authoritatively as the Son of God. He did what only God can do when he forgave a man's sins who had not so much as breathed a word of spoken penitence. Here is Christ confronting all men of all ages with his ultimate claim to be very God of very God; a claim upon the validity of which our whole salvation rests. The Pharisees spoke right to the point when they reasoned, 'Who can forgive sins but God alone?' (Luke 5: 21). For in comparison with *that* act, Christ's act of healing the paralytic was 'easier' (5).

Matthew's call and the consecration of his home (9–13). This is delightful autobiography. In 10: 13 Matthew cheerfully identifies himself as 'the publican'. He at once opens his house to Jesus (10) dedicating his all to the winning of others. We must do the same.

QUESTION:
In verse 13 and again in 12: 7 Jesus quotes Hosea 6: 6. What is the basic truth he is driving home?

TWO MIRACLES

Christ's presence should bring not the *fasting* of unsatisfied yearning, but the *feasting* of present joy and fulfilment. The disciples of John were like so many of us, keen to run the lives of others while our own perspectives are all wrong. The 'new' (unshrunk) cloth and the new wine skins (16–17) point to the 'fundamental incompatibility between the old Israel paralysed by self-righteousness and overloaded with petty regulations, and the new Israel humbled by the consciousness of sin and turning in faith to Jesus' (Tasker).

Two miracles (18–26). The father's faith in making this request on behalf of his dying child (cp. Mark 5: 23) points to Jesus' power and willingness to give spiritual life to our sons and daughters in response to the believing prayers of parents (cp. Acts 2: 39). Verse 25 suggests that there are secret works of Jesus which are not for the ears and eyes of the merely curious and casual (cp. 7: 6). When death (24) is spoken of as sleep in the Bible, the reference is to the body, not to the soul. The case of the healed woman shows us that shy faith, faith without words, can still be saving faith (21); that salvation, like her cure, can be instantaneous (22); and that this salvation is not a psychological pick-me-up but a real partaking of the healing virtue of Christ (see Mark 5: 30).

MEDITATION:
'*Faith is the hand of the soul which lays hold of the Cross.*' (*Luther*)

CHRIST'S COMPASSION AND OURS

The burden of the multitudes never left Jesus, and should never leave us (33, 36). How often we read of the 'compassion' which Jesus felt for these shepherdless sheep! He saw them 'harassed and helpless' as if worried by predatory dogs. 'Compassion' is the Latin form of the Greek word for sympathy which means to suffer with another. The Lord's miracles in verses 27–33 illustrate this kind of compassion, a compassion which felt deeply for all human misery, injury and wrong, and laboured to bring relief of body and release of spirit. This vast need in unnumbered lost men and women moved Jesus to say to his disciples: 'Pray ye, therefore, the Lord of the harvest, that he will send forth labourers into his harvest'. The church of Jesus Christ today witnesses in a world of four billions of people and is harassed by the magnitude of its task. We hear of insufficient youth workers, of too few ministers and of the shortage of missionary candidates. A demoralized church resorts to panic measures to plug the gaps in its manpower. And all the time Jesus reiterates his simple and sole remedy for our disorder, 'Pray ye therefore . . .' Have you begun to pray this prayer in your church?

GO!

'Go' is the title which a well-known missionary society has chosen for its magazine. Underline the occurrences of the word in today's portion. 'Go' means that the first twelve missionaries were not confronted with an appeal, but with a command (5). The 'go' of Jesus called not for deliberation but for obedience. The Lord's *'go not'* (5) first defined the field of missionary service negatively. The Twelve are all Jews and they are charged with a mission to Israel (6). They are to work to the Lord's priorities and not to their own. Perhaps some of them were keen to be pioneer missionaries to the Samaritan and Gentile races and had to be checked by these unromantic words of Jesus. Certainly there is no more difficult missionary task today than that of taking the good news to the Jews. The Lord then defines the field of service positively: *'go rather . . .'* (6). It is sad that Jesus should have to describe as 'lost sheep' those who lived under the ritual of temple and synagogue. The Lord's words *'as ye go . . .'* define the content of their message (7), the scope of their ministry (8) the terms of their service (9–10) and the pattern for their daily provision (11–14). The scrip of verse 10 is our hiker's pack or ruck-sack.

INTERPRETATION:
'The salutation mentioned in verse 12 was the Semitic 'Peace be unto you'. The benediction is to be withdrawn from the house that has shown itself unworthy of it' (Tasker). This surrounds Christian hospitality with the holiest of sanctions.

THE MISSION OF THE TWELVE

Every Christian is called to be a witness to his Lord and Saviour. Our witness belongs to the very nature of our calling (Acts 1: 8). But it is obvious that the church's testimony fluctuates from generation to generation. In the three centuries which followed immediately upon these words of Jesus, great waves of persecution swept over the early church, backed by the powerful Roman Empire. At the commencement the church was only a tiny company of believers. In the persecutions hundreds of thousands of Christians were martyred. At the end of the persecutions Christianity emerged strong and with tremendous vitality and missionary zeal. In times of comparative quietness and indifference the church sinks into complacency, and whispers where it is called to shout (27). In today's reading we are carried back to realities – the realities of the first-century environment for the church's testimony. Notice the varied forms of opposition; from the crowds (16), from a corrupt religion (17), from the civil authorities (18), and even from one's home (21). Notice too the varied reactions which Jesus urges upon us under these conditions: wariness with simplicity (16), trusting the Spirit to guide us (17–20), flight, which will result in a wider ministry (23), sharing consciously the reproach of Christ (24–25), dauntless preaching (26–27), a clear view of time and eternity (28), and dependence upon our Father's infinite power and love (29–31).

QUESTION:
'When they persecute you . . . flee' (23). Find examples of this from the Apostle Paul's life (Acts 9: 25; 14: 6 etc).

Matthew 10: 34–42

THE CHRISTIAN AND HIS FAMILY

On the difficult and perplexing verses which open today's reading Prof. Tasker comments: 'Consequences are often expressed in the Bible as though they were intentions. So here the divisive result of Jesus' coming, particularly in the sphere of family relationships, is described as though He had deliberately come to bring this about'. A young man said to me, 'My wife does not want me to go to church; she thinks that religion brings trouble into the home'. This young woman was afraid that her husband might become a Christian. I watched him as he gradually dropped off until he ceased to attend worship. The whole of Bunyan's *Pilgrim's Progress* is a true commentary upon verses 34–39. Pilgrim's burden drove him to Christ. His wife could not understand his daily pre-occupation with his sins and God's certain judgment. He travelled the whole of his pilgrimage without any flicker of response from wife or children. But part two of the allegory is profoundly true. Christiana believed in Christ after her husband's triumphant death, and with her went her boys on pilgrimage to the same Celestial City. Not one was lost. It has often happened that a boy or girl has accepted the Saviour only to bring bitter ridicule and opposition upon him from those nearest and dearest. But, sustained in a quiet and consistent testimony by the indwelling Saviour, this boy or girl has lived to see the home transformed and the rest of the family yielding their hearts to Christ.

FOR SELF EXAMINATION:
Am I making it easier or harder for my loved ones to believe in Jesus?
(1 Cor. 7: 16; 1 Peter 3: 1–2).

SHUT UP IN DOUBTING CASTLE

When Christians are in the dungeon of doubt, tormented by
misgivings and sick with despondency, even God's greatest
mercies grow grey and lifeless. This was so with John the
Baptist; it can be so with us. Recollect John's meeting with
Jesus at Jordan, his ardent preaching as the forerunner and his
recorded testimony after he had baptized Jesus, 'I saw, and bare
record, that this is the Son of God' (John 1: 34). Now, walled in
by dark events, and likely to die for his testimony, John seems
to falter. It took courage to communicate his doubts. It is so
easy to give the impression of an iron-clad, unwavering faith
which is subject to no tremors and no moments of despair.
John's hour of despondency called forth Jesus' noblest tribute
(11). A few miles below the traditional site of Jesus' baptism the
Jordan river broadens and reeds grow freely along its banks.
They are lank and leafy and rooted only in the soft mud. They
do not grow erect, but bend as the wind bids them in all
directions. Here Jesus found his perfect metaphor for the man
John was *not* (7). In his darkest hour John took the right course;
he went to Jesus with his doubts – in the persons of two
unnamed disciples. A little later those disciples will bury the
headless body of the prophet, and then they will go to Jesus
again (14: 12).

QUESTION:
*Is this not evidence that the answer of Jesus in chapter 11: 4–6
reassured John and put an end to his terrible uncertainty?*

IMPENITENCE, OR REST

Here we are face to face with the two radical aspects of the gospel: it is 'judgment' for the impenitent (20–24), and it is 'rest' for the heavy-laden (28–30). Between these strangely diverse words lie the golden verses (25–27) which lift the veil of mystery enough to show us that our repenting (20) and our coming (28) are both secret works of God, wrought in us by the Holy Spirit. Jesus says that these secret works of God are 'hid' from those who think they know most, and 'revealed' to those who become as little children (25, cp. 18: 3–4). Impenitence is most terrible in those who have had most opportunity to repent. To hear the Saviour speaking, to see his miracles of love and power, to come near enough to touch the hem of his garment, is all so critically decisive. Chorazin, Bethsaida and Capernaum could pass for your town and mine. They differed from Sodom, Tyre and Sidon in their opportunity to hear and obey the gospel. This opportunity involved decision. Their decision was manifest in their indifference. We are today more privileged than any of these cities which Jesus upbraided. We are therefore more solemnly responsible for the way we react to the Saviour.

WHAT TO DO:
'To escape the wrath and curse of God due to us for sin, God requires of us faith in Jesus Christ, repentance unto life, with the diligent use of all the outward means whereby Christ communicates to us the benefits of redemption' (The Westminster Shorter Catechism. Q.85).

[324]

THE LORD'S DAY

'How dull the sabbath day, without the sabbath's Lord! (William
Cowper). When spiritual life languishes among the people of
God two parallel processes make this decay evident – laxer
behaviour and stricter ritual. Jesus confronted both of these
tendencies in the Jewish church of his day. He exposed its lax
behaviour in the Sermon on the Mount when he dealt with the
sixth and seventh commandments (5: 21–32). Now he deals
with the second tendency, the drive for a stricter ritual. This
conflict centres on the abuse of the fourth commandment, upon
which the rabbis had erected a Taj Mahal of neatly-chiselled
regulations. Over this shrine they stood guard with fanatical
zeal. A Jewish rabbinical tract on the sabbath dealt in detail
with what might or might not be done on the sabbath. In this
tract the plucking of corn was forbidden because this amounted
to reaping and threshing! Healing was permitted on the sabbath
only if the person were critically ill; the rest could wait. 'Have
ye not read?' (3, 5) is Jesus' way of drawing the Pharisees'
attention to their moral blind spots. Of course they had read
these incidents; but, blinded by their love of the ritual and the
external regulations, they could not discern the spiritual
principles or the moral obligations of God's sabbath law in the
Old Testament.

MEDITATION:
*Sunday is a holy day; Sunday is a day of worship; Sunday is a day
of rest; Sunday is a day of service; Sunday is a family day (from
Bishop Maurice Wood's foreword to the 1956 edition of Bishop
Daniel Wilson's* 'The Lord's Day').

THE UNPARDONABLE SIN

The Pharisees, though vipers, believed in the devil. There are those who do not. Jesus also believed in the devil and has taught us to pray 'Save us from the evil one' (6: 13). The Pharisees, in their ugly mood of hate and misrepresentation, told the crowd 'It is only by Beelzebub, prince of devils, that this man drives the devils out' (6: 24). This was the ultimate act of blasphemy which provoked Jesus' searching words about the sin which shall not be forgiven (31–32). Following Abraham Kuyper (*The Work of the Holy Spirit*) we affirm that to commit this sin two things are required which belong together: *first* close contact with the glory which is manifest in Christ or in his people; *second*, the declaration that the Spirit who manifests himself in that glory is a manifestation of Satan (cp. Mark 3: 30). There is hope of pardon in the day of judgment for the men who crucified Christ. But he who despises and slanders the Spirit (who speaks in Christ, in his Word, and in his works) as though he were the spirit of Satan, is lost in eternal darkness. This betrays systematic opposition to God. Hence this word of Jesus is divinely intended to put men on their guard – Christians, lest they treat the Word of God coldly, carelessly, indifferently; false shepherds; and all who have forsaken the way.

MEDITATION:
'No child of God could or ever can commit this sin . . . Those mentioned in Hebrews 6 and 10 are never said to have had a broken and contrite heart' (Kuyper).

[326]

JONAH AND CHRIST

Jesus here warns us of three perils. (1) *The peril of resting in lesser signs* (38–42). The ultimate sign to every generation is the saving work of Jesus Christ. The very heart of this sign is his death, burial and resurrection. To those who remain unmoved by this supreme sign, the demand for other signs – more spectacular, more personal, more convincing – is evidence of perverseness and insincerity. (2) *The peril of resting in lesser experiences* (43–45). The ultimate experience which seals the soul's relationship with God is the new birth. There are 'conversions' which fall short of this. They may give good evidence of a change of life and of heart; they may consist in the tidying up of a man's behaviour. But there is no deliverance from the demons of sin merely in a resolve of the sinner's own crippled will. Deliverance is rooted in union with Christ, in death and resurrection, and leads to real newness of life (Col. 3). (3) *The peril of resting in lesser relationships* (46–50). Tender and strong though all human ties are meant to be, the deepest human bond is between those who are one in Christ as members of his mystical body. We may not rest until we are members of that family.

A COMPARISON:
The 'sign of the prophet Jonas' (39) has a parallel in the sign of Isaac; see Hebrews 11: 17–19 as the Holy Spirit's commentary on Genesis chapter 22.

THE PARABLE OF THE SOWER

The parable of the sower is meant to be a Divine encouragement to sowers. Here is Christ's clear statement of what preachers, teachers and personal workers may expect in the way of response to the gospel message. This is the best known of all the parables, yet we easily miss some of the obvious teaching. Note that there is no reflection upon *the sower* for the mixed response to his sowing and the limited success of his work. Nor is there any reflection upon *the seed*. The whole attention is directed to the diversity of hearers. The parable is a diagnosis of congregations, not of ministers. Christ warns us that in this work of sowing the good seed we are face to face with a powerful enemy, 'the wicked one' (19). 'How natural it would have been to interpret "the fowls" impersonally, as signifying in a general way worldly influences hostile to the truth . . . Not so, however, the Lord! He beholds the kingdom of evil, as it counterworks the kingdom of God, gathered up in a personal head, "the Wicked One" (Matthew) "Satan" (Mark) "the devil" (Luke)' (Trench, on the Parables). The 'wayside' hearer is interpreted in verses 12–15. The 'stony place' hearer has the longest explanation (20–21) and is the least regarded. This tells us in advance why some of the most exciting 'conversions' prove unreal. Every preacher sees these cases of 'fading', and vexes his soul over them. Yet Jesus plainly tells us to expect them.

MEDITATION:
'*It is a carrying of men in prayer until the image of Christ be formed in them, and how many of them prove abortions!*' (*Comment by James Gilmour of Mongolia on Galatians 4: 19*).

[328]

WHEAT AND TARES

In the grab for land in the New Hebrides islands nearly a century ago fierce rivalries were kindled. The writer of these notes has seen thousands of acres of good land spoilt by an evil-smelling bean which flourishes as a noxious weed. This, it is said, was broadcast by an enemy on the land of his successful rival. From that small beginning it has spread far and wide. Some such motive doubtless goaded the enemy in this parable. Satan thus busies himself over every good plot of land, planting a Jezebel here and a Judas there and a whole crop of Demases somewhere else. He slinks into the pioneer mission outpost in the shadow of the missionary. He sets up his tape-recorder in the church prayer-room. 'When Satan is doing his greatest mischief he studies most to conceal himself' (Matthew Henry). The firm refusal of the farmer to encourage his well-meaning servants to weed out the tares is remarkable. On this vexed point Matthew Henry, the shrewd Puritan divine, says, 'It is not possible for any man infallibly to distinguish between tares and wheat.' John Calvin, in his treatment of the question of church discipline, quotes Augustine, 'Christians should correct in mercy whatever they can; what they cannot they should patiently bear and affectionately lament, till God either reform or correct it, or, at the harvest, root up the tares and sift out the chaff'.

THE HIDDEN TREASURE
AND THE PEARL OF GREAT PRICE

The parables of the mustard-seed and the leaven have shown us the world-wide growth of Christ's kingdom (31–33). Here in the parables of the hidden treasure and the pearl we are shown that the kingdom of heaven is something which each one of us must possess for himself by deliberate choice. Thus these two parables point to the need for our personal appropriation of Christ as Saviour and Lord. Yet even here God's ways differ. The tenant farmer stumbled upon his treasure by chance, as we say. He did not seek it. He did not know it was there until the plough-share turned it up. The treasure came to him all of a sudden as an exciting discovery. There are those who discover the long-hidden loveliness of Jesus in this way, and the sheer joy and wonder of salvation render the cost and self-denial of no consequence to them. There are others again who seek long and earnestly, gathering pearls of beauty and value. But they never satisfy. When at last they find 'one pearl of great price' those lesser pearls are freely parted with in order that the most precious one may be theirs. This is the truest, deepest aspect of self-denial.

MEDITATION:
'As a child cannot hold two apples in his little hand, but the one putteth the other out of its room, so neither can we be masters and lords of two loves'. (Samuel Rutherford, in a letter dated Aberdeen 1637)

TWO KINGS

Here we have two kings whose lives and conduct are set side by side in startling contrast. Let us follow out the contrast in all its sharpness.

King Herod (1–10) is Herod Antipas, cruel (10), superstitious (2), dominated by his *de facto* wife Herodias, the New Testament Jezebel. Cowardly alike before John the Baptist and before the popular movement for reform which John's preaching had aided, he temporised, only to be forced by the vindictive plotting of Herodias into giving the final order for John's execution. John rises to royal dignity in his death, while Herod wraps himself in the cloak of a toad.

King Jesus is a royal mourner for his faithful forerunner (13), but solitude is denied him and he is pressed by compassion to become again a royal physician (14). Before the day is out he is to be a royal provider (19).

One or other of these kings finally wins our life's allegiance. The choice lies between living for self or living for others. Only the King of Glory can teach us how to mourn, how to heal and how to give the hungry bread (16).

MEDITATION:
It is written of Hugh Latimer, the English Reformer, that 'he watered with good deeds whatsoever he had before planted with godly words'.

WALKING ON THE WATER

Three miracles blend in this portion; where we thought there was only one:

1. *The miracle of Jesus walking on the water* (25). No stormy winds and breaking waves limit his sovereignty to work his will in the world of his creation. 'All things were made by him'. 'He plants his footsteps in the sea, and rides upon the storm' (William Cowper).

2. *The miracle of Peter walking on the water.* Jesus never ministered to mere curiosity. However rash the fisher-disciple's request may look in our eyes, the Lord took it for sincere faith, faith that ventures all in the power of Christ. Like Peter's faith, ours too rides out the storm better when in the boat than out of it.

3. *The miracle of both Jesus and Peter walking on the water.* This is implied in verse 32. The winds and waves were unabated, but Peter no longer sank. The Hand that caught him a few seconds before, now clasps him and brings him across the breaking waves to the boat. Only then did the wind cease.

QUESTION:
In his trials of faith what firm facts save a Christian from sinking?

MEDITATION:
> *'Fear not, I am with thee, oh be not dismayed!*
> *For I am thy God, and will still give thee aid:*
> *I'll strengthen thee, help thee, and cause thee to stand,*
> *upheld by my righteous, omnipotent Hand'.*
>
> (*Richard Keen*)

'UNCLEAN'

The righteousness of the Pharisees was only skin-deep (2). Evil
thoughts cannot be cleansed with soap and water, nor can the
other sicknesses of man's soul to which Jesus here refers (19).
All external religion fights the truth of man's inner rottenness.
It is part of our own infirmity that we join in the fight against
such honest, searching words. Only a deep personal experience
of the deceitfulness of our hearts, of the blackness of our sins,
and of the justice of our condemnation can bring us to affirm the
truth of man's radical sinfulness (Rom. 3: 10–23), and experience the wonder of what John Newton called 'amazing grace'.
Is the shallowness of much that goes for gospel preaching due to
its failure to stress these death-dealing words of Jesus? Of
course folk will take offence (12) and our best friends will
tremble for our reputation (12a). But it is better to plant gospel
trees with real roots than avenues of sawn-off palms which
wither in a few days' sun (13).

MEDITATION:
*'There is a vital connection between soul-distress and sound doctrine.
Sovereign grace is dear to those who have groaned deeply because
they see what grievous sinners they are'. (C. H. Spurgeon)*

Matthew 15: 21–28

'LORD, HELP ME!'

This Syrophenician mother knew the demonic when she saw it at work in her daughter. She did not tolerate it, she did not excuse it, she did not console herself with the thought, 'young people are different nowadays', nor did she make an appointment with a specialist. She went to Jesus. This is obviously the first and proper thing for believing parents to do who have troublesome sons and daughters. It is so very easy to substitute bad temper for prayer and to watch the rapid deterioration of family relationships under these stresses. Let us lay the root blame where Jesus lays it and where it belongs – with Satan. He is out to disrupt the Christian home horizontally, through husbands and wives, and vertically, through parents and their children. The fact that Jesus tries our faith with inexplicable delays (23) and that good Christian friends do not seem to understand our anguish (23) is no reason to desist from our mission to his throne of mercy. Her faithful pleading made her will his will (18) and Jesus defined that as 'great' faith.

QUESTION:
Write down the discouragements which met this mother's love and pleadings. How many were there? From what surprising lips? With what ultimate consequences?

MEDITATION:
'Continued importunity may be uneasy to men, even to good men; but Christ loves to be cried after.' (Matthew Henry)

'ALL ATE AND WERE SATISFIED'

A miracle occurs when God draws aside the veil of our limited vision and shows us himself. Naïve doubt and half-belief look anxiously at every gospel miracle for suspected flaws in the workmanship. Some there are who assert that the miracle of the feeding of the 4000 is but a varying account of the feeding of the 5000 (ch. 14). Yet Jesus himself carefully distinguishes these two occasions and refers to both as complementary in his curriculum of divine instruction for his disciples (16: 9–10). What obvious differences can you jot down as regards the location of these two miracles, the reaction of the disciples, the food available to Jesus, and the application of the miracles to his disciples? 'In the first story He seems to be concerned that the disciples should understand how utterly dependent upon Him they must always be . . . In the second He seems to be indirectly reproving them for their lack of sympathy with the needs of the Gentile world' (Tasker).

QUESTION:
Which of these two lessons do I stand most in need of myself?

MEDITATION:

> '*If I have eaten my morsel alone,*
> *The patriarch spoke in scorn,*
> *What would He think of us, were He shown*
> *Heathendom huge, forlorn, with souls unfed,*
> *While the church's ailment is fulness of bread,*
> *Eating her morsel alone!*
>   *(Wm. Alexander, Bishop of Derry.)*

AN ADULTEROUS GENERATION

The blindness of the sign-seekers (1–5). Here the conservative
Pharisees and the liberal Sadducees sink their differences in
order to trip up Jesus. The former believed in resurrection of
the just but not of the unjust. The latter scouted any idea of a
resurrection. Thus the Lord's answer focuses upon his own
resurrection, typified in the historical experience of Jonah. All
sign-seekers miss the obvious. For those who have eyes to see,
God's final Word is 'nigh' (Rom. 10: 6–9). The demand for a
new Bethlehem and a new Resurrection (Rom. 10: 6–7) to
gratify the critic and the curious will never be granted.

   The dullness of the disciples (6–12). Unhappily the blindness of
the signseekers is matched by the dullness of the bewildered
disciples. By the 'leaven' Jesus means that which is corrupt and
corrupting: the leaven of the Pharisees is their hypocrisy and
religious showmanship; of the Sadducees, their unbelief,
worldliness and go-getter opportunism. Many of the Lord's
present-day disciples seem unable to see this leaven at work.

QUESTION:
*'O ye of little faith' (8) also occurs at 14: 31 (compare 17: 20).
Distinguish the circumstances which evoked these words of Jesus.*

MEDITATION ON VERSE 4:
*'Christ calls them "an adulterous generation" because while they
professed themselves of the true church and spouse of God, they
treacherously departed from him' (Matthew Henry).*

'THOU ART THE CHRIST!'

The great question was not, 'Whom do men say that I am?' (13), but 'Whom say ye that I am?' (15). The first question requires only information; the second, personal faith. The first can be answered from hearsay knowledge of the Son of man; the second searches the heart for a personal confession. Men still give the most varied and contradictory answers to the first question. This is as true of the theologians as of the common man. We cannot find any real unanimity of testimony in what we read about Jesus from the books in the religious section of our public libraries. Only among the circle of his true disciples is there a humble, forthright and consistent testimony to the person of our adorable Lord. Peter's answer (16) implies that Jesus is no less than God manifest in the flesh, the promised Messiah, the Redeemer of the people of God. Jesus immediately erects upon Peter's confession the statement of his life purpose (21). Not a throne but a cross awaits the Lord of Glory. Many, besides Peter, have petulantly taken Peter's role (22–23) in demanding a 'successful' Saviour, a Redeemer without the print of the nails and the crown of thorns. To all such earth-born views of his work the Saviour replies, 'You are looking at things from man's standpoint, and not from God's' (23b Phillips' trans.).

INTERPRETATION OF VERSE 28:
'Not a reference to the Lord's second advent, but probably to his coming back from the dead after the resurrection' (Tasker).

THE TRANSFIGURATION

Peter, James and John never lost the wonder of the transfiguration of Christ. Peter refers to it in his second letter (1: 16–18).
John has it clearly before him as he writes 'We beheld his glory'
(John 1: 14). On Patmos he was to see in fuller view this same
glory (Rev. 1: 13–16). The *language* of the transfiguration (2–3)
links such words as 'shine' 'white' 'light'. Mark and Luke add
that even his homespun garments became 'glistening', 'exceeding white', and 'dazzling'. These words are rays of reflected
light from Jesus' full deity, sinless purity and searching
holiness. The *audience* of the transfiguration (2, 4) could then be
counted on the fingers of one hand. But that audience has
grown with the flow of the faithful to a great multitude which no
man can number. They enjoy an undimmed vision, without
cloud or intermission, for they 'all, with unveiled face,
beholding as in a mirror the glory of the Lord, are transfigured
into the same image, from glory to glory, as by the Spirit of the
Lord' (2 Cor. 3: 18). The *meaning* of the transfiguration is
threefold: The Son of God here confirms his earlier words about
his approaching death and resurrection (16: 21; cp. 17: 9). The
presence of Moses (the law) and Elias (the prophets) validates
Jesus' words as to the consistent testimony of the Old
Testament Scripture (cp. verse 3 with Luke 9: 31). The spoken
word of the Father (5) confirms to the three disciples, and to the
church ever since, that the atoning work of Jesus upon the cross
was his central work, his true vocation.

MEDITATION:
*The Father is well-pleased with such a Son. I am well-pleased with
such a Saviour.*

'WHY COULD NOT WE?'

Into the languishing life of our congregations and assemblies there is being injected shot after shot of pick-up drugs. For prayer we have substituted programmes; for fasting, frequent suppers. We ministers are partly to blame. We have allowed the popular image of success to rule us. That activity is good which brings plenty of people about the church. Especially is this so in youth work. 'What has happened to all our young people?' is a question which is sure to put any minister on the defensive. But why? Here the disciples cannot even cope with one needy lad (15, 16), how much less with a hall full of them! How searchingly does Jesus expose our error by reminding us of the central place of prayer (21). Prayer is too slow, too difficult, too other-worldly for bustling, ulcer-ridden Christians of today, ruled by the cult of numbers and incapable of dealing with souls one by one. Would to God we could come to Jesus with the same sense of impotence as these disciples felt in the face of this boy's need. 'They could not cure him'. Demon-dominated boys and girls are made subject to Christ when Christians learn to 'move men, through God, by prayer alone' (J. Hudson Taylor).

RECIPE FOR THE RENEWAL OF A YOUTH GROUP:
Make time for a regular season of prayer each week; begin with the two or three who know Christ; pray for the unconverted young people by name; be ready to speak with them when the Spirit works; then add them to the prayer-group when they are converted.

PRIDE OF PLACE

Here we learn how different is Christ's idea of greatness from our own, and how prone Christ's disciples are to become calculating place-seekers. The disciples' question struck a jarring note. From Mark 9: 37 we learn that Jesus had just been unveiling to them the fact of his approaching betrayal and death. But, as if this were mere frivolous chatter, the disciples plunged into a noisy argument as to 'who should be the greatest'. Jesus challenged their self-seeking with the acted sermon of the little child. 'He set him in the midst of them, not that they might play with him, but that they might learn by him' (Matthew Henry). Jesus speaks to every company of his disciples when he links greatness with humility, simplicity, transparency, guilelessness and trust. As Lord of the church he still notices the argument at the women's guild as to who shall be president. He observes the flushed face of the deacon who is accustomed to having his own way. And he listens to the talkative youth-leader who enjoys the sound of his own voice so much more than the voice of anybody else. Charles Simeon of Cambridge twice wrote in his diary for 1797, at the age of 28, 'Talk not about myself, speak evil of no man'. And when, in his forties, he was struck by the remark of a visiting preacher to Trinity Church, 'Let me be an errand boy for Christ, if I can be nothing more.'

INTERPRETATION:
'Offend' (verse 6) translates Gk. 'skandalizo'. Calvin comments, 'If anyone, through our fault, either stumbles or is drawn aside from the right course, or retarded in it, we are said to offend him'.

CHURCH DISCIPLINE

Today's reading is on forgiveness. It is a plain fact of experience that the wrong-doer finds it harder to forgive than the person wronged. Therefore Jesus requires the innocent party in any such situation to take the first step towards reconciliation (15). 'It is not every kind of sin which is here under consideration, but the personal wrong done by one brother to another' (Tasker). The pattern laid down in verses 15–17 has passed into the disciplinary practice of the Christian church. The writer of these notes had to learn among the congregations of one of the very young churches of an island in the Pacific how positive, health-giving and indispensable these counsels are. Yet he also had to learn how easily church discipline hardens into a loveless severity which looks to punishing rather than to redeeming the wayward Christian. It is against that persistent tendency that Jesus speaks as he does to Peter (21–22) and gives the unique parable, recorded in verses 23–35. Tasker points out that the 'seventy times seven' of forgiveness enjoined upon Peter parallels the 'seventy and sevenfold' of Lamech's unforgiving threat in Genesis 4: 24. We all know people who go through life nursing a hurt, a smouldering resentment, which finally blinds them to God's pardon in Christ. The warning of verse 35 is to reinforce the fact, which we light-heartedly forget, that such cherished heart-hatred is a fatal barrier to grace.

QUESTION:
Link with verse 35 the following verses: Matthew 6: 12–16, Colossians 3: 13, James 2: 13.

DIVORCE

It is said that in the whole history of the Puritans there is not the record of a single divorce. The problem of the unhappy home, the broken home, which is epidemic today in western society, is a spiritual problem which has its basic solution in knowing and doing the will of God. The Bible is and always will be the best book on marriage guidance. The Pharisees' question (3) runs, 'Is it lawful for a man to divorce his wife on any and every ground?' This question arose from the contrary schools of thought within the Jewish church of our Lord's day. The party of Hillel held that anything at all that upset a husband gave him the right to divorce his wife. The conservative party of Shammai restricted the right of divorce to cases of adultery. Both parties appealed to Deuteronomy 24: 1. Jesus' answer took the latter position. Nothing but adultery should be allowed to break up a home. This implies the right of the innocent partner to re-marry; but we need to note that, in every situation of unfaithfulness, the innocent partner, if a true Christian, will not first fly to a lawyer for legal remedies but will pray earnestly for the Holy Spirit to bring true penitence to the sinner, receiving him (or her) back as Christ has received us.

MEDITATION:
'The corruption of man is such as is apt to study arguments unduly to put asunder those whom God hath joined together in marriage' (Westminster Confession chapter xxiv.).

'WHAT ARE WE TO GET?'

Today's reading is introduced with a charming scene in the
Lord's kindergarten, where sophistry is unknown (13–15).
From this little window we look out upon a sophisticated and
prosperous society, where well-to-do folk bargain for salvation
at not too demanding a price (16–22), and where astonished
disciples hastily conclude that avarice erects fatal barriers to the
sovereign Spirit of God (23–26). The sophistry of the disciples
is saddest of all (27). The genius of discipleship is self-denial,
and here are disciples who have listened to the words of the
Master for so long, now demanding 'What are we to get out of
it?' (27). The Master suffered their hardness of heart for the
time being, and pointed them to the 'regeneration', 'the world
to be' as the true sphere of a Christian's rewards (28). But he
added what every believer finds abundantly true, that he who
follows Christ at the cost of the loss of old ties will find himself
one hundred times richer in human friendships and fellowship
than he was before (29).

INTERPRETATION:
*'It is clear that this command of Jesus in verse 21 is a personal
command addressed on a particular occasion to a particular
individual, a victim of the covetousness equated by Paul with
idolatry'. (Tasker)*

THEY BEGAN TO GRUMBLE

Jesus said to the dying thief, 'This day shalt thou be with me in paradise'. He had been a believer for only a few hours yet he received from Christ the crown of life. To unenlightened folk this is very unfair. They protest that the thief was received much too easily. Such a protest is identical with that of the labourers hired for a decent daily wage (2, 11). All such protests miss the genius of the Christian message, namely, that we cannot earn the crown of life if we live and labour for the Lord for a thousand years. Eternal life is a gift of God's free grace. Calvin writes, 'Men have no right to complain of the bounty of God, when he honours unworthy persons by large rewards beyond what they deserve . . . He is at liberty to bestow upon those whom he has lately called an undeserved reward.' This is the great truth in the parable. Concerning the details we accept Calvin's warning: 'If any man should resolve to sift out with exactness every portion of this parable, his curiosity would be useless.'

MEDITATION:
> '*Love is not pedlar's trumpery, bought and sold;*
> *He will give freely – or he will withhold*'.
> *(William Cowper)*

SERVANT AND SLAVE

Have you ever found yourself with wandering thoughts at the
Lord's Table, during the very act of communion? That is
comparable with the opening incident of today's reading. The
Lord speaks confidentially to his beloved disciples, and in more
solemn detail than ever before, of his approaching death (17–
19); Salome and her sons accost him only to press their worldly
claims with the greatest boldness (20–21) and arouse the stormy
indignation of the ten (24). A recent translation gives the heart
of the Lord's patient lesson in these words, 'Among you
whoever wants to be great must be your servant, and whoever
would be first must be the willing slave of all – like the Son of
man' (26–28a). Servant is the Greek word 'diakonos'; slave is
the Greek word 'doulos'. We should notice our Lord's use of
the term 'ransom' concerning his sacrificial death (28). This
translates the Greek 'lutron' which carries the meaning of
substitution. 'Christ was to die in the place of sinners the death
which they, but not he, deserved' (Tasker). Dr James Denney
used to say that this central fact of substitution is perfectly
expressed in the hymn of P. P. Bliss:

> 'Bearing shame, and scoffing rude
> In my place, condemned, he stood;
> Sealed my pardon with his blood;
> Hallelujah, what a Saviour!'

THE EPISTLE OF LOVE

For many Christians, this is their favourite book. It meets us at its threshhold with the living Saviour and his cleansing blood. It leads us into the household of faith where we are taught the blessings of Christian fellowship. It warns us of a world which is dying and points us to the life which is eternal. It draws a trenchant line between the love that withers and the love that endures. It is full of simple words and deep truths, of sharp contrasts and searching questions. At some time or other in our Christian life we are sure to linger gratefully among the flower-plots of this fragrant letter. In John's old age God used the last of the twelve apostles to place the golden crown upon the New Testament revelation. His clear memory of the blessed fellowship with his Lord, in the days of the Lord's earthly life, has been enriched by the deep spiritual understanding which the Holy Spirit has given to the apostle. Heartfelt devotion to his Saviour, tender concern for all believers, and a clear knowledge of the dangers which are threatening the church shine through each chapter. The three enemies of the church were the Roman government, now turned persecutor (Rev. 2: 10, 13), the pagan world with its coarseness and seductions (Rev. 2: 14, 15, 20), and the gnosticism which was to prove 'the most deadly enemy of Christianity' (G. G. Findlay). This gnosticism has never died out and strongly impregnates much that is called theology today.

[346]

THE IDEAL, AND THE REAL

The basis of Christian fellowship is the blood of Christ and this
bond is never broken. But the practice of fellowship turns on
the believer's obedience and this bond is often broken. The
ideal set before us is that of an unbroken walk with God; the
reality which we all face is our frequent betrayal of Christ.
Between me in my sin and God in his holiness stands Christ the
Mediator pointing the Father to his sprinkled blood upon the
mercy seat *for redeemed ones.* John includes himself. All God's
blood-bought children stand in need of the daily cleansing and
the daily advocacy of their glorified Lord.

Fellowship tied to obedience (3–6). Bengel in three words sums
up the results of this fellowship: Knowledge (cognitio) verse 3;
Union (communio) verse 5; abiding purpose (constantia) verse
6. These relate to mind, heart and will.

Love or hatred (7–11). Verse 7 begins in at least one
translation, with 'beloved' and this word sets the tone for the
verses which follow. How old is this 'old' commandment? See
John 13: 34, Matthew 22: 39 and Leviticus 19: 18. The death-
blow to this heavenly gift of love is ill-will among professing
Christians. Hatred exacts a terrible price in the soul. First, we
become blind to its presence, we do not notice ourselves hating;
then we become blind to its consequences for ourselves, we lose
our spiritual bearings; finally we become blind to its consequences for others, we trip them up (10 cp. Matt. 18: 5, 6).

MEDITATION:
*'Love in the New Testament always means a Christian's awareness
of his responsibilities.'*

LOVE THAT WITHERS, LOVE THAT LASTS

A word to the family (12–14). To children two things matter supremely; forgiveness (12) and assurance of a Father's favour (14). To young men facing life two things matter supremely; victory over the evil one (13, 14) and the Word of God abiding powerfully in them (14). To fathers, facing the setting sun, two things matter supremely; mature knowledge of the God of all grace (13) and settled assurance of salvation (14).

The world (15–17). Underline the five occurrences of this word. What is it? Not the world of nature which was created by God (Gen. 1: 31); nor the world of orderly daily life (John 17: 15, 16); but the world which is dominated by the Evil One (5: 19) and is passing on its way to the slag-heap (17).

The love that withers (15, 16) has three faces and can wear them all with accomplished and seductive skill. The lust of the flesh and the lust of the eyes and the pride of life point us back to the temptations of Paradise Lost (Gen. 3: 6) and the blessings of Paradise Regained (Matt. 4: 1–11).

The love that lasts (17). Two present tenses sharpen the contrast in these two verbs. While the world rolls on to the slag-heap, bearing its flotsam and jetsam into the darkness, the 'little children' of the Father's heart abide secure in the fellowship of the life eternal.

[348]

ANTICHRISTS

The birth of Christ set all the underworld in commotion. Herod was Satan's agent in seeking Jesus' destruction as a child (Matt. 2). Judas was Satan's agent in securing Jesus' death on the cross. Christ's coming in incarnation, death and resurrection inaugurated 'the last time' (18), called in Hebrews 1: 2 'these last days'. The Satanic opposition mounted and became more intense, and this will continue until the final victory of Christ at the last advent. Meanwhile many antichrists have set themselves up as critics and despisers of the Lord's Christ. They had a favoured start in the believing fellowship (19). This fact explains their use of the holiest names and most precious words of the household of faith, yet with a subtle difference. They taught little lies which made great differences to the faith (21, 22). And their lies had Christ as their target. This is the essence of every antichrist. He is against the full scriptural truth concerning Christ. How can the average believer hope to recognize the antichrists of our day? The answer is given in verse 20 and repeated in verse 27. Can you work it out for yourself? It is of the first importance that you should know your secret weapon and use it. The anointing is God's gift of His Holy Spirit at our new birth. He illumines our mind, and imparts spiritual perception and discernment which prevent us from being taken in by mere talk. He enables us to abide in Christ, content and nourished by his saving life. He keeps us childlike, and free from the venom of pride (28). He fills our souls with longing for his second advent (28).

[349]

SONSHIP

Like Christ (1–3). Yes, nothing less than this will satisfy the heart of God and the purpose of the cross. Verse 1 states the privilege of our sonship, verse 2 the purpose of our sonship, and verse 3 the price of our sonship.

Why Christ came (4–8). Two reasons are given: He came to take away our sins (5a). The Sinbearer had to be sinless (5b). And he came to destroy the works of the devil (8). The first purpose is individual and personal, the second universal and cosmic. The word 'destroy' suggests the loosening of masonry, or the unravelling of a tangled rope. Christ came to pull the devil's work to pieces. The Gospels show him doing this at Gadara and at the tomb of Lazarus. Especially does he liberate men from Satan's vice-like grip when he strikes off the fetters of guilt and the handcuffs of sinful habit.

A Christian no longer sins by nature. Verse 4 defines sin as a life which has thrown away restraint and accepts no obligations, no restrictions, no responsibilities. A Christian has his principle of action entirely changed. He abides meekly and gratefully in the saving and satisfying life of Christ. Here he finds his motivation for all his behaviour. He has no love for sin, and reckons himself dead to its suggestions. Though he may slip (2: 1) he does not make sin his life (9). This great miracle is the best evidence that he is a new man (10).

LOVE: THE MARK OF A CHRISTIAN

We should love one another (11–18). On Sunday August 19, 1688 Bunyan preached at Whitechapel (London) his last sermon, based on John 1: 13: 'Dost thou see a soul that has the image of God in him? Love him; love him; say "This man and I must go to heaven one day". Serve one another; do good for one another; and if any wrong you, pray to God to right you, and love the brotherhood.' Love is the mark of a Christian (10b); love is the manifestation of life (14) as hatred is the evidence of death; love is the heart of our message (11, 23); love is practical in outgoing mercy (17). There is spurious love (18), easily recognized by its talkativeness.

A Christian's way to assurance of faith (18–24). Assurance springs from the genuine practice of Christian love (14). Assurance springs from Christian service to others in need (18, 19). Assurance springs from a clear conscience (20, 21), not through any merit in our good works, but because these are the evidence of our spiritual health. Assurance springs from answered prayer (22, 23), not on some rare occasions in the past, but as the day-to-day experience of the life of faith. Assurance springs from the Holy Spirit (24). This is the first clear reference to the Holy Spirit in this Epistle and should link us with Romans 8: 15–17. Thus assurance is shown to be not a perpetual high tide of buoyant feelings, but an abiding communion with Christ through the ungrieved presence of his Holy Spirit.

HOLY SCEPTICISM

Christ and antichrist, the Holy Spirit and the spirit of antichrist (3), the spirit of truth and the spirit of error (6). Here is the situation which faced John's readers two generations after the founding of Christ's church. Is it surprising that nearly two millenniums later we face the same confusion? It has been suggested that we sense in this passage a background of charismatic extravagance. The apostle calls us to a holy scepticism concerning some manifestations of the supernatural. G. G. Findlay warns, 'To identify the supernatural and the Divine is a perilous error'. What can a young Christian do in the face of such confusion? First he is commanded not to believe every person who claims to speak and act by the Holy Spirit. He is to exercise his enlightened powers of discernment (2: 27), and 'test the spirits' to discover whether they are true or false, from Christ or from antichrist, Divine or diabolical. The certain test is: Where do these 'spirits' put Jesus? They put him out of our reach by denying his true incarnation. Our true confession (2) must be that the Man, Jesus of Nazareth, is himself none other than the Christ, the incarnate Son of God. Far from coming upon Jesus at his baptism (as these false prophets taught) Christ came in the flesh and has never laid it aside. Our whole salvation depends upon our confession of the real incarnation of the Christ of God.

GOD'S LOVE TO US AND
GOD'S LOVE THROUGH US

'Beloved' introduces verses 1–6 and the test of true doctrine. 'Beloved' also introduces verses 7–21 and the test of true character. 'Beloved' in verse 11 is a plural noun to remind us that there is nothing selfishly individualistic about God's love to us. God's love is transmitted through us to others. Verse 13 shows us the resources of love; they are found in the Holy Spirit's indwelling in the loving heart of the Christian (cp. Gal. 5: 22). Lovelessness grieves the Spirit; love is the sign of the Spirit quietly at work. The Holy Spirit bears his inward witness to us only so long as we love God and our neighbour. Verses 14 and 25 suggest that faith and love are twins. In verse 16 John re-affirms what he has been saying right through this Epistle, that God is love. 'This is the essence of God's character' (James Orr). 'Does this not sum up the whole of the gospel, just as diamonds reflect the whole sky from one facet?' (Vinet). Yet we need the reminder that, while John insists that God is love, he does not say that love is God. 'Many say that God is love but measure his love by the love of men' (Kuyper). This error is widespread today. Verses 17–21 reveal *the activity of love*. It inspires confidence (17), it casts out fear, including diffidence, distrust and doubt (18); it evokes love, as the emphatic pronouns in verse 19 so clearly declare, and it moves our self-centred hearts to love the brethren (20, 21).

'THIS IS THE VICTORY'

The self-styled intellectuals of John's day (the Gnostics) rejected the biblical truth that Jesus of Nazareth was and is the Christ of God. John therefore makes the confession of Christ's true humanity one of the tests of life. This is the verse which César Malan of Geneva used with a young Church of Scotland minister, John Duncan, in leading him to faith and assurance. He made it his practice to use verse 1 in personal discussions to get at the root of people's spiritual need. The threefold cord is this: life comes through faith (1a); love comes through this new life (1b), 'for everyone who loves the parent loves the child'; love comes through loving (2). The fires of love are fed by the Holy Spirit and fanned by the vision of God's love for us; thus love makes light of its burdens (3). As a result we are able to overcome (3–5), instead of losing heart. *Who* overcomes? 'Every child of God is victor over the godless world'. *What* do we overcome? The world, that is, 'Everyone and everything around us apart from life in God' (Griffith Thomas). *How* do we overcome? By faith (4b) in the victory of Christ our Lord (5) as the power of God (4a).

The threefold witness (6–9) brings the reader back to the sound historical basis of our living faith. 'By water and blood' means by Christ's baptism and crucifixion. The whole of verse 7 may be regarded as a gloss.

THOUGHT:
Either we overcome the world or it overcomes us.

ASSURANCE

Believing and knowing are meant to go together. Thus John describes the purpose of his Gospel in John 20: 31, 'that ye might *believe*', and the purpose of his Epistle 'that ye may *know*'. There is a moment in our life when, for the first time, our justification is published to our conscience. Many would say that this is the way to understand John Wesley's Aldersgate Street experience in 1738. The results of this assurance are far-reaching, as they were in Wesley's case. We have new confidence in our approach to God. Wesley himself speaks of having found the faith of a *son*, no longer of a *servant*, as a result of the Aldersgate experience. The 'boldness' of verse 14 means frankness of speech, an absence of fear in meeting God (cp. 2: 28 and 4: 17), a reverent boldness in prayer. The difficult question about the sin unto death (16) is best resolved by linking it with blasphemy against the Holy Spirit as spoken of in Matthew 12: 31–32. Underline the 'we know' of verses 18–20 and write out what we know who have our assurance of salvation. Verse 18b may be read, 'He who was born of God [i.e. Jesus Christ] keeps him' (RSV). Only by being thus kept can the Christian hope to keep the commandments of God (3: 24; 5: 3).

JOHN, THE MIRACLE BABY

With many, the birth of the Lord Jesus is now in full view and our daily readings take note of this fact. If Luke was as careful a physician as he was an author we can understand Paul's description of him as 'beloved'. Verse 3 underlines the diligence of his search for the facts and verse 4 the moral and spiritual purpose which urged him on. Theophilus is you and me. It means Lover of God. We are this because he first loved us. Luke tells us in sensitive prose how God made John 3: 16 happen. Notice that God worked from within the framework and fellowship of Judaism. All the significant actors in the great drama of Luke Chapters 1 and 2 were men and women reared in a God-fearing tradition and exhibiting deep reverence and spirituality. The Old Testament Scriptures came easily to their lips and the Old Testament prophecies were ever before their eyes. Despite its deformities and corruptions Christ was born into the organized church of the Old Covenant to secure its continuity with the organized church of the New Covenant.

There are *two* miracle babes to prove God's sovereign power in grace. Elisabeth and Zacharias had now no human expectation of a child. That is one reason why God chose them. It was also the reason why the devout Zacharias doubted the word of the angel (18). Yet he doubted in the very matter for which he had patiently prayed (13). His dumbness lasted many months. All doubt cripples our witness and puts a muzzle over our mouths. The most serious doubt of all is to doubt the Word of God (19, 20).

MARY'S CHILD

The mother is introduced (26, 27). Notice the four significant links. Mary was linked to Elisabeth as cousin (36), to Galilee in North Palestine with homely Nazareth as her 'city' (26), to Joseph to whom she was promised in marriage as her future husband (27), and to a great King David through Joseph (27) and also probably through her own father (32).

The message is announced (28–33). The salutation (28) 'highly favoured' means that she was endued with grace: 'not a mother of grace, but a daughter' (Bengel). Her agitation arises not from fear of the angel (contrast Zacharias, 12) but from perplexity over the import of the message (29). The angel's explanation (31–33) removed her fear and deepens her wonder and adoration. She will be first to celebrate Jesus as her Saviour (31, 47), with an awareness of what the Messianic mystery, veiled in verses 31–33, means for Israel's past (54, 55) and mankind's future (48, 50).

The mystery is indicated (34–38): 'that Holy Thing' (35) is not a new being, but One who had existed from eternity. Today's biologist is totally unable to pry into the mystery of the incarnation of God's Son. This was not the conception of a human *person* but of a human *nature*, nourished by Mary's blood in the womb, and a true man (Heb. 2: 14, 17).

THE MEETING OF ELISABETH
AND MARY

Our friendships alter imperceptibly if we change from single to married and from married to parents. Mary felt that if anyone would understand her situation it was Elisabeth, and the angel's hint confirmed her action (36). Elisabeth heard *three* voices: (1) the voice of her cousin Mary (39, 40). It brought deep consolation to her, for both women now held secrets for each other. (2) The voice of the mother of the Lord (43); the face and form of rare beauty, grace and goodness were those of the virgin Mary; the voice and greeting were those of the mother of the Lord. This was attested to Elisabeth by a double miracle; she was filled with the Holy Ghost (41) and her now viable child leapt in her womb (44). (3) The third voice was that of the Father of her Lord, for in Mary's salutation the voice of Mary coincided with the voice of God (44). In this way the Father bore witness to his own holy action in sending the eternal Son to be clothed in human flesh. This is why Elisabeth spoke out with such promptness, clarity and authority.

Mary's Song (46–56). She sings from the heart (46, 47a). She sings of her Saviour (47b). 'Mary, by this mode of expression, reckons herself among those who had been lost; even she had her salvation from Jesus' (Bengel). She sings as a servant girl (48). She sings of a great God (49, 50a) whose works are wrought in power (49a), holiness (49b) and mercy (50a). She sings as part of the living church (50). She sings as a daughter of grace (51–53). She sings of a God who keeps his promises (54, 55).

THE CHILD JOHN

This child stands at the watershed of history, the last prophet of
the old order, the forerunner of the Messiah. His name means
'Gift of God'. It was given by heaven (13) to confirm John's
unique calling and to point to his miraculous birth. His
separated life, as a man consecrated from the womb of his
mother (15), never fell from its high and holy standards of
personal behaviour (80). Already at his birth the hill country of
Judea was alert with expectations concerning the child: 'What
manner of child shall this be?' (66). Doubting brought on
dumbness in Zacharias (20) Now obedience is instantly followed by a clear testimony to God and man (64). If our tongues
have not yet been loosed it is chiefly because we doubt God's
power to speak through us. The Benedictus of Zacharias flows
easily from his glad heart. He was inspired in his utterance by
the Holy Spirit who now moves freely through his surrendered
life (67). True Spirit-inspired utterance puts God first and is full
of the truth of his redemption of his covenanted people.
Thinking of the expected Messiah (69) as well as of his own son
(76), Zacharias praises God for fulfilling his promise. Then
addressing his own little son he declares his mission as the
herald of the Divine Saviour.

THOUGHT ON VERSE 75:
Holiness *is the Godward and inward side of the Christian;*
righteousness *the manward and outward side.*

A SAVIOUR WHO IS CHRIST THE LORD

When Jesus was born the world took no notice. There was no room in the inn, no reception for the Son of David in the city of David, no excitement among the descendants of David at the birth of great David's greater Son. There in the manger he lay, and the world knew him not. But the world was asleep, and the time was dead of night.

God planned his Son's advent ceremony. It must not be that at Christ's first advent all should be cold and silent, since at his second advent there will be angels and archangels, and ten thousands of his saints, and the trumpet of the Lord calling his people home.

And so it came to pass, on that first advent night, that the Good Shepherd of the sheep was welcomed by watchful shepherds in the fields of Bethlehem. God's angel was Christ's herald, not *an* angel but *the* angel; and no doubt this angel was the Gabriel of the annunciation (1: 26) come to tell the sleeping world of men that every word of God has its exact fulfilment. How personal the angel's message was! He came from heaven to tell *them*, a few shepherds, that the Saviour's coming was for them, just as if he had no other lives in mind. His birth is his personal overture of love to every man and woman, every bright-eyed teen-ager, every boy and girl who hears heaven's broadcast today. The angel choir swept in with its anthem, long rehearsed in the concert halls of eternity; and now heard for the first time on earth. When God became man, heaven touched earth and man's heart has since found no peace except in Jesus.

THE CHRIST-CHILD IN THE TEMPLE

The circumcision of Christ (21) is surely the least noticed event in his life. On that day his first drops of blood were shed for the salvation of sinners. On that day, appropriately, he officially received the name JESUS. The symbolism of this vicarious circumcision is meaningful for every one who is 'in Christ' (see Colossians 2: 11). The guilt and tyranny of our old sinful self has been removed. After forty days Jesus was taken to the temple, under the law of Leviticus 12. The poverty of Joseph and Mary is evident in their sacrifice of two young pigeons instead of a lamb. Old Simeon was led into the temple at this precise moment. How completely the Holy Spirit was in control of every event and every detail of the incarnation! See the references in verses 25, 26, 27. Simeon saw beyond the poverty of the sacrifice to the wealth of the Lamb of God and burst into the Nunc Dimittis. The thought underlying the song is that of a slave who is told by his master to keep watch through the long dark night, on a high vantage point. He is to await the rising of a special star and then to announce it. After long dreary hours of unrelieved gloom he at last sees the star rising in all its glory. He makes his announcement, then is discharged. 'Let now thy servant depart in peace; mine eyes have seen thy Salvation'. While Joseph and Mary marvelled at the grandeur of Simeon's prophecy, Mary alone was to feel the sharp point of that sword (35) which later pierced her heart in the hour of her Son's crucifixion (John 19: 25–27). Old Anna's words did not fall on deaf ears (38). Thank God for all who today are looking for final redemption at the glorious second advent of this heavenly Lord.

MY FATHER'S BUSINESS

Of all the crowded memories of Jesus' boyhood, youth and early manhood, this alone has been confided to us by Mary. Mothers need no diaries to remember the quaint sayings of their children, and especially of their firstborn sons. But Scripture hastens on to record Christ's saving life and death and resurrection. The silent years have been filled in with imaginary incidents by the writers of the apocryphal gospels. We should be grateful for the studied reserve of the Holy Spirit's record in the Four Gospels. Among the Jews, when a boy turned 13, he was called 'a son of the law' and was initiated into its observances. This visit to Jerusalem must have served as a helpful anticipation of the visit a year later. We should notice the *humanity* of Jesus, stressed in verses 40 and 52. In our eagerness to safeguard our Lord's full deity we can overlook the truth, equally essential to our redemption, of his real humanity. There was, in Christ's human nature, a growth and development from the less to the greater. He passed through a natural development of body, mind and spirit, so that at every stage he was perfect for that stage. At twelve he stood on the threshold of his teens fit, pure in heart, observant, alert, reverent, loyal. His questions and answers in the temple were not those of a prodigy but of a well-instructed and devout son of the covenant. His reply to his mother and Joseph was a frank confession of his faith and of his sense of his holy vocation.

CHRIST'S SECOND ADVENT

The controlling thought of this letter is disciplined Christian living in view of the coming of the Lord (2: 1). His coming should be as real, as welcome and as imminent to us today as it was to the Apostle Paul when he wrote to this persecuted church in the year 51 A.D. The violent opposition which marked the planting of the church in Thessalonica (Acts 17: 1–10) continued unabated (1: 4). It served God's kingdom well, bracing the Christians to steadfastness and binding their hearts in outgoing love (3). Verses 6–10 seem to accent a severity which we are too slow to recognize in Scripture and in the words and actions of the Saviour. They recall the incident in Scottish history where Andrew Hislop, a shepherd lad of 18, whose mother was a widow, was shot by the dragoons of Graham of Claverhouse for giving shelter to a refugee covenanter. The guns were loaded and the boy was told to pull his 'bonnet' (cap) over his eyes. But he refused and stood confronting his slayers with his Bible in his hand. 'I can look you in the face', he said; 'I have nothing of which I need to be ashamed. But how will you look in that day when you shall be judged by what is written in this Book?'

[363]

TRUE AND FALSE TEACHING

The first fact to notice here is that the truth of the Lord's Advent is the happy hunting ground of false teachers (1–3) who even resort to spurious letters to bolster their deceptions. There is a cult today which teaches that 'the Day of the Lord is already here' (2). St. Paul's ministry in Thessalonica included such controversial questions as a means of forewarning the Christians (5). They are forewarned, and 'not soon shaken in mind' when confronted by error in the form of some exciting doctrinal novelty. The 'tiny apocalypse' of verses 3–12 uncovers the fundamental conflict of history. 'Past defection and corruptions are but precursors of a more awful apostasy yet to come, which shall be headed by one person, the Man of Sin, the Antichrist!' (C. H. Irwin). The closing verses (10–12) remind us that 'the truth' stands in opposition to 'the lie'. Both are ultimately personified in the Lord Jesus (8) and Satan (9). There is no real possession of 'the truth' apart from personal faith in Jesus Christ (John 14: 6); and there is no escape from delusion and deception so long as a man is drugged by the devil.

FALSE MIRACLES (VERSE 9):
Calvin refers to 'these miracle-mongers' of verse 9 and states this important principle. 'It is wrong to esteem those as miracles which are directed to any other end than the glorification of the name of God alone.'

'STAND FIRM'

It is no small comfort to a Christian to learn that his salvation was neither an accident, nor an after-thought. It was a planned and premeditated act of God 'from the beginning'. But the election which effectually called our dead souls into life is not content with any limited salvation. God's loving purpose is our total conformity to Christ. Hence salvation includes sanctification and both are effected by the Holy Spirit (13). In this hidden process the Spirit does a profound work upon our mind and will, dissolving old prejudices against the Word of God and binding our souls to its every utterance (15). He makes Christ more real, encouragement more substantial and our well-settled character the evidence of his indwelling (16–17). He implants the impulse to pray for one another (3: 1). The 'unreasonable and wicked men' of verse 2 'were the Jews who gave the apostle such trouble in Corinth as elsewhere . . . Paul wishes his friends to pray for him to be delivered from wicked men who would oppose the gospel and harm its ambassadors'. (Leon Morris) (Cp. Rom. 15: 30–31).

A GUIDE TO PRAYER:
'We should pray for the safety of gospel ministers . . . They are as the standard-bearers who are most struck at' (Matthew Henry).

COME, LORD JESUS!

The truth of the imminent advent of the Lord had shouldered out all other considerations and had produced in certain weaker brethren 'eschatological fever' (Cullmann). They could think of nothing else, talk of nothing else, plan for nothing else. They had dropped their jobs. They went the rounds of each other's houses exchanging the latest intelligence on the Advent 'signs'. It was impossible to get them to settle down to regular work and face the disciplines of normal daily life in home, church and community. Thus a kind of Christian vagrancy emerged and grew to such proportions that Paul had to devote to the problem the greater part of a chapter. 'Disorderly' (6, 7, 11) translates three Greek words with a common root, frequently used of soldiers marching out of line, or quitting the ranks. This implies neglect of proper duties and that kind of individualism which despises authority and brushes off all correction with a text of Scripture. One translation brings out the play on words in verse 11b, 'busybodies instead of busy'. Their fault lay, not in their holding fast to the doctrine of the Lord's imminent advent, but in their failure to lead obedient, disciplined, useful lives in the sight of God and men.

TRUE PERSPECTIVE:
'Our business is to go on, living upon the promise of Christ's coming. Upon our so doing depends the exercise of every Christian virtue' (J. A. Bengel, died 1752).

LIVE: A HISTORY OF CHURCH PLANTING IN VANUATU

J. Graham Miller

Three volumes of this unique series are already published in paperback. Beginning with the first stormy days of missionary entrance into the New Hebrides, they contain a wealth of historical detail and of inspiring spiritual instruction. Dr. Miller writes primarily to give the present-day islanders 'the largely lost facts about the coming of Christianity and the planting of the Church'. This perspective, and his undisguised love for 'man Vanuatu', keeps the approach in the best sense popular. We begin to feel why the years with his wife, Flora, in Vanuatu (1941–52 and in the 1970's) are so happy in their memories. At the same time the *Live* volumes are a serious attempt to bring the Christian world at large up to date with these Pacific islands which were once so well-known on account of the sufferings of missionary martyrs and early pioneers. Graham Miller believes in the necessity of the Church knowing her history: next to the Bible itself, nothing so stimulates.

Live I, II AND III may be purchased from
Vanuatu: The Presbyterian Church Office, PO Box 150, Vila.
United Kingdom: The Evangelical Book Shop, 15 College Square East, Belfast, N. Ireland.
New Zealand: The Vanuatu Association, 32 Hinemotu Ave, Kawerau.
Australia: Presbyterian Christian Education Dept, GPO Box 100, Sydney 2001.
  Rev. Dr. J. Graham Miller, 14 Franklin St. Wangaratta, Vic. 3677, Phone (057) 21 2610.